# Profiling and Criminal Justice in America

Recent Titles in the

# CONTEMPORARY WORLD ISSUES

Series

*World Energy Crisis: A Reference Handbook*
David E. Newton

*Military Robots and Drones: A Reference Handbook*
Paul J. Springer

*Marijuana: A Reference Handbook*
David E. Newton

*Religious Nationalism: A Reference Handbook*
Atalia Omer and Jason A. Springs

*The Rising Costs of Higher Education: A Reference Handbook*
John R. Thelin

*Vaccination Controversies: A Reference Handbook*
David E. Newton

*The Animal Experimentation Debate: A Reference Handbook*
David E. Newton

*Steroids and Doping in Sports: A Reference Handbook*
David E. Newton

*Internet Censorship: A Reference Handbook*
Bernadette H. Schell

*School Violence: A Reference Handbook, Second Edition*
Laura L. Finley

*GMO Food: A Reference Handbook*
David E. Newton

*Wind Energy: A Reference Handbook*
David E. Newton

Books in the **Contemporary World Issues** series address vital issues in today's society such as genetic engineering, pollution, and biodiversity. Written by professional writers, scholars, and nonacademic experts, these books are authoritative, clearly written, up-to-date, and objective. They provide a good starting point for research by high school and college students, scholars, and general readers as well as by legislators, businesspeople, activists, and others.

Each book, carefully organized and easy to use, contains an overview of the subject, a detailed chronology, biographical sketches, facts and data and/or documents and other primary source material, a forum of authoritative perspective essays, annotated lists of print and nonprint resources, and an index. Readers of books in the *Contemporary World Issues* series will find the information they need in order to have a better understanding of the social, political, environmental, and economic issues facing the world today.

# Profiling and Criminal Justice in America

## A REFERENCE HANDBOOK, SECOND EDITION

Jeff Bumgarner

## ABC-CLIO

Santa Barbara, California • Denver, Colorado • Oxford, England

15-165

**Library of Congress Cataloging-in-Publication Data**

Bumgarner, Jeffrey B.
  Profiling and criminal justice in America : a reference handbook / Jeff Bumgarner. — 2nd edition.
      pages cm. — (Contemporary world issues)
    Includes bibliographical references and index.
    ISBN 978-1-61069-851-1 (hard copy : alk. paper) — ISBN 978-1-61069-852-8 (ebook)   1.  Criminal justice, Administration of—United States.   2.  Racial profiling in law enforcement—United States.   I. Title.
    HV9950.B86   2015
    363.2'308900973—dc23        2014028899

ISBN: 978-1-61069-851-1          15-16
EISBN: 978-1-61069-852-8

19   18   17   16   15      1   2   3   4   5

This book is also available on the World Wide Web as an eBook.
Visit www.abc-clio.com for details.

ABC-CLIO, LLC
130 Cremona Drive, P.O. Box 1911
Santa Barbara, California 93116-1911

This book is printed on acid-free paper ∞

Manufactured in the United States of America

*Preface, xiii*

**1   BACKGROUND AND HISTORY, 3**

Introduction, 3

Definitions, 6

Importance of Studying Criminal Justice Profiling, 9

The Criminal Justice System, 13

Profiling and Political Philosophy, 14

Pluralism: The American Ideal, 16

Elitism: The American Reality?, 17

Applications of Criminal Justice Profiling, 21

Profiling by the Police, 21

The Origins of Police Institutions, 22

Slave Patrols, 28

Emerging Theories of Crime and Profiling, 29

Common Police Profiles, 33

The Hijacker, 33

The Serial Killer, 34

Drug Courier, 35

Proactive and Reactive Profiling, 36

Prosecutorial and Judicial Profiling, 42

References, 42

2    **PROBLEMS, CONTROVERSIES, AND SOLUTIONS, 47**

Stereotyping and Profiling, 47

Police Discretion, 51

Charging Decisions, 55

In Court, 58

At Sentencing, 65

Constitution and Civil Rights, 69

Pros and Cons of Criminal Profiling, 81
        Arguments against Profiling, 81
        Arguments for Profiling, 87

Remedies, 91

Profiling after September 11, 96

References, 99

3    **PERSPECTIVES, 105**

On Racial Profiling: Thorvald O. Dahle, 107

Criminal Behavioral Profiling—A Critical
Perspective: Penny R. Shtull, 112

Media Influence on Perceived Offender-Victim
Relationship: Paige Heinrich, 116

Going beyond "Flying While Arab"—
Islamophobic Profiling in the Era of
Homeland Security: Connie M. Koski, 120

Profiling as a Positive Intervention for
Managing People with Mental Illness in
the Criminal Justice System: Pat Nelson, 128

Negative Stereotypes, Discrimination, Poverty,
and Anger—The Enduring Factors Leading to
African Americans' Overrepresentation in Prison:
Lauren Kientz Anderson, 132

Epidemic Proportions: How Person and
Environment Combine in the Overrepresentation
of African Americans in the Criminal Justice
System: Raphael Travis Jr., 140

4    PROFILES, 155

Personalities, 157
        Freda Adler (1933–), 157
        Joe Arpaio (1932–), 157
        Harry A. Blackmun (1908–1999), 158
        Julian Bond (1940–), 159
        Henry Brown (1836–1913), 160
        Warren E. Burger (1907–1995), 160
        William J. Clinton (1946–), 161
        Morris Dees (1936–), 163
        John Douglas (1947–), 164
        W.E.B. DuBois (1868–1963), 164
        Franz Gall (1758–1828), 165
        Ruth Bader Ginsburg (1933–), 165
        Herman Goldstein (1931–), 166
        John M. Harlan (1833–1911), 167
        Thomas Hobbes (1588–1679), 167
        J. Edgar Hoover (1895–1972), 168

Jesse Jackson (1941–), 169
Martin Luther King Jr. (1929–1968), 170
Rodney King (1965–2012), 171
John Lewis (1940–), 172
Cesare Lombroso (1835–1909), 173
Thurgood Marshall (1908–1993), 173
Kweisi Mfume (1948–), 174
Rosa Parks (1913–2005), 175
Lewis Powell (1907–1998), 176
William H. Rehnquist (1924–2005), 176
Janet Reno (1938–), 177
Jean-Jacques Rousseau (1712–1778), 178
Margaret Sanger (1879–1966), 178
Antonin Scalia (1936–), 179
Al Sharpton (1954–), 180
Roger Taney (1777–1864), 181
August Vollmer (1876–1955), 182
Earl Warren (1891–1974), 183
Ida B. Wells (1862–1931), 184
Byron White (1917–2002), 184
Christine Todd Whitman (1947–), 185
James Q. Wilson (1931–2012), 186
O. W. Wilson (1900–1972), 187

Organizations and Agencies, 188
Private Organizations, 188
Federal Government Agencies, 202
State Government Agencies, 204

5   DATA AND DOCUMENTS, 209

Government Documents, 209
Civil Rights Complaints in U.S. District Court:
1990–2006, 210
Confronting Discrimination in the Post-9/11 Era:
Challenges and Opportunities Ten Years Later, 210

Contacts between the Police and the Public,
2008, 211
Correctional Populations in the United States,
2012, 215
End Racial Profiling Act of 2013, 215
Guidelines Regarding the Use of Race by
Federal Law Enforcement Agencies, 220
Immigration Offenders in the Federal
Justice System, 2010, 221
Police Behavior during Traffic and Street Stops,
2011, 221
Prisoners in 2011, 222
Probation and Parole in the United States,
2011, 225

Protecting Civil Rights: A Leadership Guide
for State, Local, and Tribal Law
Enforcement, 227
Protecting the Rights of Lesbian, Gay,
Bisexual, Transgender, and Intersex
Individuals, 228
Protecting Women's Rights, 228

Racial Profiling: Legal and Constitutional
Issues, 229
Racial Profiling Factsheet, 229

Key Supreme Court Cases, 229
Documents, 230
*Korematsu v. United States,*
323 U.S. 214 (1944), 230
*Hoyt v. Florida,* 368 U.S. 57 (1961), 235
*Delaware v. Prouse,* 440 U.S. 648 (1979), 240
*Batson v. Kentucky,* 476 U.S. 79 (1986), 245
*United States v. Sokolow,* 490 U.S. 1
(1989), 251
*Whren v. United States* (1996), 257

**6    RESOURCES, 267**

Academic Studies, 267

Books, 303

**7    CHRONOLOGY, 321**

*Glossary, 343*
*Index, 353*
*About the Author, 377*

*Profiling and Criminal Justice in America: A Reference Handbook* offers readers an introduction to the issue of profiling within the criminal justice system in the United States. The term *profiling* has come to mean different things to different people. When the term is mentioned, many people immediately conjure up images of detectives hard at work developing psychological sketches of unknown offenders who have left "calling cards" at crime scenes. Although this type of profiling does exist as an investigative tool and is addressed in some portions of this book, the bulk of this publication runs in a different direction. This book, in its second edition, is primarily concerned with the use of race and other potentially objectionable identifiers by criminal justice officials in making decisions about enforcement, prosecution, guilt, and punishment.

The nation's views regarding the use of profiling along racial, ethnic, religious, and other dimensions has changed over time. In the 1980s, it wasn't on anyone's radar. In the 1990s, it became a major public policy concern and profiling was dimly viewed. After the terrorist attacks of September 11, 2001, many people, including public officials, started to retreat from an absolutist position against profiling—at least along ethnic and religious lines which might be implicated in the war against terrorism. Criminal justice institutions, and their political masters, have attempted to strike a balance between civil liberties and public safety—but it has frequently been messy. The traveling public, for its part, collectively rolls its eyes and complains under its breath when observing the random screening of an elderly white woman for extra scrutiny at an airport while the Middle Eastern men behind her proceed unmolested. But at the same time, the public, when asked, does not think that a person's race or religion should doom that individual to a lifetime of chronic suspicion and inconvenience.

Of course, most complaints about profiling have nothing to do with the fight against terrorism, but rather involve the routine responsibilities of the various components of the criminal justice system. To be sure, profiling is a tough issue. The public wants to be safe from crime, but does profiling deliver safety? What about mistakes? Invariably, when well-meaning criminal justice officials consciously or unconsciously engage in profiling, there is considerable room for error.

This book attempts to present both sides of the issue of profiling, and to explain the context that binds it. My hope is that readers will find *Profiling and Criminal Justice in America: A Reference Handbook* to be a useful and balanced introduction to the topic and a springboard for further research about profiling within the context of our criminal justice system.

# Profiling and Criminal Justice in America

## Introduction

On July 27, 1996, in the early morning hours and amid well-attended all-night festivities in Atlanta's Centennial Olympic Park, a security guard named Richard Jewell came across a green, military-style backpack placed under a bench. This bench was located next to a row of additional benches; it was also next to the NBC Sound Tower that had been erected to manage the sound from a stage nearby, where one band after another performed for the crowds in attendance. Even though it was 1:20 A.M., the park was crowded with bystanders in town to enjoy the Olympic events and associated celebrations.

To Jewell's horror, the backpack contained an apparent bomb. Immediately, Jewell radioed law enforcement officers of his situation and started clearing the area of people. Another security officer arrived on scene, and Jewell informed him of the bomb. Jewell said, "Let's get out of here." A few seconds later, the bomb exploded. The explosion killed one woman instantly, caused a fatal heart attack for another individual, and seriously injured more than 100 others. Immediately after the bomb, Jewell, who aspired to a career in law enforcement, began administering aid to the wounded. By all accounts, Jewell had acted heroically before and after the explosion—by all accounts except that of the Federal Bureau of Investigation (FBI).

---

Washington, DC, Police Superintendent Daniel Sullivan (left) and an unidentified officer, 1924. (Library of Congress)

Almost immediately after the FBI investigation began, federal authorities began to focus their suspicion on Richard Jewell. According to their profile of the likely offender, Jewell measured up. FBI profilers suspected that the bomber was white, male, in the 30-something age group, politically conservative, a relative loner, and a Southerner. Additional information received by the FBI further solidified their suspicions. For example, former coworkers of Jewell described him as wanting to be in the middle of the action if anything happened at the Olympics. He was characterized as an "adrenaline junkie." His passion for a career in law enforcement was read by FBI investigators as Jewell's possessing a "hero complex"—in other words, they thought Jewell relished the idea of coming in and saving the day during some crisis. The FBI believed this about Jewell, despite the fact that Jewell himself never claimed to be a hero or to be doing anything other than his job—even in the immediate hours after the incident when everyone else believed that he was, indeed, a hero.

On July 30, 1996, the *Atlanta Journal-Constitution*, which is Atlanta's major daily newspaper, ran a front-page story identifying Jewell as a suspect of the FBI in the bombing. The paper cited several unidentified law enforcement sources. This was a huge national and international story. From that point on, every major media organization referred to Richard Jewell as the Olympic Park bombing suspect. For over 80 days, Richard Jewell was officially a suspect of the FBI in the Olympic Park bombing. Although no physical evidence was ever found tying him to the bombing, the FBI clung to Jewell and his remarkable resemblance to the suspected profile of the bomber. The facts (as opposed to the profile), however, simply could not sustain long-term suspicion against Jewell. After search warrants were executed on his car and at the residence of Jewell and his mother, and after countless interviews, the FBI could not tie Jewell in any way to the bombing or even produce evidence of a motive. In late October 1996, the U.S. Department of Justice sent Jewell a letter stating that he was no longer a suspect in the bombing.

Indeed, in November 2000, Eric Robert Rudolph was indicted on 21 counts related to the Olympic Park bombing by a federal grand jury. He was also indicted for a bombing at an abortion clinic in Birmingham, Alabama, in which an off-duty police officer was killed. In some ways, the FBI profile held up with Rudolph. He was white, male, 30-something, ultraconservative politically, and a Southerner. But given the misdirected attention by the FBI toward Jewell and the apparent unwillingness early on to look elsewhere given Jewell's fit with the profile, can it be said that the profile worked?

FBI profilers would have a chance to redeem themselves in another high-profile terrorist attack, a half-decade later. In 2001, just days after the 9/11 terror attacks, several letters laced with anthrax were mailed to government officials and media personalities. In total, over 20 people were infected and 5 people died. Although on the surface, the letters appeared to be penned by individuals for whom English was not a first language, and the content of the letters expressed Muslim extremist views, the FBI profilers zeroed in on a former U.S. government scientist, Steven Hatfill. For years, Hatfill was considered a "person of interest" as he fit a profile of a disgruntled and disaffected government contractor. However, after several years of attempt and failure to link him to the anthrax mailings, the FBI in 2005 then shifted its focus to another government scientist—Dr. Bruce Ivins. Dr. Ivins, who was a bacteriologist, denied involvement. In 2008, just as the FBI was going to seek an indictment against Dr. Ivins, he committed suicide by overdose. His family stated that the pressure of the investigation overcame him.

The FBI remains convinced that Ivins was the lone perpetrator. However, many scientists are skeptical of this conclusion. Meanwhile, in 2008, the Department of Justice agreed to pay Steven Hatfill nearly $6 million for the cloud of suspicion the government created over him. Few would argue that the anthrax investigation was a triumph in any sense of the word for the quasi-science of behavioral profiling. If anything, journalists, the courts, and even many in law enforcement are more suspicious than ever of its utility.

## Definitions

There is no disagreement in the United States today that criminal justice profiling is a controversial and sensitive issue. The presence of controversy implies that there is more than one side to the issue. Indeed there is. In this handbook, we will examine the issue of criminal justice profiling from what I hope is an objective, nonjudgmental perspective. The goal is to simply provide you, the reader, with information about the issue and expose you to all sides of it.

As criminal justice profiling is controversial, it should not be surprising that there is more than one definition that governs the topic. What is criminal justice profiling? In its plainest sense, criminal justice profiling occurs when criminal justice officials strategically consider characteristics such as race, gender, religion, or sexual orientation as they make discretionary decisions in the course of their duties. In considering such characteristics, criminal justice officials may select some action or actions over others, in part because of the profile of the suspect, convicted offender, victim, witness, or other relevant party under consideration.

Although many writers on the subject use the expression *criminal profiling*, this handbook will regularly refer to *criminal justice profiling* because it is not necessarily suspects alone who are profiled by the criminal justice system.

It is easier to imagine legitimate uses of profiles by law enforcement than it is to imagine legitimate prosecutorial or judicial uses. This does not mean, however, that profiling does not take place at some level or another in the prosecutorial and judicial realms. This handbook will present in a later chapter some scholarly evidence that decisions are made by prosecutors and judges, at least in part, on the basis of race, gender, and other offender characteristics. For example, a prosecutor may attempt to strike an individual from consideration for jury duty during jury selection (voir dire) because of the gender of that potential juror. Prosecutors may believe, for example, that women will be less likely to invoke the death penalty, and so the more men on the jury, the better (from the prosecutor's standpoint).

Although this book concerns itself with profiling throughout the criminal justice system, it is incontrovertible that the most pressing profiling debates revolve around the use of profiles by law enforcement. This fact was true prior to the suicide hijackings on September 11, 2001; it is even more true afterward. The impact that 9/11 and the subsequent war on terror had in breathing new life into the pro-profiling movement cannot be overstated.

Just when it seemed politicians were in agreement that race or ethnicity had been receiving too much weight by law enforcement in decision making and that it must stop, the terrorist attacks took place. Today, some policy makers are asking why airport security personnel are randomly selecting passengers for searches, including elderly ladies from Nebraska, when the most likely threat is going to come from a male young adult—perhaps of Middle Eastern descent.

Profiled characteristics can certainly include race, ethnicity, gender, sexual orientation, and religious affiliation. These are not the only characteristics considered in profiling, however. Things such as travel patterns, socioeconomic status, geographic location, age, clothing, and many other factors can weigh into a profile that is used by criminal justice professionals. What is so controversial, however, about race, sex, and religion being utilized in profiling is the fact that these characteristics are all explicitly protected statuses, or classes, in our laws. Further, these are not behaviors; these are characteristics that simply "are."

Although a neutral definition of profiling may be simply the consideration of certain characteristics in criminal justice decision making, less neutral definitions also exist. For example, some may define criminal justice profiling as the targeting of racial, sexual, and religious minorities for criminal justice action on the basis of their class or group affiliation. Such a definition is by and large a negative portrayal of profiling. Indeed, profiling that results in criminal justice action solely on the basis of these characteristics is illegal, as we shall see.

Others (especially within the criminal justice system) may choose, however, to define profiling as the consideration of racial, sexual, or religious characteristics, when relevant, along with other characteristics in a law enforcement officer's decision to stop, question, arrest, or search someone, in a prosecutor's decision to prosecute someone, or in a judge's decision of how to adjudicate someone. This definition, although a little unwieldy, allows criminal justice professionals some flexibility and freedom to account for any number of obvious observations of, or association with, criminal tendencies.

Daniel Carlson, author of the book *When Cultures Clash* (2002), distinguished between rational and irrational profiling. He noted that rational profiling is a legitimate investigative tool in the fight against crime, and police officers, relying on a commonsense analysis of the observed environment and the activities of suspicious people in context, use the tool frequently.

Irrational profiling, by contrast, is when a police officer decides to stop and question someone when the sole rationale for the stop is the person's race or some other protected classification (Carlson 2002).

Although there are numerous instances of irrational profiling in the criminal justice system, past and present, most profiling advocates argue that legitimate and proper criminal justice profiling actually guards against random harassment and discrimination by law enforcement. This is because profiling offers criminal justice officials the opportunity to pool together collective criminal justice experience into comprehensive and accurate information, as opposed to selectively remembered war stories of individual officials (Harris 2003).

## Importance of Studying Criminal Justice Profiling

The importance behind the issue of criminal justice profiling is as plain as the commonsense arguments for and against the use of profiling. First and foremost, it is important because fighting crime and ensuring the safety of all people in a community is among the chief purposes of government. Any tool that can be enlisted in that fight has got to be thoroughly considered prior to any decision to disregard such tool.

Likewise, another purpose of our government—perhaps a greater purpose than fighting crime—is to ensure the equality of all people before the law. The image of Lady Justice blind-folded while holding her scale is rooted in a very important American (and generally Western) concept: that all people, re-gardless of class, race, sex, religion, disability, and so on, are of fundamentally equal worth and should therefore be treated as equals. Class should not have its privileges before the bar of justice.

American history teaches that this concept of equal justice, although lauded from our beginnings, has been in fact a work in progress. But progress has been made. More than ever before, it has become the goal of the criminal justice system, and gov-ernment generally, to treat men and women; blacks and whites; Jews, Muslims, and Christians; and heterosexuals and homo-sexuals as equals. The extent to which criminal justice profiling negatively impacts the steady movement in the United States toward equality of all before the law necessitates that the issue be carefully thought out and studied—certainly before any final verdicts about its legitimacy as a criminal justice tool are made at the public policy level.

There are arguably no two greater aims of government than to protect its citizens from other citizens who would do peo-ple harm and to protect its citizens from government itself, by abiding by constitutional and statutory restrictions and through self-restraint. In the case of criminal justice profiling, these two aims appear somewhat at odds with each other. As with any issue having two or more compelling sides to it, only the possession of an informed understanding of the issue by policy makers and the public will result in the proper balance being struck.

The issue of criminal justice profiling and its potential discriminatory effects was hotly debated in a number of statehouses in the early 2000s. Many state politicians wanted to reiterate, after the 9/11 attacks, that they would not tolerate law enforcement acting as if it was open season on particular groups or classes of people. In the state of Virginia, the legislature passed a measure to require and expand cultural diversity training for law enforcement officers in part because of perceived racial profiling. West Virginia's legislature passed a measure outlawing any stop or search of a person solely on the basis of his or her race or ethnicity. Such a stop was already unconstitutional, but legal redundancy rarely gets in the way of good politics. The measure also established procedures for investigating claims of biased policing and for disciplining officers found to engage in it.

In South Carolina, the state senate passed a bill that would require police officers to collect data on traffic stops to determine if law enforcement is engaging in racial profiling. Similar requirements already exist in several other states. The state of Utah passed legislation requiring driver's licenses and state identification cards to record the holder's race, so that the race of individuals being checked in the system by law enforcement can be tracked. Additionally, officers are required to record why a person is being checked every time the officer runs someone in the system. The information of race is then matched up with the reasons people are being stopped and which officers are stopping them. The aggregate information is passed on to the departments and to the state legislature. Utah law enforcement agencies are also required under the law to adopt policies against bias-based policing (International Association of Chiefs of Police 2003).

In 1994, the National Commission on Crime Control and Prevention was established by the Violent Crime Control and Law Enforcement Act. This commission, like national crime commissions in the past, was tasked with the responsibility to make broad and realistic recommendations to improve the U.S. criminal justice system. Among the mandates given to it by Congress, the commission was to:

1. develop a comprehensive proposal for preventing and controlling crime and violence in the United States;
2. bring attention to the successful models and programs in crime prevention and crime control;
3. reach out beyond the traditional criminal justice community for ideas for controlling and preventing crime;
4. recommend improvements in the coordination of local, state, federal, and international crime control and prevention efforts, including efforts relating to crime near international borders;
5. make a comprehensive study of the economic and social factors leading to or contributing to crime and violence, including the causes of illicit drug use and other substance abuse, and to develop specific proposals for legislative and administrative actions to reduce crime and violence and the factors that contribute to it;
6. recommend means of utilizing criminal justice resources as effectively as possible, including targeting finite correctional facility space to the most serious and violent offenders, and considering increased use of intermediate sanctions for offenders who can be dealt with adequately by such means;
7. examine distinctive crime problems and the impact of crime on members of minority groups, Native Americans living on reservations, and other groups defined by race, ethnicity, religion, age, disability, or other characteristics

and to recommend specific responses to the distinctive crime problems of such groups;

8. examine the problem of sexual assaults, domestic violence, and other criminal and unlawful acts that particularly affect women and to recommend federal, state, and local strategies for more effectively preventing and punishing such crimes and acts;

9. examine the treatment of victims in federal, state, and local criminal justice systems and to develop recommendations to enhance and protect the rights of victims;

10. examine the ability of federal, state, and local criminal justice systems to administer criminal law and criminal sanctions impartially without discrimination on the basis of race, ethnicity, religion, gender, or other legally proscribed grounds and to make recommendations for correcting any deficiencies in the impartial administration of justice on these grounds; and

11. examine the nature, scope, causes, and complexities of violence in schools and to recommend a comprehensive response to that problem.

Interestingly, two of the aforementioned mandates concern the issue of race, ethnicity, religion, and other protected classifications. Mandate number 7 implores the criminal justice system to concern itself with the specific and unique problems associated with particular classes of people; the 10th mandate, however, essentially demands that the criminal justice system ignore the variety of classifications in pursuit of justice, lest it be unequal in its application. In other words, the former mandate proposes consciousness regarding groups and classes, whereas the latter proposes neutrality.

This seeming, and certainly unintentional, contradiction exemplifies in a broad way some of the dilemmas felt in the more narrowly framed issue of criminal justice profiling. In the following sections, criminal justice profiling will be examined for what it is and is not and for the contradictory aims and achievements it yields.

## The Criminal Justice System

In understanding criminal justice profiling, it is important to know something about the criminal justice system in the United States. In particular, what are its goals? Criminal justice scholars are not in agreement on the degree to which American criminal justice operates as a system to begin with. Generally, when we speak of the criminal justice system, we think of the police, the prisons, and the courts as the triad comprising the system. It could be argued, however, that American criminal justice is distinctly a "nonsystem," as the police, prisons, and courts have different, and sometimes competing, goals. In a true system, the component parts of the system are all designed to work toward the bigger objective. Instead, the component criminal justice parts are working frequently at odds with each other and, in any case, rarely act in concert with each other.

Add to the differing goals of these 3 criminal justice components the fact that the United States has 1 federal and 50 state criminal justice systems existing at the same time, and you will have the epitome of decentralization that marks our federalist approach to the government. Calling it a "system" that can be universally characterized as "racist" or "nonracist" or "sexist" or "just" may be giving it too much credit, or discredit.

This point notwithstanding, most criminal justice professionals and scholars believe there are some overall objectives of all who work in the U.S. justice system. These broad objectives can be said to be the goals of the American criminal justice "system." And it is within the context of these goals that profiling takes place. The overarching goal of the U.S. criminal justice system is to "do justice" (Cole, Smith, and DeJong 2014). There are two values associated with doing justice. Although these values are somewhat in competition, they are not mutually exclusive. The first is that of crime control. This value requires our free society to make every effort to allow law-abiding citizens to live in freedom and safety by repressing crime that would otherwise be perpetrated against them. This means there is an emphasis placed on efficiency, speed, and finality in the prevention, apprehension, and punishment of criminals.

The other value characterizing U.S. criminal justice is that of due process. This value requires us to make every effort to ensure that our criminal justice decisions and actions are based on fair and reliable information. There is an emphasis on the adversarial process, the rights of defendants, and formal decision-making procedures over ad hoc, impulsive, or emotion-driven decisions. Those who stress crime control tend to support the expansion of police numbers and police powers; they tend to want to limit the ability of judges to be lenient on defendants; and they tend to oppose probation and parole, preferring instead to build more prisons and jails. Those who stress due process, on the other hand, make every effort to ensure that individual rights are protected; they tend to prefer treatment and rehabilitation efforts over punishment for punishment's sake; and they insist that the system err on the side of offenders rather than risk unjustly depriving innocent people of their rights or their liberty.

The relative value one places on crime control and due process will likely shape one's view on the worthwhileness of criminal justice profiling. Those who value crime control over due process will find profiling to be an invaluable crime-fighting tool that is not used enough or to great enough lengths to preserve law-abiding citizens' safety and security from criminal elements. Those who value due process above crime control will find profiling to be an oppressive and illegitimate tool of government to single out some of its citizens for action. Even if it works, the cost to individual dignity and rights is too high to warrant its use.

## Profiling and Political Philosophy

The issue of criminal profiling has broader implications than those just for the law enforcement community, or the criminal justice system for that matter. Profiling raises questions that are the heart of the political philosophies of the United States. Indeed, exactly what America's philosophies and core values are continues to be debated to this day. At the root of the debate are the models of "consensus" and "conflict."

The debate of consensus versus conflict amounts to two competing models of explanation as to where our laws (and the enforcement mechanisms that follow) come from. The consensus model holds that criminal law, as an expression of the social consciousness of the whole society, reflects widely shared values and beliefs (Cole, Smith, and DeJong 2014). In other words, the laws of American society reflect a consensus that has been arrived at by society's members.

The main principles commonly associated with the consensus model are that (1) the law reflects the need for order; (2) the law results from a consensus on the values that are widely shared in society; (3) the law is an impartial system that protects the public interest; and (4) the law provides a neutral means for resolving disputes.

Crimes that tend to be emphasized by those adhering to this model are known as *mala in se* offenses. These offenses are thought to be wrong by their very nature, with or without a criminal code telling us so. Offenses such as murder, assault, rape, and so on are considered *mala in se* crimes. The fact that there are criminal codes against these offenses reflects the fact that society's members widely agree that committing these acts is wrong.

The conflict model rejects the notion that most of the criminal laws are written as a result of widespread consensus. Instead, subscribers of this model hold that the criminal laws and enforcement mechanisms have been crafted by powerful political groups. The model assumes that people act in their own self-interests; therefore, people who have power are the ones whose preferred wishes will be codified into law (Cole, Smith, and DeJong 2014).

The conflict model emphasizes crimes known as *mala prohibita* offenses to prove its point. *Mala prohibita* crimes are prohibited by law but are not necessarily evil or wrong in and of themselves. These offenses include gambling, vagrancy, prostitution, and drug use. Many critics of the notion of consensus in our criminal laws point out that the statutes articulating *mala prohibita* offenses tend to be largely enforced against the lower classes in society—especially against racial and sexual minorities.

## Pluralism: The American Ideal

Often associated with the criminal justice notion of consensus is the broader political philosophy of pluralism. Pluralism postulates that self-rule by all the people of a society can be achieved through competition among multiple organized groups and that individual members of society can genuinely participate in societal and political decisions through group memberships and elections (Dye 2010). Things get done, including the crafting of the criminal justice system, by debating, bargaining, and compromising among various interest groups in competition.

Public policy that emerges from a pluralistic system is generally thought to be rationally derived. Through open and free debate, all policy options are aired and considered according to their relative costs and benefits. In the end, policy is crafted according to the maximum social gain, which is consistent with the consensus model.

That the government has the right to do this is based on the long-standing adherence of the United States to social contract theory. The notion of social contract in America can be traced back to 17th-century political philosopher John Locke, among others. Social contract is the idea that government originates as an implied contract among individuals who agree to obey the law in exchange for the protection of their rights. Locke argued that government is based on consensus. It exists because the people have allowed it to and for good reason. As Thomas Hobbes said in his classic work *Leviathan*, life without any government would be "solitary, poor, nasty, brutish, and short" (Hobbes 1651, 65). Indeed, we the people have consented to the existence of our government. In doing so, we have agreed to give up some of our liberties and responsibilities, such as to avenge ourselves (and to a lesser degree protect ourselves), and have delegated them to the government instead. As the Preamble of the U.S. Constitution says, we have agreed to delegate to the government our national defense, the preservation of our welfare, the establishment of justice and tranquility, and the securing of our liberties. If the government lives up to its portion of the contract and provides these things, then the people will continue to let the government exist and rule. Locke suggested, however, that when government—any government— fails to deliver in these—its essential responsibilities—then the government can and should be dissolved by the people and replaced with a new one.

Clearly, John Locke's social contract served as the justification for the American Revolution. American colonists had decided that the British Crown no longer deserved power over them as it no longer (if it had ever) met its contractual obligations. Hence, Locke's language appears practically verbatim in the American Declaration of Independence.

## Elitism: The American Reality?

The political philosophy of elitism is generally aligned with the conflict model of criminal justice. Elitism posits that public policy of all types boils down to the preferences and values of the governing elite. Those who argue that the United States is an elitist society note that most policy makers are drawn from the upper socioeconomic strata of society. What's more, so are those who have access to the policy makers. It is estimated that half of the nation's total assets are concentrated in the 100 largest corporations and 50 largest banks in the United

States (Dye 2010). Leaders of these businesses have regular access to politicians and high-ranking bureaucrats. C. Wright Mills coined the term *power elite* to describe those leaders in government, the military, and private corporations who comprise the decision makers in U.S. society. He noted that they tend to be white, male, wealthy, educated, and Protestant and together form the pinnacle of a pyramid of power, with the masses positioned below (Mills 1956).

Elitism manifests itself in the criminal justice system with two types of discriminatory laws. Historically, many laws in this country were designed to treat people differently based upon their minority racial, ethnic, gender, sexual orientation, or religious status. A well-known example would be the Jim Crow laws of the South, which well into the 20th century enforced racial segregation.

In recent years, however, the Supreme Court has scrutinized laws that were directed against particular classes of people. Most laws specifically directed against a particular class of people— favorably or unfavorably—have been found to be violations of the Equal Protection Clause of the Fourteenth Amendment and therefore unconstitutional. But many people point out that elitism also manifests itself in laws that are classification neutral but are enforced in a way that causes an adverse impact on a class or group of people (Schott 2001). In these instances, the law applies to everyone equally, but the impact tends to be greater among a particular group because of that group's tendencies or because of selective enforcement. For example, possession or sale of crack cocaine carries a harsher penalty in many jurisdictions than does powder cocaine. African American cocaine users tend to prefer crack cocaine, whereas white users favor powder.

Supporters of such laws note that crack cocaine is more dangerous and more addictive. Critics point out, however, that blacks and other ethnic minorities tend to use crack cocaine because it is cheaper, whereas middle- and upper-class whites can afford the more expensive powder cocaine. Although a white person using crack cocaine may be subject to the same penalties as minorities who use it, the net effect is that harsher penalties tend to be doled out to black cocaine users more than white cocaine users because of the preference and affordability of crack cocaine over powder among the black population. Perceiving that drug sentences historically have not been fair and have resulted in a disproportionate number of black drug offenders spending more time in prison than others, the U.S. Justice Department under Attorney General Eric Holder announced that his department supported a number of sentencing reforms that would be implemented in 2014 and apply retroactively to crack cocaine sentences handed out as far back as 2010 (Halloran 2014).

Another example is the existence of antisodomy laws that remain on the books in many states. Although heterosexuals and homosexuals alike live under such laws, homosexuals are more likely to engage in sodomy—and therefore, historically, be prosecuted for it—because sodomy is the preferred sexual activity among homosexuals. Therefore, antisodomy laws, which in appearance are neutral when it comes to sexual orientation, generally impact one particular group more than others. The Supreme Court struck down these laws in 2003. Many see such laws as prima facie evidence of an elitist society and an elitist criminal justice system. As is the case in so many social contexts, the polar extremes may not reflect the reality that is our criminal justice system. Instead, we may think of the degree of fairness or unfairness in criminal justice as a continuum. Samuel Walker, Cassia Spohn, and Miriam DeLone conceptualized discrimination in the American criminal justice system as existing along a continuum ranging from "systematic discrimination" to "pure justice" (Walker, Spohn, and DeLone 2012).

The view that the criminal justice system is discriminatory at all stages, at all times, and in all places throughout the United States is one that holds to "systematic discrimination." It is the view that the criminal justice system, as presently constituted, is hopelessly flawed with bias against all types of people. Next along the continuum is the notion that the criminal justice system is characterized by "institutional discrimination." This position asserts that disparities in outcomes along racial, ethnic, gender, or other lines are due to the application of otherwise neutral factors, such as criminal record or family status, but these factors nevertheless adversely impact some groups more than others. The previously mentioned crack cocaine and anti-sodomy laws are also examples.

"Contextual discrimination" is next on Walker, Spohn, and DeLone's continuum. People believing that this level of discrimination exists in the system hold that discrimination is not "system" wide. Rather, discrimination surfaces in particular contexts and circumstances, such as regions of the country or in regards to specific kinds of crime. Discrimination does exist, but it is not so pervasive that context is irrelevant. If you want to treat discrimination, it stands to reason that you treat the contexts that give rise to it.

Finally, at the end of the continuum opposite to systematic discrimination is the notion of "pure justice." Those who believe "pure justice" exists, and there are not many who do, believe that there is no discrimination of any type affecting any group or groups at all—ever. This position on the continuum represents the ideal of American criminal justice. Again, few argue that it represents the reality. But, as the ideal, it is always the horizon toward which we should move.

It is debatable what role criminal justice profiling plays in fixing the criminal justice system somewhere on the aforementioned continuum. Some see profiling as evidence of systematic discrimination and as a tool of maintaining systematic discrimination. Others see profiling more as a manifestation of institutional or contextual discrimination. Still others argue that profiling simply is a symptom of where crime is; to not go where the crime is, through profiling or other means, is to unfairly leave vulnerable potential victims who live with crime all around them—usually in lower-income, minority neighborhoods. By that logic, profiling is evidence of a desire on the part of the criminal justice system to protect all people, including the poor and minorities, and therefore reflects no discrimination. Whatever significance one places on criminal justice profiling in gauging the true level of fairness and equality in the United States, it clearly has become a cause célèbre—whether anecdotal or substantive—in the debate over "doing justice."

## Applications of Criminal Justice Profiling

Profiling within the criminal justice system is most often associated with law enforcement. Most of the scholarly (and almost all of the popular) literature that focuses on criminal justice profiling emphasizes the law enforcement piece of the justice system. Criminal justice profiling can and does take place at various stages of the criminal justice process including, but not limited to, police work. To the extent that profiling is defined broadly as the practice of justice officials directly or indirectly taking into consideration various characteristics of suspects or known offenders as they make decisions in their official capacity, profiling can occur in the law enforcement, prosecutorial, judicial, and correctional functions in the justice system.

## Profiling by the Police

To place profiling by the police in context, we must at least consider what the goals of modern police agencies are. The police have three primary functions in American society: order maintenance, service, and law enforcement. Order maintenance refers to the prevention of behavior that disturbs the public peace. Service involves the provision by police of assistance to the public in matters unrelated to crime. Services the police may provide include medical assistance, helping citizens locked out of their vehicles, public relations activities, and so on. It is estimated that 71 percent of police calls do not involve crimes (Roberg et al. 2012). Finally, law enforcement refers to controlling crime by intervening in situations in which the law has been or is being broken and there exists a need to identify and apprehend those guilty of breaking it. It is this latter function of law enforcement that we have come to equate with the "profession" of policing. That has not always been the case. Policing as an occupation has come a long way.

## The Origins of Police Institutions

From the late 13th century through the 18th century, England and its colonies utilized the parish-constable watch system of law enforcement (Samaha 1994). Under this system, each parish or town would appoint at least two unpaid constables, usually selected by lot. Constables in turn selected night watchmen to assist them in their duty. When a constable or night watchman, who later came to be called a "bailiff," would come across a crime in progress, the practice was to call out for help to any and everyone who could hear him. In fact, English law made it a crime for able-bodied citizens to ignore the "hue and cry" and required citizens to keep weapons in their homes for the purpose of rendering such assistance. These same citizens were also expected to join a posse, if necessary, to capture offenders. Posses were led by a leader of the shire—or county—in question. This leader was known as the shire reeve, from which the modern term *sheriff* is derived (Schmalleger 2012; Archbold 2013).

In the 1700s, particularly after the advent of gin, which was amazingly cheap for an intoxicating beverage, English urban areas became frequent sites of riots. Huge numbers of people living in London's industrial ghettos began binge drinking and rioting to drown out their troubles. The night watchmen proved to be woefully incapable of dealing with the riots and, in fact, became targets of mob violence to the point of frequently being beaten for sport (Schmalleger 2012).

The alternative to the watchmen when things were out of control was to turn to the military. Under the English Riot Act, troops could be called out "in aid of the civil power"

(Deakin 1988). In 1818, soldiers were called out to quell a riot in Manchester and in the process killed 11 and wounded over 500 in the crowd. After this incident and others with similar consequences, the notion of forming a police force to handle disorders became increasingly appealing to the British government. After all, the objection to creating a police force because it would constitute putting troops in the streets was negated by the fact that real troops were frequently put in the streets for lack of a police force. Probably the single most significant event in police history was the passage of the Metropolitan Police Act of 1829. That piece of legislation, submitted to Parliament by Sir Robert Peel, created the first modern police force. Within a year of the act's passage, the Metropolitan Police force, commonly called the Met, employed over 1,000 officers. Officers were equipped with a uniform, a short baton, and a rattle, the latter being used to raise an alarm when necessary. Each constable, nicknamed "bobby" in Peel's honor, was issued a number that he had to wear on his collar, making the bobbies immediately identifiable to the public (Peak and Glesnor 2012).

Although establishing a police force was controversial, as it resembled to some a standing army in the streets of London, the alternative of continuing to use the military was more problematic. The Met was created to keep the civil order without resorting to broadly administered violence wherever possible. The Met had a four-part mandate:

1. to prevent crime without using repressive force and to avoid calling out the military to control disturbances;

2. to maintain public order by nonviolent means, using force only to obtain compliance as a last resort;

3. to reduce conflict between the police and the public; and

4. to show efficiency through the absence of crime and disorder rather than through visible police actions.

In the United States, modern police departments arose owing to circumstances remarkably similar to those that had existed in England. From the 1830s to the 1870s, there was an unprecedented amount of civil disorder occurring throughout the industrial United States. Very few cities escaped serious rioting and mob violence. The civil upheaval was often rooted in ethnic fighting due to the massive influx of immigrants during this time period. There was also violence rooted in economic issues, resulting in banks and businesses being ransacked by angry customers or employees (Walker 1977).

As had been the case in England, there was no continuous police presence in the urban centers of the United States in the early 19th century. The night watch was largely the only official mechanism in place, short of troops, to confront the frequent mob violence—and only then at night. In one major city after another, the response was the same. Police departments began to be formed throughout the middle of the 19th century in America's urban centers to keep the peace. Policing in the United States paralleled policing in England. Some of the similarities between American and British police in the 19th century included (Uchida 2001):

- common legal tradition;
- civilian workforce (not soldiers) with a military-style command structure;
- crime prevention as the main mission;
- random patrol of fixed beats as the main strategy against crime;
- restrained police powers; and
- paid, uniformed police officers.

Although police forces in the United States were modeled after London's metropolitan force, there were some significant differences between the English and American models. Chief among the differences was the political orientation of the police. The Met was a creation of the national government in England, whereas in the United States police departments were installed by city governments. This made U.S. police officers much more a part of the political machinery than their London counterparts. Police officers were usually recruited by political leaders of a given ward or precinct and served at the pleasure of the political leadership. For example, in Cincinnati, after an election in 1880 changed the party in power, 219 of the 295 members of the police force were dismissed. Six years later, after another political power shift, 238 of the 289 patrolmen and 8 of 16 lieutenants were removed (Walker 1977).

Police in the United States in the 19th century were characterized by cronyism and endemic corruption and conducted themselves by a set of informal processes that had little to do with the official mandate of the police, namely to protect and to serve. But police were not up to no-good and nothing else. Police departments in that time period, commonly dubbed the political era of policing, spent much of their time engaged in services.

Departments, as extensions of politics, were routinely tasked with providing ambulance services, running soup kitchens, running shelters, and other benevolent activities. American policing around the turn of the century was more oriented toward service than any other police function. With the 20th century came the Progressive era. From 1900 to 1914, there were widespread reform efforts directed toward the criminal justice system. The reforms were consistent with efforts being made in government generally—namely, the depoliticization of the civil service and the birth of public administration as a distinct profession based on technical competencies and practices. The reforms directed toward police agencies included centralization of power by concentrating most authority in an autonomous chief; rational administrative procedures; upgrading personnel by means of selection, training, and discipline; and restricting the police role to enforcing the criminal law (Walker 1977; Samaha 1994; Archbold 2013).

Initially, the reform efforts toward the police were met with hostility from the police rank-and-file. They viewed reformers who sought to sever the police connection with political bosses as making their jobs more difficult, more dangerous, and less popular with the public. As one police scandal was publicly paraded after another, however, many officers began to see the police corruption and incompetence as conduits toward making all policemen laughing stocks; consequently, internal pressure began to swell for reform (Sparrow, Moore, and Kennedy 1990).

Gradually, over the years that followed the first decade of the 20th century leading into the modern era, police departments around the country began to change. To be sure, corruption and incompetence plagued many agencies and in some cases exist systematically even today. But in totality, a genuine paradigm shift relating to policing began to take place in the collective and individual minds of officers, their managers, and the public. The quality and character of police officers began to matter as never before. For example, officers in departments undergoing reform were required to declare financial interests and remain debt free as a condition of employment, in order to minimize the temptation of corruption. Indeed, in an effort to ensure that bribery and protection rackets had seen their last day, many departments went so far as to forbid unnecessary or casual conversation with the public (Sparrow, Moore, and Kennedy 1990). This obsolete rule has survived police culture in many cases to this day in the form of officer aloofness. In other words, the courteous but nonfriendly, businesslike demeanor we often observe in police officers as we try unsuccessfully to get out of a ticket does not necessarily originate in officer bias or rudeness. Rather, it is an unforeseen consequence of professionalization and countercorruption efforts.

Another reform in the police field was the use of motorized vehicles. This created an ability to cover more area of an assigned beat within a shift. This ability was further enhanced by the widespread use of radios in patrol cars by 1950. Reformers saw the radio-squad car as huge plus. Not only did the cars help keep officers separated from the public, thus minimizing the potential for corruption, but they gave officers the ability of preventive patrol and rapid response.

The "reform" or "professional" model of policing as it emerged during the first two-thirds of the 20th century remains mostly intact today even as a new model—community policing—is championed in name. Modern police deeply resent political interference. They find their legitimacy and methods in the ideas of police science and crime control, not community sentiment. And further, the ideas of professionalism have been reinforced through the advent of specialized police procedures and advanced forensic techniques.

Some developments in the professional era included the advent of the police code of ethics, merit selection and promotion, training standards, the use of management science, a new emphasis on impartiality in enforcing the law, advances in transportation, and scientific crime fighting. It is this last development that really serves as the parent of modern criminal profiling.

During the professional era, the primary mission of police departments became law enforcement, as opposed to service or even order maintenance. The supremacy in importance of fighting and solving crime was solidified in police culture. Additionally, isolation from the public was inevitable during this time period. The advent of the patrol car meant that officers were covering more ground while interacting less with the public. It is this professional, crime-fighting model of policing that has by and large survived to this very day. Although police departments increasingly adopt community policing policies, which seek to form partnerships with the communities to solve rather than salve community problems, modern law enforcement still primarily serves as a reactionary, crime-fighting force.

In the professional model of policing, the overriding mission of law enforcement is to suppress criminal activity. Profiling, to the extent that it enables law enforcement to successfully identify potential criminal activity and perpetrators of such activity, is entirely consistent with the professional model. Perhaps this is why profiling has flourished in recent years and has been legitimized in law enforcement as a quasi-science through training and practice. The bottom line in the minds of many professionally oriented police officers is that profiling tends to work.

It also makes sense that with the growth of community policing, the comfort level of society with profiling is diminishing—particularly among citizens in the subcommunities most affected. Say those citizens: How can we partner with the police when they view us as potential violators based on objective criteria over which we have no control, such as our race?

## Slave Patrols

The English origins of American policing serve as the primary source for understanding U.S. police history. The model for urban law enforcement given to us from the Met, or even the traditional notion of the office of county sheriff, derived from the British "shire reeve," who was responsible for tax collection and process service in the English countryside, does not, however, explain the police practices of the 19th-century American South.

Indeed, policing in the southern United States, particularly as policing related to black Americans, has a sad history of its own. Many historians recognize today that policing in the American South during the 18th century and first half of the 19th century was inextricably tied to slavery. Owing to a fear of violent slave uprisings, along with fearing the lesser offenses of refusing to work, escape, killing livestock, and destroying equipment, formal slave patrols began to form in the Southern colonies (Samaha 2005). South Carolina established the first slave patrol in 1704. Virginia followed in 1727 and North Carolina in 1753 (Hadden 2001). Those formal slave patrols established legislatively by the colonies constitute some of the earliest formal police operations in America. Patrollers were usually white men between the ages of 16 and 60. These men were often chosen from the rosters of the militia. They had three main duties: (1) searching slave quarters, (2) dispersing slave gatherings, and (3) safeguarding communities by patrolling the roads (Hadden 2001).

The slave patrols continued to exist throughout the South until the Civil War. In the wake of the Civil War and the emancipation of slaves, the slave patrols gave way to vigilante groups that continued to troll for blacks with an eye toward submission through intimidation at the least and downright terror for terror's sake at the worst. The Ku Klux Klan (KKK) was organized as one of these vigilante groups. Given the common heritage of organizations such as the KKK with elements of modern policing, it is little wonder that many African Americans have an antipathy for aggressive, contact-intensive police patrol tactics.

## Emerging Theories of Crime and Profiling

Just as law enforcement, as an occupation and practice, has developed over time, so have the theories of crime often relied upon by the criminal justice system. There have been many theories advanced as to the cause of crime and criminality. Obviously, the same explanations people use to explain crime can be used to predict it as well. And people, once they believe themselves capable of predicting crime, will necessarily engage in profiling to do so. The degree to which race, ethnicity, gender, sexual orientation, or religion are pieces of those explanations relates to the degree that people will tend to be profiled along these lines.

As George Cole and Christopher Smith have noted, philosophies of crime in America and elsewhere in the West prior to the 18th century were inseparable from the prevailing theologies of the day. Under this worldview, mankind is fallen and inherently sinful. Crime is a natural manifestation of mankind's sinful nature. Formal indictments for criminal offenses in colonial times would include language such as "[John Doe] not having the fear of God before his eyes but being seduced by the instigation of the Devil, did commit [some offense]" (Cole and Smith 2001, 68).

The 18th century, however, ushered in rational approaches to explaining criminality in people. In particular, Cesare Beccaria (1738–1794) published *Essay on Crimes and Punishments* in 1764, which contained the tenets of what is now known as classical criminology. He claimed that the explanation for crime is not generally rooted in theology; rather, it is rooted in rational thinking. He argued that when criminals commit crime, they do so out of their free will, having made a rational choice weighing the costs of possibly getting caught against the benefits of succeeding.

Beccaria's basic principles were as follows:

1. Crime is caused by the individual rational exercise of free will.
2. Pain and pleasure are the two central determinants of human behavior.
3. Crime disparages the quality of the relationship that exists between individuals and society.
4. Punishment is a necessary evil and is sometimes required to deter criminal choices and serve as an example to others.
5. Crime prevention is possible through swift and certain punishment, which offsets any gains to be had through criminal behavior.

Although many in history have looked at Beccaria's principles as an excuse for harsh punishment, Beccaria himself was actually a staunch opponent of excessive punishment. He believed that disproportionate punishment was counterproductive and unjust. The profiling implication of classical criminology is that crime may be predicted by identifying those most likely to find the benefits of committing a crime greater than the costs. If other people's rational choices regarding crime can be anticipated, then the criminal justice system may use that during enforcement to avert crime or during adjudication and sentencing to avert recidivism.

In the 19th century and first part of the 20th century, another theory of crime became very popular. During that time, it was common to believe that crime was at least in part due to biology. In other words, adherents to this theory argued that some people are predisposed to committing crimes. That theory of crime—the theory that some people are born criminal—is the criminogenic theory of crime.

Criminogenics' most famous champion was Cesare Lombroso (1836–1909). Lombroso and others argued that people who were born criminal had some telltale biological and physiological features. For example, they claimed that criminals tended to have primitive physical features such as strong canine teeth, huge jaws, and high cheekbones. Indeed, the cartoon cliché of criminals having "slack jaws and beady eyes" came from this school of thought.

Lombroso's theory of crime was tied to naturalism and Charles Darwin's theory of evolution. If some people exhibited features that were common to a more primitive version of man, that is, a version appearing earlier in the evolutionary chain, then it was logical to assume that the behavior of those people would tend to be more primitive.

Although few serious scholars today advance Lombroso's criminogenic theories, many do believe that genetics, physiology, and heredity may play a part in determining criminal behavior. Studies continue to be done by biologists and research psychologists in attempts to identify genetic and physiological features that are associated with people who commit various types of crime—particularly violent crime.

The implications that the biological theories of crime have for profiling are plain. If criminals are likely to have certain physical features, then the criminal justice system, many would argue, should give proactive attention to people possessing those features before all others. Or, if criminals will likely have certain genetic features, then perhaps the criminal justice system should give proactive attention to those whose deoxyribonucleic acid (DNA) fits a certain profile.

For example, homosexuality is widely believed today to be a born-trait; in other words, most gays and lesbians do not choose to be attracted to people of the same sex, but rather it comes naturally to them. Some researchers have published findings in medical and social science journals which suggest that sexual orientation has an association with pedophilia. In particular, it is claimed that homosexual men (generally assumed to constitute less than 2% of the total population) are responsible for a third of all child molestations. This disproportionate representation of homosexuals among sex offenders against children, if true, would have significant profiling implications. For example, people meeting the profile—namely, homosexual and male—might not be permitted to work unsupervised with children. Nor might they be permitted to adopt. Or, when male children went missing, homosexual males would be the first people law enforcement would look at for suspects. Other researchers point out that, although male-on-male molestations account for a significant percentage of total child molestations, the offenders rarely are identified as having an exclusively homosexual orientation. Therefore, they note, focusing inordinate attention on this population in preventing or investigating these crimes is unjust and, in any case, poor strategy.

Today, the most prevailing types of theories to explain crime are sociological ones. Sociological explanations of crime—and there are many—emphasize the role that society and social conditions (e.g., poverty, prestige, family structure or lack thereof, role of institutions such as church, lack of education, etc.) have on individual offenders. Theorists along these lines claim that we are products of our environment. Consequently, treating undesirable social conditions is the best way to address criminality in our society.

Profiles that rely on sociological theories of crime would suggest that the criminal justice system could expect crime from those quarters of our society that are run-down, impoverished, lacking traditional family households, lacking socioeconomic opportunities, and so on. A profile of "typical" violent offenders in a particular city might be juveniles who have no father figures at home, who live in poverty with drug use all around them, and who receive no moral instruction from those over them. Although many of the aforementioned elements in the profiles are associated with crime in America's urban areas, the practical application would require people to be treated differently on the basis of these conditions. This is a point already alleged by many—specifically, that the poor and minorities in this country are treated differently than others by the criminal justice system. As all are supposed equal before the bar of justice, inequitable treatment on the grounds of social status is offensive to most. Such profiling might be used, however, to identify needed points of intervention before the bar of justice is ever approached.

## Common Police Profiles

Criminal justice profiling by law enforcement has been extensively represented and glamorized in books and films. Many Americans with no connection to criminal justice professions could tell you about common types of criminal adversaries that are targeted by profiling. David Harris, in his book *Profiles in Injustice* (2003), described three of the most common police profiles categories that have been used with regularity: (1) the hijacker, (2) the serial killer, and (3) the drug courier. None of the profiles is in essence about race, gender, religion, or sexual orientation, but some of these classifications carry weight within the profiles.

## The Hijacker

Although much attention of law enforcement has been given to hijacking after the September 11 attacks, concern over the forcible commandeering of airliners has been with us for many years. In the late 1960s, U.S. airliners were successfully hijacked by the dozens. In 1968, 18 American airliners were hijacked; in 1969, more than 30 airliners were hijacked (Harris 2003).

Throughout the 1960s, many hijackings involved people from either the United States or Cuba fleeing one country and seeking asylum in the other. In the 1970s, hijackings continued, but took on a more violent character. In a few high-profile hijackings and attempted hijackings in the early 1970s, pilots were shot and commercial aircraft and their passengers were held for ransom (Bumgarner, Crawford, and Burns 2013).

In an effort to put a stop to this epidemic problem of air piracy, U.S. authorities developed a profile of potential hijackers. It was hoped that hijackers would be spotted by alert law enforcement officials before the hijackers ever got onto the airplanes. The hijacker profile was behavior driven and relied on observations made by airline personnel, starting at the ticket counter. Those individuals who acted suspiciously or in some way met the profile would be screened in greater detail. The screening would involve having flagged passengers pass through metal detectors and answer questions about their identity and destination. Hijacker profiling had limited success, and by 1973, the Federal Aviation Administration scrapped the program and simply began to require all passengers to pass through metal detection devices. Many believe it is time, in lieu of searches of randomly selected passengers, to bring hijacker profiling back and concentrate our limited security resources at airports on those most likely to pose a threat.

## The Serial Killer

The ability of law enforcement officials to profile serial killers and rapists is among the most glorified of law enforcement activities. Serial offender profiling is a relatively new police tactic that simply built upon the standard deductive reasoning process of traditional police investigations. Serial killer profiling really took root at the FBI Academy's Behavioral Science Unit. FBI special agent John Douglas and other FBI profilers became legendary in law enforcement circles for their ability to predict detailed characteristics about serial offenders based on patterns within the offenders' modus operandi (i.e., the methods, times, locations, and victims drawn from in committing the offense). As suggested earlier, profilers have generated much interest in the popular culture, thanks to fictional novel and motion picture portrayals of law enforcement profilers, as in Thomas Harris's *Red Dragon*, *Silence of the Lambs*, and *Hannibal* and in true crime reenactment television shows.

The premise of serial profiling is that much can be learned about violent serial offenders by talking to and analyzing previously identified serial offenders. Through interviewing identified serial killers and sex offenders, patterns and themes have in fact emerged concerning the upbringing, general background, and modus operandi of these offenders. The information is then used to predict (although not prove) the types of people that offenders may or may not be. Today, the FBI and many large state and local police agencies employ profilers whose knowledge and expertise about violent serial offenders can be drawn upon whenever suspicions arise that a serial or bizarre offender has committed crimes in their respective jurisdictions.

## Drug Courier

The development of drug courier profiles by our nation's drug enforcement agencies and police divisions in the 1980s war on drugs marked the beginning of widespread police profiling at the patrol officer level. After all, serial killings and hijackings are relatively uncommon criminal offenses, but drug trafficking is all around us. It was thought that if profiling as a police tool could be oriented toward drug traffickers, a significant dent in the drug trade through interdiction might be achieved (Harris 2003). Drug courier profiles initially were utilized primarily in airports by drug agents. Law enforcement officials would use profiles, that is, characteristics commonly associated with drug couriers, for screening arriving and departing passengers. Those passengers who fit the courier profile would then be temporarily detained and questioned. The passengers would not be under arrest. Rather, the detention merely amounted to an investigatory stop.

The U.S. Supreme Court upheld the use of drug courier profiling at our nation's ports of entry in the case *U.S. v. Sokolow* (1989). In that case, the defendant paid for his ticket with cash; he traveled under a name different than that which was listed with his telephone number; he made a round trip to Miami; he stayed in Miami only two days, although the travel time alone took 24 hours; he appeared nervous; and he did not check any luggage. The Supreme Court recognized the right of the police to be drawn to the obviously suspicious circumstances of Sokolow's traveling.

In time, the drug courier profile no longer was confined to the nation's international airports. Law enforcement, having perceived a level of effectiveness in profiling drug couriers at the ports of entry, developed profiles of couriers and traffickers on the roadways. Law enforcement began to ask, "What are the similarities among those motorists who transport drugs on the highways?" Volusia County (FL) Sheriff Bob Vogel, who was instrumental in mainstreaming the practice of profiling on the highways in the 1980s, used the term *cumulative similarities* rather than *profiles*. These similarities will be discussed later, but suffice to say here that the perceived success of the practice of courier profiling on the highways led to law enforcement's widespread use of it, which in turn led to its widespread criticism and incumbent controversy.

## Proactive and Reactive Profiling

Profiling by law enforcement officials can be thought of as either proactive or reactive, depending on the context. Proactive profiling occurs when officers on patrol utilize profiling as a tool to detect and prevent crime in the field. Reactive profiling is a tool used by criminal investigators to apprehend those who have already committed crimes. In other words, proactive profiling attempts to interdict and foil crime; reactive profiling seeks to solve crime.

Darin Fredrickson and Raymond Siljander defined proactive criminal justice profiling as the process whereby police officers "make judgments about another, relative to possible criminal activity, based on a number of overt and subtle factors which may or may not include things such as the person's race, manner of dress and grooming, behavioral characteristics, when and where the observation is made, the circumstances under which the observation is made, and relative to information the officer may already possess" (Fredrickson and Siljander 2002, 15). When discussion ensues about proactive criminal justice profiling done by patrol officers in the field, the discussion usually becomes one about racial profiling, as opposed to concern about other characteristics being singled out. This is because many of the voices of criticism concerning the tool of profiling come from community leaders in urban areas where the majority of residents are racial minorities— that is, African Americans, Hispanics, Asian Americans, and so on. In those urban areas, profiling is just one debate of many over various police strategies and practices that have been employed.

One especially controversial debate concerns that of the "broken windows" approach to patrol work. This approach, first proposed by James Q. Wilson and George E. Kelling, is based on the theory that if a neighborhood is allowed to run down, that situation breeds bigger problems. In fact, many crime prevention programs rely on the same assumptions. Vandalism, graffiti, broken windows in buildings, abandoned cars, and ill-kept properties are all thought to contribute to the image that people don't care in a particular neighborhood and that therefore crime can flourish. By contrast, neighborhoods that take care of the little things, such as running out the prostitutes and petty drug dealers, condemning drug houses and other substandard buildings, will broadcast a message that crime is not welcome here; take it somewhere else.

Broken windows, and its aggressive patrol tactics of questioning anyone raising suspicion and arresting people for minor offenses, was first practiced by the New York Transit Police and later by the New York Police Department (NYPD), both under the leadership of Bill Bratton. The use of broken windows policing is credited with dramatically reducing crime in the subway system in the early 1990s and then dramatically reducing crime in the City of New York in the mid- and late 1990s (Cleary 2000). Critics of broken windows' zero tolerance approach to the minor offenses point out, however, that the strategy puts the officers in the position of an occupying military force. Police have little opportunity to form partnerships with the community and build trust among the residents when they are preoccupied with stopping every suspected minor offender with the hopes of turning the case into something bigger. These critics tend to view profiling, however successful it may or may not be in detecting crime, as ultimately counterproductive because it alienates the police from the community; it sets the police against the community by suggesting that people who fit a stereotype are probably up to no-good.

In August 2013, in the case of *Floyd, et al. v. City of New York*, a federal district court judge ruled that the NYPD's policy of aggressively seeking opportunities to stop and frisk suspects whenever possible was unconstitutional. Evidence presented at the trial indicated that almost 90 percent of the 4.4 million people stopped and questioned by the police under this policy between 2004 and 2012 had done nothing wrong (Wise 2014). However, in October 2013, a panel of federal appellate judges blocked the lower court's decision and removed the district judge from the case on the basis that she exhibited bias against the NYPD. Finally, in November 2013, the same appellate court ultimately upheld the ruling that the NYPD's policy of "stop and frisk" was unconstitutional. The City of New York, under newly elected mayor Bill De Blasio (who campaigned against the police tactic as a candidate), chose not to appeal the decision.

As mentioned earlier, uniformed officers who engage in profiling are frequently attempting to snare drug offenders. Profiling for drug offenders—particularly drug couriers—involves consideration of the race of the motorist, the gender, age, route of travel, and the vehicle being driven.

In the 1980s, law enforcement began to identify certain interstate highways from points of origin such as Miami that served as main arteries for transporting drugs up the East Coast and into the interior of the country. What's more, police officers noted that offenders were frequently minorities, were young males, and utilized rental cars. Rental vehicles were ideal in that they were mechanically reliable (Fredrickson and Siljander 2002). With the advent of computer terminals in squad cars, rental cars offered added protection against detection by the police in that a license plate check by officers while driving would show the registered owner to be the rental company, rather than the driver—who might or might not have a warrant or be suspended or revoked. Indicators that a vehicle might be carrying drugs are many.

In profiling, it is the totality of the facts that generates sufficient suspicion to warrant further inquiry by the officer. These indicators, with regard to the vehicle, include (Fredrickson and Siljander 2002):

- rear end riding low (because of the weight of the drugs);
- spare tire or luggage in the back seat to make room for drugs in the t runk;
- tinted windows, or windows down during unusually hot or cold weather;
- modifications or alterations to the vehicle;
- very little, if any, luggage for out-of-state travelers;
- "good guy" decals such as religious symbols, pro-police stickers, or antidrug stickers;
- lifestyle statements, such as drug paraphernalia, decals of drugs, and decals of known drug-using rock bands;
- multiple deodorants in the vehicle to mask the smell of drugs;
- dirty vehicle with clean plates; and
- unusual driving,. especially perfect driving or driving too slowly.

Obviously, an individual may signal any number of these indicators and not actually be carrying drugs in his or her vehicle. But profiling plays the odds, and police note that the odds frequently pay off.

Profiling by patrol officers has frequently targeted other criminal activities as well. Profiling has been used very successfully to combat auto theft. Once again, race, age, and gender of the offender are pieces of a larger profile that also includes make of vehicle, number and type of occupants (a family, for example, would not fit the profile), direction of travel, and time of day.

The more glamorous and less controversial type of criminal justice profiling relates to reactive profiling—generally a tool of investigators rather than patrol officers. This type of profiling attempts to take facts and clues garnished from one or more crime scenes and develop a composite sketch of the likely type of person who committed the crime(s).

Today, the FBI is among the most noteworthy of agencies to employ criminal investigative profilers. The FBI's Behavioral Analysis Unit (BAU) and the Violent Criminal Apprehension Program are both organized under the FBI's National Center for the Analysis of Violent Crime (NCAVC), located at the FBI Academy in Quantico, Virginia. Both units are staffed with criminal profilers. The BAU's mission is to provide behavioral-based investigative and operational support to the FBI's own field agents as well as other law enforcement agencies. Each year, the NCAVC responds to over 1,500 requests for assistance from law enforcement agencies in the United States and from around the world (Bumgarner 2007).

Criminal investigators who are profilers, such as those who work in the FBI's Behavioral Analysis Unit, perform their services in the pursuit of three goals (Holmes 1989):

1. to provide the criminal justice system with a social and psychological assessment of the offender;

2. to provide the criminal justice system with a psychological evaluation of belongings found in the possession of the offender; and

3. to provide interviewing suggestions and strategies.

The first goal relates to identifying the offender. The assessment will include basic information that is hypothesized about the offender in a particular case. The information will include a guess as to the offender's age, sex, race, religion, employment, marital status, education, and any other relevant factors that can be reasonably inferred.

The second and third goals of the criminal investigator/profiler are geared toward shoring up the case against a suspect once identified. Souvenirs and mementos taken from the victims and from other sources that are found in a suspect's possession can provide greater psychological insight as to what motivated the offender to offend in the way he or she did. Profilers will also help the primary investigators with strategies for questioning suspects. Based on the profile developed, it might be thought that certain points of conversation might be hot buttons worth pushing. Or it might be supposed that the suspect would love to tell his or her story, and therefore a more congenial approach would be fruitful.

Investigative profiling is generally reserved for the most serious types of offenses, such as rape and murder. Those who are experts in profiling are few and therefore their efforts tend to be channeled in that direction. As suggested earlier, criminal profiling is simply an extension of deductive reasoning utilized by police for ages. Some critics say that profiling murderers and rapists is a practice that requires no special expertise and exists as a science only in the minds of those who do it. One psychologist suggested that most profiles submitted for consideration in an investigation are either too vague and ambiguous to be useful or simple statements of common sense that did not require an expert from Quantico, Virginia, to make (Holmes 1989).

## Prosecutorial and Judicial Profiling

Profiling is generally thought of as a law enforcement issue. There is growing attention, however, to profiling in prosecutorial and judicial venues of the criminal justice system as well.

Although law enforcement has an argument that profiling is a tool that helps identify criminal suspects, there is significantly less rationale for considering race, gender, or other characteristics when it comes to prosecution decisions or rulings from the bench. And yet, evidence does suggest that racial, gender, and other differences among people seem to matter as, in the aggregate, they are treated differently. In the next chapter, an examination of the discretion criminal justice officials have includes segments on prosecutorial and judicial discretion. Also, in a later chapter, summaries of several studies concerning real and alleged unequal treatment of various groups under the law by prosecutors and judges will be presented. You will have the opportunity to draw your own conclusions as to the legitimacy of charges of bias in the criminal justice system, whether it exists intentionally or not.

## References

Archbold, C. A. 2013. *Policing: A Text/Reader.* Thousand Oaks, CA: SAGE.

Bumgarner, J. 2007. Criminal Profiling and Public Policy. In: R. Kocsis (Ed.). *Criminal Profiling: International Theory, Research, and Practice.* Totowa, NJ: Humana Press.

Bumgarner, J., C. Crawford, and R. Burns. 2013. *Federal Law Enforcement: A Primer.* Durham, NC: Carolina Academic Press.

Carlson, D. P. 2002. *When Cultures Clash.* Upper Saddle River, NJ: Prentice Hall.

Cleary, J. 2000. *Racial Profiling Studies in Law Enforcement: Issues and Methodology.* St. Paul: State of Minnesota, House of Representatives Research Department.

Cole, G. F., and C. E. Smith. 2001. *The American System of Criminal Justice.* 9th ed. Stamford, CT: Wadsworth.

Cole, G. F., C. E. Smith, and C. DeJong. 2014. *The American System of Criminal Justice.* 14th ed. Belmont, CA: Wadsworth.

Deakin, T. J. 1988. *Police Professionalism: Renaissance of American Law Enforcement.* Springfield, IL: Charles C. Thomas.

Dye, T. R. 2010. *Politics in America.* 9th ed. London: Pearson/ Longman.

Fredrickson, D. D., and R. P. Siljander. 2002. *Racial Profiling.* Springfield, IL: Charles C. Thomas.

Hadden, S. 2001. *Slave Patrols: Law and Violence in Virginia and the Carolinas.* Cambridge, MA: Harvard University Press.

Halloran, L. 2014. New Climate for Drug Sentencing, Guidelines Expected to Change. *NPR: It's All Politics,* March 13. Retrieved from http://www.npr.org/blogs/itsallpolitics/ 2014/03/13 /289817341/ew-climate-for-drug-sentenc ing-guidelines-expected-to-change.

Harris, D. A. 2003. *Profiles in Injustice.* New York: The New Press.

Hobbes, T. 1651. *Leviathan.* Reprint, London: J. M. Dent and Sons, 1965.

Holmes, R. M. 1989. *Profiling Violent Crimes.* Newbury Park, CA: Sage.

International Association of Chiefs of Police. 2003. Legislative Updates section. Retrieved from http://www.theiacp.org/ leg_policy.

Mills, C. W. 1956. *The Power Elite.* New York: Oxford University Press.

National Commission on Crime Control and Prevention. 1994. *Final Report.* Washington, DC.

Peak, K. J., and R. W. Glesnor. 2012. *Community Policing and Problem Solving: Strategies and Practices.* 6th ed. Upper Saddle River, NJ: Prentice Hall.

Roberg, R., K. Novak, G. Cordner, and B. Smith. 2012. *Police and Society.* 5th ed. New York: Oxford University Press.

Samaha, J. 2005. *Criminal Justice.* 7th ed. Belmont, CA: Cengage.

Samaha, J. 1994. *Criminal Justice.* 3rd ed. St. Paul, MN: West.

Schmalleger, F. 2012. *Criminal Justice Today.* 12th ed. Upper Saddle River, NJ: Prentice Hall.

Schott, R. G. 2001. The Role of Race in Law Enforcement. *FBI Law Enforcement Bulletin,* November, 24–32.

Sparrow, M. K., M. H. Moore, and D. M. Kennedy. 1990. *Beyond 911: A New Era for Policing.* New York: HarperCollins.

Uchida, C. 2001. The Development of the American Police: An Historical Overview. In: R. G. Dunham and G. P. Alpert (Eds.). *Critical Issues in Policing.* 4th ed. Prospect Heights, IL: Waveland, 18–35.

Walker, S. 1977. *A Critical History of Police Reform.* Lexington, MA: Lexington Books.

Walker, S., C. Spohn, and M. DeLone. 2012. *The Color of Justice: Race, Ethnicity, and Crime in America.* Belmont, CA: Wadsworth.

Wise, D. 2014. "Removing the Judge Who Ruled 'Stop and Frisk' Unconstitutional Is a Blow to Justice." *The Nation,* January 27. Retrieved from http://www.thenation.com/issue/january-27-2014

## Stereotyping and Profiling

Many policy makers, and a broad swath of society in general, view stereotyping and profiling as synonyms for one another. In doing so, all the negative connotations of profiling are thereby attached to stereotyping. When Neighborhood Watch member George Zimmerman shot and killed teenager Trayvon Martin in Sanford, Florida, in 2012, many pundits and community leaders focused on the stereotyping that Zimmerman, in their minds, surely must have engaged in. They weren't alone. The State Attorney's Office charged Zimmerman with murder and manslaughter because it too believed that Martin died as a result of Zimmerman's stereotyping. Martin was a black teenage male, wearing a "hoodie" sweatshirt with the hood pulled over his head while he walked through yards in Zimmerman's neighborhood. The prosecutors alleged that Zimmerman improperly stereotyped Martin on the basis of his race, gender, age, and clothing to conclude that Martin was a prospective criminal up to no good (when in fact, Martin was just walking from a convenience store to his father's fiancé's home located in the neighborhood).

At his trial in 2013, Zimmerman was acquitted of all charges because evidence was presented that supported the defense

---

The shooting death in Florida of Trayvon Martin by neighborhood watch captain George Zimmerman in 2012 sparked protests all around the country. Demonstrators, such as these in New York City's Union Square, regularly donned hoodies to commemorate Martin and to show that the presence of a hoodie does not mean the wearer is a hoodlum. (AP Photo/ Mary Altaffer) team's assertion that Martin was the initial aggressor. However, what was not in dispute was the fact that Martin was thought by Zimmerman to be a suspicious character. After all, Zimmerman called the police about Martin and followed him on foot while he was on the phone with the police dispatcher. So, how much did Zimmerman's assessment of Martin, based on Martin's appearance, play into a fight that would result in injuries to Zimmerman and a fatal gunshot wound to Martin? Would this confrontation have happened if Martin had been white, middle-aged, and dressed in business clothes while cutting through people's yards?

Profiling is certainly related to stereotyping but is not the same thing. Profiling is an act. In criminal justice, profiling involves the taking of some action by criminal justice officials based on observable conditions, behaviors, and activities. Stereotyping, on the other hand, is not action oriented; it is perception oriented (Lee, Albright, and Malloy 2001). Stereotyping is the ascription of characteristics to social groups or segments of society (Banaji and Bhaskar 2000).

That having been said, stereotypes help shape the meaning of the observations for the person doing the observing. Given the relationship of stereotyping to the formation of meaning and context for one engaged in criminal justice profiling, it is important to understand more thoroughly the concept of stereotyping. Stereotyping is essentially a shortcut to perceiving people. Stereotypes can be rooted in truth or falsehood, or somewhere in between. But whatever their veracity, stereotypes allow people, including criminal justice officials, to start from somewhere other than zero when sizing up other people. Obviously in a criminal justice system such as ours, where all people are to be treated equally and are presumed to be law-abiding, stereotyping raises ethical quandaries apart from its utility.

Stereotypes can be thought of along two dimensions: accuracy and valence (Lee, Jussim, and McCauley 1995). Accuracy relates to the question of just how much the set of inferences in the mind of the perceiver matches the objectively measured (i.e., actual) qualities of the group in question. A stereotype can be thought of as existing along a continuum, ranging from completely accurate to completely inaccurate.

Although accuracy can be objectively measured, valence is more subjective. The dimension of valence relates to the degree that a stereotype is positive or negative. Sometimes the characterization of something as positive or negative depends on the perspective of the observer. One observer says: "Wow, that glass is half full!" A second says: "Darn, that glass is half empty." The first observer clearly is happy with as much in the glass as there is; the second is clearly disappointed. Both observers are accurate—the glass contains one half of its maximum capacity.

In the case of stereotypes, when the dimensions of accuracy and valence are brought together, four realms within which stereotypical perceptions are cast emerge (see Figure 2.1). Given that stereotypes shape context and meaning for an observer (to include criminal justice officials), understanding these realms becomes important.

From Figure 2.1, it is evident that a stereotype can be accurate and positive, accurate and negative, inaccurate and

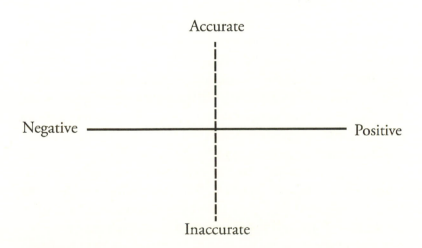

Figure 2.1    Inersection of Accuracy and Valence (Lee, et al.)

positive, and inaccurate and negative. To the extent that stereotypes are drawn upon (and all humans draw upon them), the ideal is that a stereotype is accurate and positive. By contrast, clearly the worst kinds of stereotypes are those that are inaccurate and negative. Such stereotypes can be slanderous and vicious. In the middle are those stereotypes that are inaccurate but positive and accurate but negative. For example, the stereotype that Asian Americans are really smart is positive. Who doesn't want to be thought of as "smart"? The degree to which it is accurate—particularly for all Asian Americans—is debatable and subject to further evaluation. Maybe after looking at college entrance scores for Asian American high school students across the country and comparing them to other high school students, we might come to conclude that the stereotype is more accurate than not but fail to legitimately claim that it is completely accurate. Or we might not. But it is measurable; the accuracy is verifiable. With regard to the issue of criminal justice profiling, and knowing that profiles are influenced, if not driven, by stereotypes, we can consider the combinations of accuracy and valence characterizing those stereotypes to help assess the legitimacy of a given profile.

Profiles rooted in a negative and inaccurate stereotype are unfair, unethical, immoral, and counterproductive (particularly due to the inaccuracy element). A stereotype that all urban African Americans are into drugs and crime is not only extremely negative and unfair to law-abiding African Americans, but it is wildly inaccurate, thereby resulting in false investigations and accusations of innocent people at the expense of more reasoned efforts against the genuinely guilty.

On the other hand, a stereotype that all Hispanic teenage males, in particular Los Angeles neighborhoods, who wear certain colored bandanas and have their pants hang low, exposing their boxer shorts, are gang members is one that is rooted in some truth. Although it would not be completely accurate (i.e., true for *all* such persons), it may be largely accurate despite the negative connotation of being linked to gang membership.

Law-abiding Hispanic teens wearing such clothing in the afore-mentioned way may find the negative stereotype offensive, but it largely works for law enforcement—thereby giving them a shortcut in making initial judgments of such people. When police officers in Los Angeles pay special attention to such people while ignoring others, all because of the relatively accurate stereotype, they have engaged in profiling.

In short, stereotypes that are positive and accurate are not controversial. Stereotypes that are positive and inaccurate are not useful. Stereotypes that are negative and inaccurate are harmful and not useful. Stereotypes that are negative and accurate are controversial. It is this realm that criminal justice officials, and particularly law enforcement officers, claim to occupy when they profile. They argue that it is unfortunate that this group or that group is subject to a negative stereotype, but the "shoe fits." Community leaders, on the other hand, argue that the criminal justice system is too often in the realm of the negatively inaccurate. They argue that the culture of criminal justice in the United States perpetuates myths about groups of people—blacks, Hispanics, young males, gays—that are simply not true. Consequently, acting on those stereotypes predictably results in the harassment of the innocent and overreaction to the guilty.

## Police Discretion

To the extent that criminal profiling by the police is a permitted and accepted practice in law enforcement, it is a manifestation of police discretion. Any discussion about reforming the use of profiling as a tool necessarily implies the need to curtail police discretion. Long before profiling emerged as a particular controversial issue in criminal justice, politicians, academicians, and practitioners were debating the appropriate limits of police discretion. So, exactly what is police discretion?

Discretion exists when a police officer's effective limits on his or her power leave the officer free to make a choice among possible courses of action or inaction. It is worth noting that the emphasis is on the effective limits of the officer's power, not simply what is legal or what is authorized; the range of decisions available to an officer may include options that are illegal or of questionable illegality (Evans 1978). In light of this definition, police officer discretion might simply be paraphrased as an officer having a choice in how to respond to a situation.

Discretion is what governs an officer's decision to pull over a traffic law violator or not, or to give him a ticket, or her a warning. It governs the detective's decision to work a particular case aggressively, or minimally, or whether to open the case to begin with. Discretion is everywhere in law enforcement; many police reformers and critics would like to rein it in.

Dean Champion and George Rush, in their book *Policing in the Community* (1997), presented a number of reasons that support the need for police officer discretion. The reasons include the following:

- some laws are too vague to expect that they be enforced with regularity;
- police have limited resources and therefore must pick their battles;
- enforcing all laws as written without discretion would cause community alienation;
- discretion enables officers to individualize the law (e.g., electing to take a juvenile vandal home to his parents when it is believed that this juvenile will be responsive to sanctions imposed by the parents); and
- many violations are minor.

Advocates of giving police a wide berth in decision making point to these arguments and others. There are problems with police discretion as well. Samuel Walker noted that uncontrolled discretion can result in (Walker 1999):

- denial of due process for suspects;
- denial of equal protection under the law;

- poor police-community relations, particularly when most of the discretionary decisions to enforce the law are concentrated in particular communities or neighborhoods;
- poor personnel management; and
- poor planning and policy development.

Additionally, discretionary enforcement of the law can reduce the deterrent effect of the law and, because of discretion's hidden nature, can make officer decisions difficult to review (Brooks 2001).

There are four basic categories of variables that influence police discretionary decision making. These are organizational variables, neighborhood variables, situational variables, and individual factors (Roberg, Crank, and Kuykendall 2000).

Organizational variables include things such as the bureaucratic nature of police departments and the criminal justice system. A growing number of police departments require that for every traffic stop, a form be completed to document the race and gender of the driver, as well as the reasons for the stop and outcome. Additionally, an officer would still be required to complete the initial contact report (ICR) and the citation or warning, if one is issued. For a number of officers, pulling over motorists for other than the most serious of violations is too much hassle. Consequently, the organizational variables—in this case paperwork—are an influence on officers' decisions to not pull people over (a decision within the realm of their discretion).

Neighborhood variables refer to the characteristics of a neighborhood that make policing a unique experience. Things such as the racial and ethnic homogeneity or diversity of a community could be a factor in the decisions an officer makes. Likewise, the economy and business makeup of a community will have an impact as well. If the neighborhood being policed is a suburban residential community with little more than light industry and heavy commuter traffic, then traffic enforcement might be the normal operation for officers not responding to calls. A working-class neighborhood with numerous small shops and even some manufacturing facilities, however, may require that officers spend more time engaging in preventative patrol around those businesses to guard against break-ins or holdups; that would leave less time for traffic enforcement.

Situational variables refer to specific factors relating to an incident to which the officer is responding and/or which the officer is resolving. Factors that are situational include how the officer came into the situation (was the officer dispatched or did he or she just happen along), the demeanor and attitude of the parties involved, the gender of the parties involved, the relationship between the complainant and the suspect, the type of offense, the location, and the presence of others.

For example, if an officer happens upon a dispute between neighbors, he or she might choose to handle it less formally than if the officer had been dispatched. Or if an officer responds to a misdemeanor assault, the officer may be more inclined to make an arrest in lieu of a citation if the parties have an "intimate" relationship (ironically, officers were more likely to have exactly the opposite reaction only a few years ago—prior to heightened attention given to domestic violence). Still another example of situational variables includes the demeanor of the suspect. If a motorist carries on with outrage about being stopped for speeding, he will almost certainly receive a citation. If a motorist is polite and apologetic, and the offense wasn't too serious, many officers would be inclined to give a warning instead. A bad attitude is not illegal; yet those people with bad attitudes frequently receive harsher treatment from agents within the criminal justice system. Whether that's fair or not, it is obvious evidence of discretion.

The final category of variable is that which relates to the officer's individuality. In other words, these variables are specific to the officer and include the officer's education, experience, age, race, gender, and career ambitions. Officers with less experience will make different discretionary decisions than those with more experience. Officers who treat their job as just a job, or who are cynical, will make different decisions than those who view law enforcement as their life's calling and approach their occupation with passion. Officers who are members of an ethnic or racial minority may be more sympathetic with others from that group and more understanding of their culture and their plight. Perhaps female officers may be more diplomatic than many male officers. All these factors can and do impact the decisions police officers make in the field on a daily, and hourly, basis.

## Charging Decisions

Prosecutors throughout the United States have considerable discretion in determining who is going to be charged and with what. Clearly, things such as race or ethnicity should not enter into the decision making about what charges, if any, should be brought against one subject or another. Yet there have been studies that suggest that prosecutors tend to be lenient in their decisions toward female offenders and more likely to prosecute racial minorities over whites (Schmalleger 1999) or to upgrade charges against minorities while downgrading them for whites (Robinson 2002).

Sorensen and Wallace (1999) studied the pretrial stages of prosecutorial decision making in capital murder cases. They found that racial disparity existed in prosecutorial decisions, even after controlling for legally relevant factors relating to the offense. They noted that homicides involving blacks killing whites were more likely to result in first degree murder charges than any other racial combination. The study focused on the prosecutorial decisions in an unnamed Midwestern state and county over a six-year period of time. The study, if accurate, suggested that prosecutors were indeed allowing nonlegitimate factors—race and/or other factors which themselves were significantly correlated to race—to influence their charging decisions.

But prosecutors, of course, are called upon to use their discretion and make decisions. They can't prosecute all cases brought to them. All cases are not equal in their merit, quality of evidence, severity, importance to the public, and so on. So, how do prosecutors decide which cases are worthy of their efforts, and which are less of a priority? The U.S. Department of Justice has long offered guidelines to federal prosecutors to gauge whether a particular case should be pursued or not. The guidelines ask prosecutors to consider (U.S. Department of Justice 2002):

- federal law enforcement priorities of the day,
- the nature and seriousness of the offense,
- the deterrent effect of prosecution,
- the person's culpability in connection with the offense,
- the person's criminal history,
- the person's willingness to cooperate in the investigation, and
- the probable sentence or consequences if the prosecution is successful.

Obviously, nowhere among the consideration criteria is there listed race, gender, sexual orientation, or other factors not related to the criminal activity itself.

In criminal justice literature, three decision-making models have emerged to help explain how prosecutors accept or decline individual cases: legal sufficiency model, system efficiency model, and trial sufficiency model (Jacoby 1979). The three models vary according to how strong the case must be prior to acceptance for prosecution.

The legal sufficiency model requires only the minimum level of legal elements necessary to prove a case against a suspect. Prosecutors operating under this model will tend to accept virtually all cases given to them by the police, knowing that the majority of them will be plea-bargained away before ever reaching trial. That outcome is fine with them because many of these cases are questionable as to whether proof beyond a reasonable doubt (the standard for a conviction) could be demonstrated in court. Attorneys operating under this model are comfortable with the fact that many of these cases will eventually be dismissed. The system efficiency model is a little more stringent in standards. The weak cases are screened out upon receipt from law enforcement. Then, of those that remain, the majority are disposed of outside of court. Fewer cases are expected by the prosecutor to be dismissed altogether, however, because the truly lousy cases are not pursued from the start. Although these cases are stronger, there is still an emphasis on plea bargains and diversions, given the volume of cases and the time it takes for a prosecutor to try a case.

The trial sufficiency model is the most stringent in screening cases. Prosecutors operating according to the trial sufficiency model will only accept cases that clearly have enough evidence to win at trial. In other words, the outcome of getting a conviction upon trying the case, whether before a judge or a jury, is not in doubt in the prosecutor's mind. With such cases, plea-bargaining is not common. If plea-bargaining does take place, the terms will be especially favorable to the prosecutor. Given the volume of cases generated in the urban areas, prosecutors are frequently overwhelmed with case decisions. Urban prosecutor offices often follow one of the first two models and emphasize plea-bargaining as a means to dispose of cases. Plea bargains mean convictions. Given that urban areas have large minority populations, it is not surprising to see large numbers of minority convictions. But is it fair?

In 1886, the Supreme Court addressed the question about the legality of racial motivation in bringing charges against suspects. The Court said clearly in *Yick Wo v. Hopkins* that it was impermissible for racial discrimination to be a motive in charging decisions. Since then, however, the Supreme Court has upheld in case after case the right of prosecutors to decide who and how to charge, short of breaking the law (McCoy 1998).

In *Wayte v. U.S.* (1985), the Supreme Court affirmed the government's right of prosecutorial discretion, as long as it is not intentionally discriminatory. The Court said that discretion is broad but not "unfettered." Even so, in order to quash an allegedly discriminatory prosecution, the burden of proof is on the defendant to show that:

- the government's prosecution had discriminatory effect, and

- the government intended to discriminate along illegal classification lines (e.g., race, religion, etc.).

Further, the Supreme Court has allowed prosecutors, in making the decision to prosecute or not, to consider factors outside the strict merits of the case, such as community sentiment. Consider the case against the Los Angeles police officers who had beaten Rodney King in 1992. They had been tried for and acquitted of criminal assault against King. Customarily, the U.S. Justice Department does not retry cases that were lost at the state level, unless there was a substandard prosecutorial effort made at the state level. That was certainly not the case regarding the effort of the Los Angeles County District Attorney's Office. Even so, the community's sentiment cried out for another prosecution, and the U.S. Justice Department obliged.

## In Court

The entrances and hallways to courtrooms across the United States are frequently adorned with icons of equal justice for all, such as pictures or statues of Lady Justice, blindfolded and holding her scales. Indeed, the emphasis on formal procedures to ensure due process and equal protection would make one think that profiling, that is, classification consciousness, would have no place there; regardless of how one comes to be there, all are equal upon stepping into the courthouse. However, even in the courthouse, there has historically been a place for profiling by class (race, gender, etc.). The courthouse activity most touched today by the practice of profiling is the jury selection process. Jury selection is one area in the trial process where attorneys have some latitude in their ability to discriminate. Through voir dire, which refers to the questioning of prospective jurors by the prosecution and defense attorneys to screen out individuals the attorneys believe are biased or incapable of delivering a fair verdict, attorneys can have jurors stricken from the jury pool.

During the voir dire process, prosecutors and defense attorneys are granted the ability to make a limited number of peremptory challenges and an unlimited number of challenges for cause. Peremptory challenges traditionally meant that an attorney could disqualify a potential juror for any reason or for no reason at all. The attorney needed only to feel uncomfortable with that juror, and he or she would be excused from jury duty in that case. There are limits to the number of peremptory challenges attorneys can exercise. The precise number depends on the jurisdiction, but customarily, the defense has more preemptory challenges than does the prosecutor.

Challenges for cause are when either the prosecutor or the defense attorney can convince the judge, based on objective evidence, that a prospective juror is likely incapable of rendering a fair verdict and therefore must be removed. A potential juror whose husband was killed in a robbery might be fine as juror in a tobacco lawsuit but is too likely to be biased against the defendant in a robbery or murder case. In such a case, the judge would strike the juror from service, and neither side would lose one of its peremptory challenges.

Historically and through legal imposition, juries consisted of white men. Over time, the laws changed to allow women and minorities to serve on juries. What was permissible under the law, however, was not always seen as desirable by attorneys trying the cases. Indeed, through peremptory challenges and through challenges for cause based on flimsy rationales of jury bias offered to sympathetic judges, women and minorities continued to be discriminated against when it came to jury duty. The U.S. Supreme Court has a track record of eyeing discriminatory jury pools and peremptory challenges with suspicion when a particular race or group of people is excluded from jury duty. As far back as the 1879 case of *Strauder v. West Virginia*, the Court said that a defendant who is a racial minority is deprived of equal protection under the Fourteenth Amendment when members of his or her race are purposefully excluded from the jury. The law in place that was struck down by the Court was West Virginia's 1873 law concerning who could serve on juries. It read: "All white male persons who are twenty-one years of age and who are citizens of this State shall be liable to serve as jurors, except as herein provided." The persons excepted were state officials.

As David Cole noted in his book *No Equal Justice* (1999), the Court in *Strauder* recognized that race matters. Strauder was denied equal protection through the exclusion of black jurors because there was an assumption that black and white jurors, especially in the post–Civil War era, would evaluate a black defendant differently.

Ironically, the practice of excluding jurors on the basis of race would be challenged 100 years later relying precisely on the opposite conclusion—namely, that there should be no presumption that one race is inherently biased against the other and is incapable of rendering a fair verdict. If that were true, say some, then the Supreme Court erred in *Strauder* in its reasoning by assuming that an all-white jury could not fairly evaluate Strauder. Despite the *Strauder* case, discrimination against minorities who would serve on juries continued for decades with the Supreme Court's blessing via its upholding of convictions. In *Smith v. Mississippi* (1896), the Court upheld a conviction of a black man convicted by an all-white jury, despite the fact that there were 1,300 black voters and only 300 white voters in the county and that no blacks had ever been selected to serve as jurors in that county since their emancipation (Cole 1999).

In the case of *Neal v. Delaware* (1881), however, the U.S. Supreme Court was compelled to find in favor of a black defendant because the lower courts (in particular, the Delaware Supreme Court) actually put to paper their unfettered bias against blacks. Even though the State of Delaware had a population of less than 150,000, whereas its black residents totaled over 26,000, and had never had a black citizen serve as a juror in the history of the state, the Delaware Supreme Court upheld the bias against black jurors and therefore the conviction against Neal by an all-white jury, stating in part: "That none but white men were selected is in no wise remarkable in view of the fact that—too notorious to be ignored—that the great body of black men residing in the State are utterly unqualified by want of intelligence, experience, or moral integrity to sit on juries. Exceptions there are, unquestionably, but they are rare. . . ." (103 US 370).

Even in 1881, the U.S. Supreme Court could not let that one go. In the Court's words, such a rationale excluding blacks from jury duty amounted to a "violent presumption" about the fitness of blacks to engage in jury service. Despite *Strauder* and *Neal*, however, the Supreme Court, with rare exception, let stand numerous convictions rooted in all-white juries for decades to come (Cole 1999). It was not until the latter part of the 20th century that the Supreme Court began to consistently afford relief to defendants convicted by juries derived from suspect pools or by suspect challenges.

In *Batson v. Kentucky* (1986), the Supreme Court overturned a conviction because prosecutors had used the peremptory challenge to exclude black jurors, and the trial judge did not require a rational explanation for the exclusions.

In 1991, the U.S. Supreme Court heard the case of *Powers v. Ohio*. In that case, the Supreme Court declared that it was unconstitutional to issue preemptory challenges in a criminal case if the challenge was based on race. The court declared that the very fact that [members of a particular race] are singled out and expressly denied . . . all right to participate in the administration of the law, as jurors, because of their color, though they are citizens, and may be in other respects fully qualified, is practically a brand upon them, affixed by the law, an assertion of their inferiority, and a stimulant to that race prejudice which is an impediment to securing individuals of that race equal justice which the law aims to secure to all others (499 US400).

Later in the same term, the U.S. Supreme Court declared that racially motivated peremptory challenges were likewise unconstitutional in civil cases. The Court said in *Edmonson v. Leesville Concrete Company, Inc.* (1991), that "it is clear that neither prosecutor nor civil attorneys in the future will be able to exclude minority potential jurors consistently unless they are able to articulate clearly credible race-neutral rationales for their actions" (500 US 614).

Then, in the case of *J.E.B. v. Alabama* (1994), the U.S. Supreme Court extended the logic against racially motivated peremptory challenges to those challenges motivated by gender. Gender discrimination was very common in peremptory challenges, as women were often seen by prosecutors as less likely to grant the death penalty in capital cases and, ironically, as harsher critics of female victims of sexual violence who are perceived to have contributed to their victimization by their lifestyle choices.

The Supreme Court wrote in *J.E.B.*:

> The Equal Protection Clause prohibits discrimination in jury selection on the basis of gender, or on the assumption that an individual will be biased in a particular case solely because that person happens to be a woman or a man. Respondent's gender-based peremptory challenges cannot survive the heightened equal protection scrutiny that this Court affords distinctions based on gender. Respondent's rationale—that its decision to strike virtually all males in this case may reasonably have been based on the perception, supported by history, that men otherwise totally qualified to serve as jurors might be more sympathetic and receptive

to the arguments of a man charged in a paternity action, while women equally qualified might be more sympathetic and receptive to the arguments of the child's mother—is virtually unsupported and is based on the very stereotypes the law condemns. The conclusion that litigants may not strike potential jurors solely on the basis of gender does not imply the elimination of all peremptory challenges. So long as gender does not serve as a proxy for bias, unacceptable jurors may still be removed, including those who are members of a group or class that is normally subject to . . . "rational basis" review and those who exhibit characteristics that are disproportionately associated with one gender. (000 US U10411)

The dissenting justices in the *J.E.B. v. Alabama* case, observing that a growing number of preclusions were cropping up to the historically absolute right of peremptory challenges, noted that "the core of the Court's reasoning [to ban preemptory challenges when based on discrimination against a protected class] is that peremptory challenges on the basis of any group characteristic subject to heightened scrutiny are inconsistent with the guarantee of the Equal Protection Clause. . . . Since all groups are subject to the peremptory challenge . . . it is hard to see how any group is denied equal protection."

Despite the decisions in *Batson v. Kentucky*, *Powers v. Ohio* (1991), *Edmonson v. Leesville Concrete*, and *J.E.B. v. Alabama*, discrimination against potential jurors, and by extension, defendants, did not end. As the Court said in *Edmonson*, the attorneys would have to articulate clearly credible race-neutral (and later, gender-neutral) rationales for their actions. But what is "credible"?

The lower limits of the term were put to the test in the 1995 case of *Purkett v. Elem*. In this case, prosecutors removed jurors of one particular race. The trial judge, according to the *Batson* ruling, asked the prosecutor to provide nonracially motivated reasons for removal of the prospective jurors.

The prosecutor responded:

I struck [juror] number twenty-two because of his longhair. He had long curly hair. He had the longest hair of anybody on the panel by far. He appeared to not be a good juror for that fact, the fact that he had long hair hanging down shoulder length, curly, unkempt hair. Also, he had a mustache and a goatee type beard. And juror number twenty-four also has a mustache and goatee type beard. Those are the only two people on the jury . . . with facial hair. . . . And I don't like the way they looked, with the way the hair is cut, both of them. And the mustaches and the beards look suspicious tome. (000 US U10277)

The U.S. Supreme Court, in a vote of 7–2, upheld the striking of those prospective jurors, despite the objectively silly reasons offered by the prosecutor, because the trial judge asked for, received, and accepted the nonracially motivated explanation for the exclusions. The Supreme Court left in place the use of peremptory challenges. Had it ruled otherwise, it effectively would have left only those challenges that were based on reasonable concerns about juror fitness, which is the definition of challenges for cause.

One interesting fact about the legal and illegal profiling that takes place by both prosecuting and defense attorneys during voir dire is that the prevalence of it has not drawn that much attention. Scholars who spend time exploring the fairness of the criminal justice system are certainly aware of the jury selection issue, but it has not captured the public's attention, nor that of their elected representatives, as the issue of police profiling has. Perhaps one explanation is that police profiling involves encounters between the system (in the form of the police) and citizens, guilty and innocent. By contrast, at least in the public's eye, profiling in court only affects the guilty. "Why else would they be in court if they weren't guilty, after all?"

The subtlety of this profiling, coupled with its belated position along the criminal justice chain of events, means it will likely remain an issue of interest to academic types and activists, but few others.

## At Sentencing

Still another point in the criminal justice process where profiling of a sort can occur is at the sentencing phase. Many scholars have examined sentencing for different types of bias. There have been many criminological studies which have concluded that criminal sentences handed down in the United States are routinely contaminated with bias. Scholars point to disparity of sentences between those received by blacks and whites, Hispanics and whites, men and women, minority juveniles and white juveniles, male juveniles and female juveniles, and so on.

The assertion of many of these studies, or at least the implication of them, is that the sentencing process is unfair in light of the statistics that emerge. If the sentencing patterns are disparate, that is, if they do indeed reflect real differences between groups, then is it a result of some sort of judicial profiling, or do other explanations prevail? If it is profiling at the heart of many of these disparities, then it must be judges and juries who are doing so. How can this be when procedures are supposed to be in place to ensure fairness and neutrality? Is it really possible that judges may consider things such as race or sex of the convicted when handing down a sentence?

Some inferences might be drawn from the studies highlighted later in this handbook. But first, to put those studies in context, one must understand how sentencing in the United States works. Keep in mind that differences do exist from state to state. Even so, there are some basic commonalities among most sentencing procedures in criminal courts across the country.

Upon conviction of a crime, punishment is doled out to the offender. Punishments vary because the goals of punishment vary. Indeed, there are many goals of punishment. One goal is retribution, that is, punishment for punishment's sake because it is deserved. Another goal of punishment is deterrence; it is hoped that being punished will deter that individual offender from offending again (specific deterrence) and will be a lesson to the rest of us not to engage in that same criminal behavior (general deterrence). A third goal of punishment, especially involving incarceration, is that of incapacitation. In other words, through punishment, the public will be protected from the offender for at least the duration of the punishment. A final goal of punishment is rehabilitation. This last goal is not about being punitive to the offender, but rather restorative. Rehabilitation seeks to treat the underlying causes of criminal behavior in the offender and then restore that person to society as a constructive and law-abiding member.

Depending on the circumstances of the case, a judge may seek to achieve any one or more of these goals in handing down a sentence. And it is the judge who is responsible for sentencing. In states where juries make recommendations as to the sentence, the judge has the ultimate responsibility of deciding whether to follow the jury's recommendations or to do something different. In fact, in the U.S. Supreme Court case of *Ring v. Arizona* (2002), the Court reiterated that juries are deciders of facts while judges impose sentences relying on those facts.

This does not mean that judges have absolute, unrestrained discretion in their sentences. Sentencing for crimes is usually broadly (but sometimes specifically) proscribed in the penal codes of each state. There are three types of sentences in the United States: indeterminate, determinate, and mandatory.

Indeterminate sentences are sentences for an indefinite period of time that specifies a minimum and maximum period to be spent incarcerated. This type of sentencing is generally associated with rehabilitation because it allows for an offender to be paroled and released at such time within the minimum and maximum sentencing range that the offender is sufficiently treated and reformed to return to society. Over two-thirds of the states permit judges to set indeterminate sentences for at least some offenses.

Determinate sentences are those that set a specific period of time to be served. Fourteen states rely on determinate sentences instead of indeterminate ones. Over half the states use determinate sentences for at least some offenses (Champion 2008). Even though the judge must prescribe a specific sentence with determinate sentencing, the judge often still has discretion. Determinate sentencing relies on sentencing guidelines passed by the legislature that list presumptive sentences for offenses (i.e., the sentences the judge should give to the offender absent some reason not to). An upward or downward departure from that presumptive sentence is permitted by the judge as circumstances warrant. The judge need only be prepared to explain the departure from the guidelines. Finally, a mandatory sentence is one that is required by law to be imposed upon conviction of a particular offense. For example, in many states, a first degree murder conviction requires that the offender be sentenced to life without parole. In cases involving mandatory sentences, judges have no discretion at the sentencing phase. All 50 states have mandatory sentences, or mandatory minimum sentences, for at least some offenses.

Other than in mandatory sentencing circumstances, the sentences received by offenders who commit the same crime may vary even within the same jurisdiction. This is because judges are often permitted to consider aggravating and mitigating factors (Schmalleger 2012). Aggravating factors work against the offender and include such things as (Champion 2008) the following:

- whether the crime involved death or serious bodily injury;
- whether the crime was committed while the offender was on bail;

- whether the offender was on probation, or parole;
- whether the offender is a recidivist;
- whether the offender was a leader in the commission of the offense;
- whether the offense involved more than one victim;
- whether the offender treated the victim with extreme cruelty;
- whether the offender used a dangerous weapon during the commission of the crime.

In considering aggravating factors, judges may lengthen a sentence or even invoke the death penalty in some states because of them. Judges may also consider mitigating factors in their sentences. Mitigating factors work in the defendant's favor and include (Champion 2008):

- the offender did not cause serious bodily injury;
- the offender acted under duress or extreme provocation;
- the offender's conduct was possibly justified under the circumstance;
- the offender was suffering from mental incapacitation;
- the offender cooperated with authorities in apprehending other participants;
- the offender committed the crime through motivation to provide necessities for him- or herself and his or her family;
- the offender did not have a previous criminal record.

The net effect of aggravating and mitigating factors is that convicted offenders are treated differently by judges who must assign—sometimes subjectively—weight and value to these factors in determining a sentence. Race, gender, sexual orientation, and religious affiliation are neither legitimate aggravating nor mitigating factors in any state's sentencing guidelines. Therefore, one would not expect to see profiling by the judiciary along these lines. Profiling critics note, however, that some legitimate factors may be disproportionately associated with race, gender, and so on and therefore result in de facto profiling. For example, having small children who rely on you may be a mitigating factor; that factor will favor female offenders more often than male offenders. Or, committing a crime motivated by hate is an aggravating factor in many jurisdictions and might be more associated with certain racial groups or religious beliefs over others.

In looking at sentencing patterns, some caution must be injected into assumptions based on numbers alone. The numbers may be indicative of judicial profiling, or they may be indicative of other things that happen to also correspond to groups of one kind or another. Profiling in law enforcement and even in jury selection has its defenders. But few would argue that taking into consideration race, gender, sexual orientation, or religion has any place in the activity of an unbiased and neutral judge. As profiling by the judiciary is the least defensible, we should be very aware of possible alternative explanations.

## Constitution and Civil Rights

It is important to remember that criminal justice profiling does not occur in a legal vacuum. There are parameters within which some types of profiling may legitimately occur; profiling outside of those parameters can trigger a variety of ethical, moral, statutory, and constitutional violations.

The United States is a country that explicitly imposes limits on how the government relates to its citizens, even while pursuing justice. Chief among the protections for American citizens is the Constitution of the United States. This document contains the Bill of Rights, which is the first 10 amendments to the Constitution and was ratified in 1791. The Bill of Rights was added to the original constitutional document to ensure that individuals' liberties were protected in their dealings with the government. Several of the first 10 amendments have specific relevance to the criminal justice system and are worth mentioning in the following:

### First Amendment:

Congress shall make no law respecting the establishment of religion, or prohibiting the free exercise thereof; or abridging the freedom of speech, or of the press; or the right of the people peaceably to assemble, and to petition the Government for a redress of grievances.

### Fourth Amendment:

The right of the people to be secure in their persons, houses, papers, and effects, against unreasonable searches and seizures, shall not be violated, and no Warrants shall issue, but upon probable cause, supported by Oath or affirmation, and particularly describing the place to be searched, and the persons or things to be seized.

### Fifth Amendment:

No person shall be held to answer for a capital, or otherwise infamous crime, unless on a presentment or indictment of a Grand Jury, except in cases arising in the land or naval forces, or in the Militia, when in actual service in time of War or public danger; nor shall any person be subject for the same offense to be twice put in jeopardy of life or limb; nor shall be compelled in any criminal case to be a witness against himself; nor be deprived of life, liberty, or property, without due process of law; nor shall private property be taken for public use, without just compensation.

### Sixth Amendment:

In all criminal prosecutions, the accused shall enjoy the right to a speedy and public trial, by an impartial jury of the State and district wherein the crime shall have been committed, which district shall have been previously ascertained by law, and to be informed of the nature and cause of the accusation; to be confronted with the witnesses against him; to have compulsory process for obtaining witnesses in his favor, and to have the Assistance of Counsel for his defense.

### Eighth Amendment:

Excessive bail shall not be required, nor excessive fines imposed, nor cruel and unusual punishments inflicted.

As worthwhile as these protections are, they did not protect citizens from state and local government historically. In fact, until the last half of the 20th century, the Bill of Rights served primarily to protect citizens from federal abuses alone. It is true that state constitutions had similar protections contained in them, but their interpretations were subject to the whims of state and local judicial politics.

On the heels of the Civil War, the Fourteenth Amendment was ratified in 1868. Section 1 of this amendment sought specifically to protect individuals from state and local governmental abuses of power. The Fourteenth Amendment (Section 1) reads as follows:

All persons born or naturalized in the United States and subject to the jurisdiction thereof, are citizens of the United States and of the State wherein they reside. No State shall make or enforce any law which shall abridge the privileges or immunities of citizens of the United States; nor shall any State deprive any person of life, liberty, or property, without due process of law; nor deny any person within its jurisdiction the equal protection of the laws.

In the last half of the 20th century, through a series of U.S. Supreme Court cases, the Bill of Rights in the Constitution came to be applied to state and local governments through a judicial process called "incorporation." Essentially, the Supreme Court determined that the protections of the First, Fourth, Fifth, Sixth, and Eighth Amendments apply to state and local governments because of the due process and equal protection provisions of the Fourteenth Amendment. In other words, the Fourth Amendment has been "incorporated" into the Fourteenth, and so has the Fifth Amendment, the Sixth, and so on.

In addition to protections of the Constitution by way of evolving interpretations by the courts, the Congress of the United States and state legislatures throughout the land have passed civil rights legislation affording additional protections to "protected classes." In the Civil Rights Act of 1964, the U.S. Congress outlawed discrimination in housing, employment, and other areas on the basis of race, ethnicity, religion, and gender. Discrimination legislation relating to age and disabilities was passed later. Many state legislatures have also passed civil rights laws that prohibit discrimination on the basis of sexual orientation.

Many would argue that criminal justice profiling violates these various constitutional safeguards. People who are subject to a traffic stop because they fit a profile that includes race, age, or gender as a prominent factor might claim that their Fourth Amendment right to be free from unreasonable searches and seizures as well as their Fourteenth Amendment right to be treated fairly under the law was violated by officers. Or, an offender receiving the death penalty might claim his or her Sixth Amendment and Fourteenth Amendment rights were violated when a prosecutor successfully excluded all but the most hawkish of females from the jury. To be sure, when the criminal justice system breaches potential constitutional liberties, the bar is high for the government to justify its actions. At a minimum, whenever the criminal laws and the actions the government takes to enforce them touch on constitutionally protected interests, the government must show that the laws and actions are rationally related to furthering a legitimate government interest.

Criminal laws that directly infringe upon fundamental rights found in the Bill of Rights are subject to more stringent evaluation, however. Such laws receive "strict judicial scrutiny," which means that the law is presumed by the court to be unconstitutional absent the government's ability to show a "compelling government interest" (Scheb and Scheb 2011). Likewise, enforcement actions that directly challenge our civil liberties in a way that is not explicitly endorsed by the Constitution are likely to be viewed as unconstitutional as well.

The debatable question about criminal profiling is: Does profiling rise to a level of patent unconstitutionality absent the high standard of a "compelling government interest," or is it adequate for government to show that profiling as practiced is rationally related to the legitimate government interest of fighting particular crimes, for example, drug trafficking, hijacking, and so on? To answer this question, it is worth first considering the various conditions and circumstances that permit law enforcement officers to initiate contact with citizens in the first place, and to detain them sometimes against their will.

The widely recognized police encounter that is almost universally seen as something to avoid by citizens is the traffic stop. Many people are confused as to what is exactly required for a police officer to pull a motorist over. Some people believe officers can stop people on gut feelings or hunches alone. Unfortunately, some officers believe that as well. But the standard is higher. Specifically, police officers may pull over motorists if they have reasonable suspicion that a legal violation—traffic or criminal—has taken place. Reasonable suspicion is an accumulation of observations, along with an officer's informed experience, that leads one to reasonably believe a motorist has committed a violation (Klotter, Hemmens, and Walker 2009). With reasonable suspicion, an officer may stop and temporarily detain a person to investigate that suspicion further.

Investigative stops are rooted in the landmark case of *Terry v. Ohio* (1968). In that case, the U.S. Supreme Court explained the limits of detention for investigative purposes. In that case, a plainclothes Cleveland, Ohio, police officer was walking his beat in downtown Cleveland when he saw three individuals acting suspiciously. In particular, he saw the three men peering into a store window, walking down the street a short distance, and then coming back to peer through the window again. The officer suspected that the suspects might be casing the store in preparation for holding it up.

The officer approached the subjects, identified himself as a police officer, and asked their names. The responses by the suspects were muted, and the officer decided to pat one of the suspects down. In doing so, he felt a pistol in the pocket of the suspect's overcoat. The other two suspects were also patted down for weapons and an additional revolver was found. The Supreme Court upheld the detention and search for weapons by the officer. It said that police officers may approach and detain people for the purposes of investigating possible criminal activity when the officers can reasonably conclude, in light of their experience, "that criminal activity may be afoot." And in *Delaware v. Prouse* (1979), the threshold of reasonable suspicion was extended to the stopping and searching of suspects in motor vehicles. Police officers were not permitted to conduct traffic stops on the basis of hunches or fishing expeditions.

The outcome of any investigative stop is to either develop the probable cause (if it does not already exist at the time of the stop) necessary to take action—such as write a ticket or make an arrest—or to set the person free. An example of this would be of an officer who hears of a report that a bank robbery just took place involving two men leaving the scene in a blue Camaro. Not far from the scene, the officer sees a blue Camaro with two occupants and pulls it over. The officer at this point does not have probable cause to make an arrest. Merely seeing a blue Camaro with two people inside does not yet permit the officer to say in court that those particular occupants in the

Camaro are the bank robbers. But it is certainly reasonable to investigate the possibility.

After the officer stops the vehicle, realizes that the two occupants are husband and wife with a previously unseen child in the backseat, and verifies that these people do not fit the description of the robbers and therefore lets them go, the stop in retrospect was no less reasonable—even though probable cause for an arrest did not develop. That's the purpose of an investigative stop.

With exception of truly random checkpoints in certain cases, traffic stops that are based upon anything less than reasonable suspicion are unconstitutional. Obviously, if an officer observes the subject vehicle committing a violation, then reasonable suspicion and even probable cause exist that a violation occurred and a stop is clearly warranted.

Once a vehicle is stopped, there is also some confusion—inside policing and out—of just when an officer may search a vehicle. The Fourth Amendment generally requires that the police have a search warrant if they want to search someone's belongings and possibly seize them for evidence. The U.S. Supreme Court, however, has crafted several exceptions to the search warrant requirement that police officers may use in searching a motorist's vehicle. These exceptions are explained below.

1. Consent—Consensual encounters are those interactions between the police and the citizens that are voluntary and require no legal basis for the interaction to occur. Citizens may break off the encounter with the officer at any time and may choose to forego interaction with the officer altogether. The courts have consistently held that searches of vehicles when the motorist in control of the vehicle gave consent to do so are valid searches, even if the motorist was not expressly told of his or her right to refuse to consent. Rather, the courts have looked at the degree to which a reasonable person would know that they were free to refuse the search. An officer asking permission to search a vehicle suggests to a reasonable person that the answer could be "no."

2. Terry Search—Police officers may search the passenger compartment of a vehicle for weapons if the officer has reasonable suspicion to believe weapons may be present. This is only a search for weapons. Opening a film canister or reading documents strewn about the car floor would not be permitted in a Terry search.

3. Plain View—Police officers who observe evidence or contraband in plain view may seize that evidence. In order for the search to be valid, officers must have the legal justification to be where they were when the evidence was observed, and it must be apparent that the object observed constitutes evidence of a crime. If an officer on a traffic stop sees drug paraphernalia sitting in the cup holder of the vehicle, that evidence can be seized. If it can be shown that the traffic stop was without merit, however, then the officer had no right to be where he or she was when the observation was made, and the evidence would become inadmissible.

4. Carroll Search—The most sweeping warrantless search authority given to police officers is that granted to them by the Supreme Court in *Carroll v. United States* (1925) and extended to state and local law enforcement in *Chambers v. Maroney* (1970). The Supreme Court essentially ruled that because vehicles are mobile, obtaining actual search warrants in a timely manner from a judge back at the courthouse is not always realistic or possible. Therefore, officers may search a vehicle for evidence without a warrant, bumper to bumper, if they have sufficient probable cause as to justify a search warrant had they sought one. There is still a preference for a warrant if there is time and means to get one, but it is not required when dealing with motor vehicles.

It is important to note that refusal to give permission for a search does not constitute probable cause that there is evidence of a crime in the vehicle despite certainly arousing the suspicions of the police officers. Many officers will utilize drug dogs to sniff around the vehicle, however. If the dog detects a "hit," then most officers will conclude they have probable cause that drugs are in the vehicle and conduct a Carroll search. Further, most courts will uphold that belief by the officers. Still others will develop probable cause after finding evidence during a more limited search—for example, a Terry search for weapons.

Another very important Supreme Court case that relates directly to the authority officers have in the field to engage in profiling is *Whren v. United States* (1996). This case addressed the frequent complaint of black motorists that police officers use incredibly minor offenses as the basis for their stops, knowing full well that they are looking for more serious offenses. Critics further argue that black motorists are being stopped far more often for these minor offenses then white motorists and that therefore illegal race-based profiling is taking place. In other words, minor violations are being used as a pretext for stopping African Americans and other minorities.

For example, in a North Carolina traffic study funded by the National Institute of Justice in which nearly 1,400 blacks and nearly 1,500 whites were surveyed, it was found that black motorists were twice as likely to report having experienced a traffic stop as were white motorists. Additionally, black males were more likely to have experienced a traffic stop than were black females, while there was no significant difference in the rate of traffic stops for white males and females. The authors of the study noted that at least some of the difference in likelihood of being stopped related to driving patterns, and that there were no significant differences between blacks and whites in experiences or outcomes (citation, warning, etc.) after the stop takes place (Smith et al. 2004). A more recent follow-up study in North Carolina showed that blacks and Hispanics were slightly more likely to be pulled over than whites, but were far more likely to have their vehicles searched following the stop than were whites (Baumgartner and Epp 2012).

Indeed, many states, with the support of the U.S. Department of Justice, have been examining their traffic-stop patterns since 2000. In May 2014, the Missouri Attorney General released its annual report on traffic-stop statistics. The report

showed that blacks, based on their proportion to the population, were 66 percent more likely than whites to be stopped
for traffic violations—up from 30 percent more likely in 2000
(State of Missouri 2014).

In *Whren*, the Court addressed head-on whether pretextual
traffic stops—that is, those with an objective basis for the stop
but actually rooted in ulterior motives of the officer—are constitutional. In the *Whren* case, police officers who were patrolling in a "high drug area" of Washington, D.C., observed a
vehicle stopped at a stop sign for an unusually long period of
time, then suddenly turning without signaling. The vehicle
was stopped purportedly by the officers to warn the driver
about traffic violations. Upon approaching the vehicle, however, the officers observed in plain view plastic bags of crack
cocaine.

The suspects in the case, James Brown and Michael Whren,
were convicted of federal drug crimes. They challenged their
convictions because the officers did not have reasonable suspicion or probable cause that they were trafficking in drugs, and
the traffic violation was just a pretext to stop them. After all,
the officers had been in civilian clothes and an unmarked squad
car; traffic enforcement was obviously not the officers' number
one priority, said the defendants.

Whren and Brown relied in part on the Court's decision in
*Delaware v. Prouse* (1979). In that case, a police officer stopped
a motorist without observing a traffic or equipment violation.
Rather, the officer contended he simply wanted to check the
driver for a valid license and proper vehicle registration. The
stop resulted in the officer's arresting Prouse for driving after
revocation and, incident to that arrest, finding marijuana on
his person. The Supreme Court in *Prouse* said "the permissibility of a particular law enforcement practice is judged by
balancing its intrusion on the individual's Fourth Amendment
interests against its promotion of legitimate governmental interests" (440 US 648). In the *Prouse* case, the government's legitimate interests were deemed to be outweighed by Prouse's

Fourth Amendment interests, and therefore the conviction was overturned.

Whren and Brown were hoping for a similar decision on the part of the Supreme Court regarding their case. After all, a pretextual stop based on a petty, generally unenforced traffic law, is little more than the hunch the officer had in *Prouse*. Furthermore, the Court in *Florida v. Wells* (1990) had indicated that an inventory search prior to a vehicle's being towed must not be used as a pretext for a search for incriminating evidence. The decision in that case suggested, at least to Whren and Brown, that the court looked disapprovingly at "police attempts to use valid bases of action against citizens as pretexts for pursuing other investigatory agendas" (517 US 806).

The Supreme Court in *Whren*, however, cited other cases where the motives of the officer did not adversely affect the objective basis for action. In the end, the Court ruled in *Whren* that as long as an objective basis for a traffic stop exists, including minor equipment and moving violations, then there is no unreasonable seizure in violation of the Fourth Amendment. The convictions were upheld. The Court did reiterate that stops may not be based on race or some other similarly illegal factor. But if they are, the relief is found in the Fourteenth Amendment, not the Fourth Amendment.

Justice Scalia, writing for the majority, said:

> We think these cases [cited in the *Whren* opinion] foreclose any argument that the constitutional reasonableness of traffic stops depends on the actual motivations of the individual officers involved. We of course agree with petitioners that the Constitution prohibits selective enforcement of the law based on considerations such as race. But the constitutional basis for objecting to intentionally discriminatory application of laws is the Equal Protection Clause, not the Fourth Amendment. Subjective intentions play no role in ordinary, probable-cause Fourth Amendment analysis. (517 US 806)

Put simply, reasonable suspicion that a violation of a law occurred is all that is required for a traffic stop.

The standard of reasonable suspicion figured prominently in a controversial Arizona law passed in 2010. The "Support Our Law Enforcement and Safe Neighborhoods Act," also known as Senate Bill 1070, or "SB 1070" for short, sought to expand the authority of law enforcement in Arizona to confront the illegal immigration which inordinately taxed the law enforcement and public welfare resources of the state. The law permitted law enforcement officers to stop and detain individuals believed to be in the United States, and therefore in Arizona, illegally based on a reasonable suspicion threshold. In the event that the officer would go on to develop probable cause that a person was an illegal immigrant, the person could be charged with the misdemeanor crime of being in Arizona without proper documentation.

Critics of the law immediately branded it as a permission slip for racial profiling. There was much speculation that police officers would be stopping people on the reasonable suspicion that they were in the country illegally, with the reasonable suspicion calculation having been arrived at for little more cause than the person being stopped looked Hispanic. Given that a third of the population of Arizona is ethnically Hispanic, the concern that law-abiding Arizonians would be harassed by the police under this law was palpable.

Almost immediately after passage, the law was targeted by lawsuits from both the American Civil Liberties Union and the U.S. Justice Department. As a result, federal district court and the Ninth Circuit Court of Appeals blocked key portions of the law from going into effect. Then, in 2012, the U.S. Supreme Court considered the constitutionality of SB 1070. The Supreme Court declared that law enforcement could investigate the immigration status of people with whom they came in contact if they had reasonable suspicion that the suspects were in the country illegally. However, the portion of SB 1070 which made it a misdemeanor to be in Arizona without being in the United States legally—that is, essentially to be trespassing in Arizona—was ruled unconstitutional. The Court reasoned that regulating immigration was the exclusive responsibility of the federal government under the U.S. Constitution. Consequently, if local law enforcement does ascertain that someone is in the country illegally, the most that could be done is to turn over that person to federal immigration authorities. The criminalization at the state level of the undocumented status of an alien had been at the heart of SB 1070. With that portion of the law ruled unconstitutional and therefore no state charge available, and with federal immigration authorities in Arizona largely unwilling to take custody of non-violent undocumented immigrants, the law has ultimately had very little impact on law enforcement operations or on the problem of illegal immigration in Arizona.

## Pros and Cons of Criminal Profiling

### Arguments against Profiling

There are many arguments that can be made against criminal justice profiling. One argument against profiling is really a counterargument to those who argue for profiling. Many proponents of profiling suggest that some groups more than others—certainly men more than women and often minorities more than whites—commit a disproportionate share of crime. In support of this, many statistics are presented that show, for example, that blacks are arrested per capita far more often than whites.

Jim Cleary and others have noted, however, that this reasoning is circular. They claim it is precisely because blacks are targeted disproportionately by law enforcement that they are arrested disproportionately by law enforcement. In other words, racial profiling helps create its own justification (Cleary 2000). Harvard professor Randall Kennedy, on the other hand, conceded that blacks and other minorities are committing greater numbers of crime and also conceded that most profiling is done by criminal justice officials who are well intentioned and are not racists. But he remains firmly against criminal justice profiling on principle when it is based even partly on race or some other protected classification (Kennedy 2000).

Kennedy argued that profiling results in a downward spiral of relations between criminal justice officials and members of the community. Well-meaning and courteous police officers will eventually pull over individuals who themselves had always been supportive of law enforcement but have grown tired of being stopped. When they lash out against the officers out of resentment of their plight, the officer will likely defend himself or herself, but the spiral begins. Eventually, after a number of similar encounters, the regard held by officers and citizens for each other will inevitably be low.

Kennedy's ultimate criticism of profiling is not rooted in the practical effects on police-community relations; it is rooted in principle. Regardless of the odds of a black man committing a crime compared to a white woman or some other breakdown, Kennedy posited that people should be judged solely by their individual conduct. Factors such as race or gender should not even partly be used to form opinions or suspicions about other people. The use of profiling, however successful it may be, undercuts this principle and therefore should be discarded, said Kennedy. Success is not an argument. Think how safe and crime free we would be if we dismissed the Fourth Amendment requirement against unreasonable searches and seizures. But we don't, because principle trumps even safety and success. Still another argument against profiling is the potential harm it causes individual law-abiding citizens who fall subject to it. This harm includes mental anguish and emotional distress from the degradation of a confrontational and accusatory encounter with the police. Consider the following testimony given in March 2000 by an African American to the U.S. Senate's Judiciary Committee, which was investigating the occurrence of racial profiling by law enforcement.

*My name is Master Sergeant Rossano Gerald. I am glad to have an opportunity to talk with you today about my experience in Oklahoma. The issue of racial profiling is a serious problem in this country today and I am glad to see that the Senate is beginning to take a look at it. I am coming forward to tell my story to try to prevent this from happening again. I don't want anything like this to happen to my son again.*

*In August of 1998, I was driving in Oklahoma on my way to a family reunion. At that time I was a Sergeant First class in the Army stationed in Fort Richie. My 12-year-old son Gregory was with me. As soon as we crossed the border from Arkansas, I noticed patrol cars in the area and began driving even more carefully than usual. Within minutes, an officer pulled me over for "following another car too closely." He did not give me a citation.*

*Soon after, we stopped to buy gas and use the restroom. After our break we continued driving. Having been stopped once already, I was driving particularly carefully. I was in the right hand lane when I saw two patrol cars approach on the ramp. I signaled, then pulled over to let them in. I said to my son, "Watch this, I bet they'll stop me again." Sure enough, I was pulled over again. An officer walked to the rear of my car and told me to get in the patrol car. I later learned that his name was Trooper Perry. Once he had me in the car and started questioning me, I told him that my son was still in my car. He left and got Gregory and frisked him before putting him in the back of the patrol car. He told me that I had changed lanes without signaling. I told him that I had signaled, and asked how he would have been able to see from his vantage point on the ramp. Trooper Perry started writing me a warning ticket and asking me questions. He asked me why I was nervous. I told him that I was not nervous, but upset because I had just been stopped by another trooper. He then asked me more questions about my destination, my point of origin and my military assignment.*

*Trooper Perry informed me that he had just made a drug bust and asked to search my car, and I said no. I asked him to call my Commanding Officer, Captain Rhodes, because it is standard operating procedure for the army. He refused. He would not let me call Captain Rhodes on my cell phone. I asked him again later to call my Commanding Officer and again he refused. Trooper Perry gave me the warning ticket but told me that I was not free to go.*

*Trooper Perry continued asking me questions. He badgered me about why I would not let him search my car if I had nothing to hide. I was polite but would not let him search my car. He asked me if I was carrying any weapons or contraband and I informed him that I was not. Trooper Perry then stated that it was legal for him to search my car without my consent.*

*Trooper Perry called for the K-9 unit from the second patrol car. I said I wanted to watch the search and we got out of the car. The dog walked around the outside of the vehicle. The dog did not "alert." He did not bark, scratch, whimper or sit down, although the trooper kept patting certain areas of the car and would not let the dog walk away. Even though the dog did not alert, the second trooper patted the right wheel well and claimed that the dog had alerted. He said he would conduct a full scale search now. I have been trained in using dogs and thought that the search was highly improper and unusually suggestive.*

*Trooper Perry ordered Gregory and me to get back into the car. At this point, I became really worried that the Troopers were going to plant illegal contraband in my car. Trooper Perry then got the drill and took over the search. He began drilling under the carpet at the feet of the passenger side. Trooper Perry came back to the car and stated that he had found "something." The two troopers spoke privately. I was then accused of having a secret compartment in my car that had drug residue in it. This compartment was actually a footrest that was a feature of the car.*

*I was then handcuffed by Trooper Perry who manhandled me, thrust me into his car and then strapped me in. He turned off the on-board camera and took out the tape. The second trooper continued the search of my car. At one point, Trooper Perry and the other officer lifted the hoods of their patrol cars, an action that had no obvious purpose. I was worried that they were trying to obstruct my view so that they could plant contraband in my car.*

*During the search we overheard Trooper Perry on the radio with another trooper. He told the other trooper that he was turning up nothing. The other trooper told him to keep searching and asked if he needed back up. By this point a third unit had appeared. This trooper moved Gregory into his car and asked him questions without me being present. The second trooper brought the drug dog to the car that Gregory was in and asked him some of the same questions. The dog kept barking at Gregory, who was afraid it would bite him.*

*The troopers put our luggage on the ground and had the dogs sniff it. They found airline tickets, one of which was to Chicago. When the trooper asked me about it, I answered that Gregory had flown out of Chicago. Because he had again asked me about drugs, I informed him that my car had passed inspection and received military clearance and that because of my military assignment, I was subject to random urinalysis tests and would never do drugs. Trooper Perry was angry that I would not give him details about my classified assignment. I suggested that he contact my Commanding Officer.*

*At 3:45 P.M. the Troopers let me go with nothing more than a warning ticket. I was told that I was being let go because I was "behaving myself now." I complained that my car and baggage were a mess and Trooper Perry said, "We ain't good at repacking." Trooper Perry had removed parts of the headliner, floorboards, carpet and other areas. There was over one thousand dollars of damage.*

*As soon as we were released, I called Captain Rhodes. He advised me to go to Fort Sill where the Director of Public Safety searched my vehicle in case drugs were planted in my car. An Army-certified narcotic working dog did not find any drugs or contraband.*

*This experience was very traumatic for Gregory. Throughout the interrogation, he was frightened and crying. Even before he was removed from my presence he was nervous, crying and hyperventilating. I had to watch while my son suffered tremendous physical discomfort from the heat. Trooper Perry had turned off the air conditioning when he put us in his car, despite the ninety degree heat.*

*Before we were finally released, one of the troopers asked who would come get Gregory if they arrested me. This remark made Gregory more nervous and upset. He was crying and wondering what would happen to him and I tried to calm him down. He was scared for the rest of the trip. My son has since become afraid of dogs. He continues to ask his mother why his father was treated this way.*

*I was very humiliated by this experience. I was embarrassed and ashamed that people driving by would think I had committed a serious crime. It was particularly horrible to be treated like a criminal in front of my impressionable young son.*

*I never thought I would find myself in the position of suing police officers. I am an authority figure myself. I don't want my son thinking that this kind of behavior by anyone in uniform is acceptable. I hope that by coming forward to tell my story it might prevent other people of color from being treated this way. (Gerald 2000)*

Sergeant Gerald was only one of several who testified or submitted statements for the record concerning their brushes with profiling. The witnesses included not just African Americans, but Hispanics, and included people from all walks of life, including a prominent attorney pulled over on the way home from a family member's funeral. In all cases, the testimony reflected deep resentment at having their privacy invaded and being suspected of wrongdoing without any basis. It is clear that these occurrences create lifelong memories of unpleasant and, from their perspectives, unfair encounters with the criminal justice system.

A final argument raised with frequency today in opposition to criminal justice profiling, particularly by the police, is that it is inconsistent with the new law enforcement paradigm of community policing. Many definitions of community policing exist, but they all tend to have the common theme of partnership between the police and the community. Community policing can be defined as a philosophy of law enforcement, based on the concept that police officers and citizens working together in creative ways can help solve contemporary community problems related to crime, the fear of crime, social and physical disorder, and neighborhood decay (Kappeler and Gaines 2009). This definition has serious ramifications for police-community relationships and leaves little room for preemptive, adversarial profiling of community members. Opponents of profiling point out that profiling is a tool of a by-gone policing era and that in the community policing era, officers need not and should not go it alone—them against the community. Rather, officers should seek to build relationships in the community that will yield dividends in the future.

## Arguments for Profiling

There is frankly no contest to the assertion that some groups of people commit disproportionate shares of crime. African Americans, for example, constitute 13 percent of the nation's population and yet represent 49 percent of those arrested for homicide, 55 percent of robbery arrests, 34 percent of aggravated assault arrests, and 40 percent of weapons violations, to name a few. In fact, in every category of felony crime, including both violent crimes and property crimes, blacks are arrested at rates that are no less than double their percentage in the population (Federal Bureau of Investigation 2013).

Although some critics, such as Jim Cleary, have argued that profiling is self-perpetuating, the fact that there is a disproportionate number of minorities arrested for the most serious offenses mitigates that criticism. The serious felonies are investigated until suspects, whatever their race, materialize. Investigating a homicide or armed robbery is not driven by a bias against one race or another. The crime occurred. What's more, the statistics are bound by context and do not only affect African Americans. All races are subject to light shed by statistical realities. Most individuals trafficking illegal aliens on the southern border are likely to be of Hispanic origin. Statistically, a stop of a van driven by a Hispanic male will more likely yield smuggled drugs or aliens than would a stop of a van driven by an apparent soccer mom in the same border vicinity.

Besides race, observations about gender jump out in association with criminal activity. In 2012, law enforcement made over 500,000 arrests for violent crimes and 1.6 million arrests for property crimes nationwide. Males accounted for 80 percent of violent crime arrests and 64 percent of property crime arrests (Federal Bureau of Investigation 2013). An officer responding to a violent crime, while not ruling out anything, can at least know that odds are the perpetrator is a man. Is that bias or merely a recognition of a statistical reality?

In addition to the statistical argument, supporters of profiling point out that it is common sense. In 2000, Johnny Hughes of the National Troopers Coalition, a retired major in the Maryland State Police, testified to the U.S. Senate that criminal profiling is a good, effective, and commonsensical law enforcement tool. Police trainees are taught to observe the individual characteristics or indicators for drug-courier activity and other crimes in progress. These observations are based on reason, said Major Hughes, not race (or any other class per se). He argued that common sense dictates that preventing and investigating crime in minority areas are necessarily going to involve the interaction of police with predominantly minorities.

In a hypothetical case, and officer might observe a white male motorist in an urban black neighborhood late at night with license plates that register to the suburbs. The motorist is quite possibly in the area to purchase drugs. The race of the motorist, in this case Caucasian, cannot help but be noticed in the context of a black neighborhood. Many police officers would say that to completely ignore the racial aspect of an overall profile or observation is to unrealistically hamper law enforcement from thinking.

During the trial of George Zimmerman for the killing of black teenager Trayvon Martin, Pulitzer Prize–winning columnist Kathleen Parker (2013) summarized the common sense sentiment by writing in part:

African Americans are right to perceive that Martin was followed because he was black, but it is wrong to presume that recognizing a racial characteristic is necessarily racist. It has been established that several burglaries in Zimmerman's neighborhood primarily involved young black males . . . This is not to justify what subsequently transpired between Zimmerman and Martin but to cast a dispassionate eye on reality. And no, just because a few black youths caused trouble doesn't mean all black youths should be viewed suspiciously. This is so obvious a truth that it shouldn't need saying and yet, if we are honest, we know that human nature includes the accumulation of evolved biases based on experience and survival. In the courtroom, it's called profiling. In the real world, it's called common sense.

Finally, some defenders of criminal justice profiling note that public safety and the community are benefactors. It is argued that to avoid using good and proven police techniques in the detection and prevention of crime is to do so to the detriment of the community. Doing so unnecessarily leaves the public vulnerable to criminals who might have otherwise been apprehended.

The very public harmed when profiling is disallowed are usually minorities and the poor, as it is their neighborhoods that are often overrun with the criminal element. To leave law-abiding minorities—which are the majority in such neighborhoods—to stew in a crime-ridden environment could itself be considered racist or classist. Minorities have the right to be safe too.

For example, studies show that blacks are far more likely than whites to be victims of serious crime. In 2012, blacks experienced 11.3 serious violent crimes per 1,000 people while whites experienced a rate of 6.8 serious violent crimes per 1,000. For persons age 12 and older, the rate of violent victimization for blacks was 34.2 per 1,000, compared to 25.2 and 24.5 per 1,000 for whites and Hispanics, respectively (Truman, Langton, and Planty 2013).

In 2005, blacks accounted for 49 percent of all homicide victims, and 52 percent of all male homicide victims. Studies show that most interpersonal crimes are intraracial. In other words, people tend to be victimized by offenders from their own race. Among homicides involving a single victim and a single offender in 2005, 93 percent of black victims were killed by black offenders, and 85 percent of white victims were killed by white offenders. A full 90 percent of these killers, among both blacks and whites, were men (Harrell 2007). Given that violent crime tends to be intraracial, and given the disproportionate share of victimization suffered among some minority groups, one can argue that it is minority communities who are served by effective criminal justice profiling.

## Remedies

There are two primary remedies that citizens can pursue when they feel they have been illegally profiled or in some other way discriminated against by the criminal justice system. One route is to involve the U.S. Department of Justice (DOJ), Civil Rights Division. The other route is to pursue civil litigation. The DOJ Civil Rights Division maintains a section devoted to special litigation, which includes the responsibility of suing local and state law enforcement and corrections agencies. Under authorities given to DOJ under the Civil Rights of Institutionalized Persons Act (CRIPA), violations of the civil rights of those who are incarcerated can be investigated, civilly litigated, and even prosecuted by the Department of Justice.

Additionally, under authority of the 1968 Omnibus Crime Control and Safe Streets Act, DOJ's Civil Rights Division has the authority to initiate civil litigation to remedy patterns of racial, ethnic, gender, or religious discrimination by law enforcement agencies that receive federal funds. The Violent Crime Control and Law Enforcement Act of 1994 further empowers DOJ to conduct similar investigations and seek similar remedies from agencies administering juvenile justice that demonstrate patterned illegal conduct.

A common tactic for the DOJ in recent years has been to enter into consent decrees with targeted criminal justice agencies. In exchange for the dropping of the federal lawsuit against them, agencies and departments under investigation for discriminatory conduct consent to an agreement whereby a multitude of things will be done by that department, depending on the areas identified by DOJ as needing improvement. Typically, the departments agree to such things as (U.S. Department of Justice 2003b):

- revising policies concerning citizen encounters
- instituting a reformed training program
- changing supervisory practices and protocols

- implementing systems to receive and investigate citizen complaints
- greater emphasis on minority recruiting/promotions

In the 1990s and early 2000s, several the police agencies around the country entered into consent decrees with the Department of Justice to avoid federally spearheaded lawsuits alleging pervasive racial discrimination in the departments and the use of racial profiling, including the Pittsburgh, Pennsylvania Police Department in 1997, the Steubenville, Ohio Police Department in 1997, the New Jersey State Police in 1999, the Montgomery County, Maryland Police Department 2000, the Los Angeles Police Department in 2001, the Washington DC Police Department in 2001, the Highland Park, Illinois, Police Department in 2001, and the Cincinnati Police Department in 2002.

The 2002 consent decree between the DOJ and the Cincinnati Police Department serves as a good example of how these decrees are constructed. Cincinnati had been plagued by horrible relations between the police and the black community there. This relationship deteriorated into riots following a shooting by an officer of a wanted, but unarmed, African American. The officer was prosecuted in the death of the suspect but was acquitted. With the growing national attention on Cincinnati, the DOJ took a closer look. According to a DOJ press release, among the terms agreed to by both parties were the following things that the city and the police department (CPD) would do:

- enhance policy requirements and limitations on the use of force by officers, including the use of firearms, beanbag shot guns and 40 millimeter foam rounds, chemical irritant and canines;
- improve supervisory oversight of use of force incidents; supervisors will document and investigate each incident

giving rise to a use of force for compliance with CPD policy and to evaluate the tactics used by the officer;

- implement policy revisions and training which will emphasize that de-escalation techniques, such as disengagement, area containment, surveillance, waiting out a subject, summoning reinforcements or calling in specialized units, may be an appropriate response to a situation;

- enhance and expand its risk management system that will provide CPD managers with information necessary to better supervise officers and groups of officers;

- analyze trends in uses of force, searches, seizures, and other law enforcement activities that create a risk of officer misconduct;

- create a cadre of officers who are specially trained to intervene in situations involving people with mental illness;

- improve the procedures for investigating allegations of misconduct and uses of force by CPD officers and to complete the investigations in a more thorough, fair, and timely manner;

- publicly report important data regarding CPD use of force incidents and civilian complaints; and

- implement a variety of changes in the procedures used for receiving, investigating, and resolving misconduct complaints. CPD will make complaint forms and informational materials more widely available at a variety of public locations (U.S. Department of Justice 2003a).

The U.S. Department of Justice Civil Rights Division is on the record as favoring the tool of consent decrees and expends considerable resources to combat police misconduct through investigation, litigation, and the threat of litigation. In Fiscal Year 2014, the DOJ Civil Rights Division budgeted over $12 million in this effort to support a staff of 71 positions, including 52 attorneys. The Fiscal Year 2015 budget request sought to increase the budget for the police misconduct initiative by

$1.9 million and 20 positions, including 9 attorneys (U.S. Department of Justice 2014).

In 2012, the U.S. Department of Justice entered into one of its most comprehensive consent decrees ever with the New Orleans Police Department. The agreement brought to a close a two-year federal investigation, begun in 2010, into the patterns and practices of the New Orleans Police. The investigation found that there was a pattern of excessive force and other Fourth Amendment violations. The investigation also found that discriminatory policing regularly occurred on the basis of race, ethnicity, gender, and sexual orientation. With the agreement, the City of New Orleans agreed to have a federal court monitor the operation of the police department for a minimum of two years (U.S. Department of Justice 2012).

The other common remedy available to citizens when they believe their civil rights have been violated by law enforcement or some other criminal justice entity is to pursue civil litigation themselves. Although there has long been the right to sue certain criminal justice officials, including police officers, for violating one's civil rights, the practice has become increasingly common in recent years. In the 1960s, there was an average of 6,000 such civil cases each year against law enforcement. By 1976, the number was 13,400. And recent figures have shown more than 30,000 cases each year against the police (Kappeler 2006).

The ability to sue the police and other state-level criminal justice officials is rooted in the Civil Rights Act of 1871, which was codified in Title 42 of the United States Code, Section 1983. To win a "1983" action, the plaintiff (i.e., the one bringing the suit) must show that (Kappeler 2006):

- the officer was acting under the color of law;
- the violation was a constitutional or federally protected right; and
- the violation was sufficiently serious enough to reach a "constitutional" level.

The requirement that an officer acted under the color of law simply refers to the idea that the officer used or in some way implicated his or her status as a criminal justice official during the incident that violated the plaintiff's rights. Usually, showing that the officer acted under the color of law is not difficult for profiling cases. The facts that the officer was in uniform, in a squad car, filed official documents on the case, displayed or was obviously armed with a weapon, and was working with the department's authorization are all evidence that the officer acted under the color of law.

The most common violations raised in 1983 actions are alleged violations of the First, Fourth, Fifth, Sixth, Eighth, and Fourteenth Amendments, along with the Civil Rights Act of 1964 and subsequent amendments.

Although a technical violation of one's civil rights may have occurred, the courts have been reluctant to uphold civil rights lawsuits if the offense is not sufficiently serious. Although exactly how serious the violation has to be is an issue that has been back and forth in various district and appellate courts, most would agree, for example, that an officer telling a jabbering suspect in the backseat of the squad car to "shut up" does not constitute a serious violation of the First Amendment free speech right.

Generally, 42 USC 1983 allows private citizens to sue individual officers who violate civil rights. If it can be shown, however, that the department acted with "deliberate indifference" in regulating the conduct of its employees, then the department could be liable as well. To link an employee's misconduct to the department at large, a plaintiff would need to show things such as (Kappeler 2006):

- the frequency of violations;
- extent to which the violations were routine for other employees;
- extent to which the practice was accepted by supervisors;
- number of employees involved in violation in question;

- retention of, failure to discipline, and failure to investigate employee;
- failure to prevent future violations; and
- failure to train employees adequately, properly, or at all.

Although there have been a growing number of lawsuits against officers for unlawful profiling and other alleged civil rights violations, the cases usually do not succeed for the plaintiffs. Only about 8 percent of civil cases brought against officers and departments are won. However, percentages are higher in some geographic locations. A study of over 600 lawsuits against police agencies and officers in Texas indicated that plaintiffs prevailed against the police in 22 percent of the cases (Kappeler 2006).

Officers do have defenses they can rely on. If they can demonstrate they acted in good faith (i.e., they could not have known at the time that their conduct was illegal), then they will prevail. Likewise, if it can be demonstrated that their conduct was "objectively reasonable" at that time—in other words, a reasonable officer in the same situation with the same amount of information would have acted similarly—the officer will win the case.

Some think the laws should be loosened up further to make it easier to win and sustain convictions against criminal justice officials thought to be engaging in discriminatory conduct. Others, however, point to the fact that criminal justice employees are usually just doing the best they can. To extend greater liability to them—people who are earning working-class wages at best and often enjoy no widespread public appreciation—will only make recruitment of decent officers tougher, and that is a problem that itself can cyclically contribute to the very problem of misconduct that so many criminal justice professionals, politicians, and citizens are trying to alleviate.

## Profiling after September 11

It is impossible to ignore the effects that the catastrophe that was September 11, 2001, brought to the issue of profiling in criminal justice. Prior to 9/11, it was difficult to find public officials who would defend profiling under any circumstances. As William McDonald noted, profiling had developed a "broad and almost unchallengeable public antipathy" (McDonald 2003, 232). Governors, presidential candidates, and former FBI director Robert Mueller, when a candidate for his job, all decried profiling—particularly racial or ethnic profiling—as obscene in relation to the Constitution and generally unfair and immoral.

But on September 11, 2001, 19 males of Middle Eastern descent, most of whom were from Saudi Arabia, killed approximately 3,000 people in the United States. Had law enforcement and intelligence officials ignored the obvious commonality in race and religion among the assailants, they would have been properly accused of gross incompetence or negligence. There are certain people currently at war with the United States, and their last names are *never* Jorgesen or Smith. But the opposite is true as well. Not *all* men named Mohommad are at war with the United States. Many so named are Americans and love America. So what is law enforcement to do?

In examining current federal policy, one sees a tiered approach to the use of profiles, be they based on race, ethnicity, religion, or gender which began under President George W. Bush and has continued under President Barak Obama, despite many Obama supporters on the left being critical of it. In June 2003, the U.S. Justice Department issued new policy guidelines to all of federal law enforcement that banned the use of racial and ethnic profiling. Doing so was consistent with President Bush's proclamation in February 2001 that racial profiling was "wrong and we will end it in America" (U.S. Department of Justice 2003b 1). At that time, President Bush directed the Justice Department to look at the use of race and ethnicity by criminal justice agencies and to craft policies to curtail their use.

The policy does indeed ban the use of racial profiling, absent specific suspect information that would implicate race, in traditional law enforcement activities. Such activities include general patrol functions for uniformed police services, drug investigations, and other general crimes. The policy is more permissive, however, where national security and border integrity are concerned.

Regarding traditional law enforcement activities, the policy reads:

> In making routine or spontaneous decisions, such as ordinary traffic stops, Federal law enforcement officers may not use race or ethnicity to any degree, except that officers may rely on race and ethnicity in specific suspect description. This prohibition applies even where the use of race or ethnicity might otherwise be lawful. In conducting activities in connection with a specific investigation, Federal law enforcement officers may consider race and ethnicity only to the extent that there is trustworthy information, relevant to the locality or timeframe, that links persons of a particular race or ethnicity to an identified criminal incident, scheme, or organization. This standard applies even where the use of race or ethnicity might otherwise be lawful (U.S. Department of Justice 2003b, 2–4).

This standard articulated for traditional law enforcement activities is more stringent than the Constitution requires. Indeed, the Supreme Court has made it clear that the Constitution does not concern itself with the motives of officers where an objective offense is observed; nor does the Constitution prohibit profiling for particular offenses, such as drug trafficking, where race of the suspect is one of many factors in the profile. But now, using race as a factor or acting on an observation of an actual offense when the officer is personally more inclined to do so when committed by members of a particular race is prohibited practice for federal law enforcement.

The policy might have stopped there but for 9/11. The policy goes on to state that the aforementioned standards "do not affect current federal policy with respect to law enforcement activities and other efforts to defend and safeguard against threats to national security or the integrity of the Nation's borders. . . . in investigating or preventing threats to national security or other catastrophic events (including the performance of duties related to air transportation security), or in enforcing laws protecting the integrity of the Nation's borders, Federal law enforcement officers may not consider race or ethnicity except to the extent permitted by the Constitution and the laws of the United States" (U.S. Department of Justice 2003b, 8).

It is worth noting that even where the potential harm is catastrophic, the policy pays homage to the Constitution. But that fact notwithstanding, race and ethnicity (and by extension, religion and gender) may indeed be used as factors in developing profiles of those who might do the United States significant harm.

In short, federal policy bans profiling—usually. This policy is a stark example of the dilemma inherent to profiling generally. If we concede that profiling does prevent some crime (and many say it does not), we must also acknowledge that it does so at a cost—particularly for those innocents who are subject to it. In the weeks following 9/11, many Middle Eastern men were asked to disembark from commercial airliners because passengers and pilots refused to fly with them aboard. These individuals were demeaned, inconvenienced, and embarrassed. If it turns out that just one of the dozens this happened to actually intended to do a flight harm—perhaps by blowing it up with a shoe bomb—would we say it was all worth it? And if it *is* worth it in airline security, is it not likewise worth it to get a murderous, drug-dealing gang member off the streets of Chicago?

One thing is absolute after 9/11: far fewer people are absolutely against criminal profiling than were before.

## References

Banaji, M., and R. Bhaskar. 2000. Implicit Stereotypes and Memory: The Bounded Rationality of Social Beliefs. In: D. L. Schacter and E. Scarry (Eds.). *Memory, Brain and Belief.* Thousand Oaks, CA: Sage, 139–175.

Baumgartner, F., and D. Epp. 2012. *North Carolina Traffic Stop Statistical Analysis: Final Report to the North Carolina Advocates for Justice Task Force on Racial and Ethnic Bias.* Chapel Hill: University of North Carolina.

Brooks, L. W. 2001. Police Discretionary Behavior: A Study of Style. In: Roger G. Dunham and Geoffrey P. Alpert (Eds.). *Critical Issues in Policing.* 4th ed. Prospect Heights, IL: Waveland, 117–131.

Champion, D. J. 2008. *Probation, Parole, and Community Corrections.* Upper Saddle River, NJ: Prentice Hall.

Champion, D. J., and G. E. Rush. 1997. *Policing in the Community.* Upper Saddle River, NJ: Prentice Hall.

Cleary, J. 2000. *Racial Profiling Studies in Law Enforcement: Issues and Methodology.* St. Paul: State of Minnesota, House of Representatives Research Department.

Cole, D. 1999. *No Equal Justice.* New York: New Press.

Evans, M. (Ed.). 1978. *Discretion and Control.* Beverly Hills, CA: Sage.

Federal Bureau of Investigation. 2013. *Crime in the United States 2012.* Washington, DC: UCR.

Gerald, R. 2000. Statement given to the United States Senate, Senate Judiciary Committee, Subcommittee on the Constitution, Hearing, March 30, 2000.

Harrell, E. 2007. *Black Victims of Violent Crime.* Washington, DC: Bureau of Justice Statistics.

Jacoby, J. 1979. The Charging Policies of Prosecutors. In: W. F. McDonald (Ed.). *The Prosecutor.* Beverly Hills, CA: Sage, 75–97.

Kappeler, V. 2006. *Critical Issues in Police Civil Liability.* 4th ed. Long Grove, IL: Waveland.

Kappeler, V., and L. Gaines. 2009. *Community Policing: A Contemporary Perspective.* Cincinnati: Anderson.

Kennedy, R. 2000. Suspect Policy. In: Joseph Victor (Ed.). *Criminal Justice*. Guliford, CT: Dushkin/McGraw-Hill, 102–106.

Klotter, J. C., C. Hemmens, and J. Walker. 2009. *Legal Guide for Police*. 8th ed. Cincinnati: Anderson.

Lee, Y. T., L. Albright, and T. Malloy. 2001. Social Perception and Stereotyping: An Interpersonal and Intercultural Approach. *International Journal of Group Tension* 30(2): 183–209.

Lee, Y. T., L. Jussim, and C. McCauley. 1995. *Stereotype Accuracy: Toward Appreciating Group Differences*. Washington, DC: American Psychological Association.

McCoy, C. 1998. Prosecution. In: M. Tonry (Ed.). *The Handbook of Crime and Punishment*. New York: Oxford University Press, 457–473.

McDonald, W. F. 2003. The Emerging Paradigm for Policing Multiethnic Societies: Glimpses from the American Experience. *Police and Society* (7): 232–249.

Parker, K. 2013. Unanswered Questions in the Trayvon Martin Case. *Washington Post,* July 16.

Roberg, R., J. Crank, and J. Kuykendall. 2000. *Police and Society*. Los Angeles: Roxbury.

Robinson, M. B. 2002. *Justice Blind?* Upper Saddle River, NJ: Prentice Hall.

Scheb, J. M., and J. M. Scheb II. 2011. *Criminal Law and Procedure*. 7th ed. Belmont, CA: Wadsworth.

Schmalleger, F. 1999. *Criminal Justice*. 3rd ed. Upper Saddle River, NJ: Prentice Hall.

Schmalleger, F. 2012. *Criminal Justice Today*. 12th ed. Upper Saddle River, NJ: Prentice Hall.

Smith, W., D. Tomaskovic-Devey, M. Zingraff, M. Mason, P. Warren, and C. P. Wright. 2004. *North Carolina Highway Traffic Study*. Washington, DC: National Institute of Justice.

Sorensen, J., and D. Wallace. 1999. Prosecutorial Discretion in Seeking Death: An Analysis of Racial Disparity in the Pretrial Stages of Case Processing in a Midwestern County. *Justice Quarterly* 16(3): 559–578.

State of Missouri. 2014. *Missouri Vehicle Stops Annual Report.* Columbia, MO: Missouri Attorney General's Office.

Truman, J., L. Langton, and M. Planty. 2013. *Criminal Victimization, 2012.* Washington DC: Bureau of Justice Statistics.

U.S. Department of Justice. 2003a. Civil Rights Division Section. http://usdoj.gov/crt.

U.S. Department of Justice. 2003b. *Guidance Regarding the Use of Race by Federal Law Enforcement Agencies.* Washington, DC.

U.S. Department of Justice. 2012. Justice Department Announces Consent Decree with City of New Orleans to Resolve Allegations of Unlawful Misconduct by New Orleans Police Department. *DOJ Press Release,* July 24.

U.S. Department of Justice. 2002. *United States Attorneys' Manual.* Washington, DC.

U.S. Department of Justice. 2014. *U.S. Department of Justice FY 2015 Budget Request.* http://www.justice.gov/jmd/2015factsheets/civil-rights.pdf.

Walker, S. 1999. *The Police in America.* Boston: McGraw-Hill.

MUSLIM + AMERICAN = NO PROBLEM!!
MY HIJAB DOES NOT MAKE ME A CRIMINAL

# 3    Perspectives

This chapter offers readers an opportunity to hear from different voices on the issue of profiling the criminal justice system generally, and on specific facets or angles regarding criminal justice profiling in particular. The authors of the essays that follow are scholars in the areas of criminal justice, criminology, social work, history, and related fields. The viewpoints offered in the essays are those of the authors themselves, although each make compelling observations and arguments that will hopefully nudge the reader toward contemplation.

The first essay, authored by Thorvald Dahle of North Dakota State University, provides a general overview on racial profiling and on the media coverage of profiling as a public policy issue worthy of attention. In his essay, he revisits the zenith of coverage and awareness of racial profiling in the 1990s.

Penny Shtull of Norwich University in Vermont provides readers with a thorough introduction to behavioral profiling and its intended role in helping to solve violent crimes—typically, homicides. The essay provides a solid explanation of this type of profiling, thereby distinguishing it from more nefarious types of profiling (i.e., based on race, religion, etc.).

Paige Heinrich of Marshall University in West Virginia delivers an essay exploring the influence of media on perceptions of crimes characterized by particular offender-victim

---

Muslim students on the steps of New York City Hall, protesting against "Islamophobia" and the alleged use of racial and religious profiling by the New York City Police Department. (AP Photo/Richard Drew)

combinations. Specifically, the difference in coverage of violent crimes when race or gender of the offender and victim are different is examined.

Connie Koskie at Longwood University in Virginia explores the perils of profiling along religious lines. In particular, her essay addresses the history and continued presence of Islamophobia in the wake of the 9/11 terror attacks. Special law enforcement initiatives to monitor Arab and Muslim Americans, along with their questionable benefits and diminished public support, are discussed.

Pat Nelson of Minnesota State University, Mankato, approaches profiling from a different angle by focusing specifically on the profiling of mental illness. She argues that profiling techniques for law enforcement can be developed and refined in order to equip them to better deal with citizens suffering from mental illness during encounters on the streets or while handling a call. In this vein, she supports the rational construction of mental illness profiles that law enforcement can draw upon to minimize danger to themselves, suspects, and others.

The last two essays, given their scope, were permitted to be a bit longer than the preceding ones. Lauren Kientz Anderson, a historian at Luther College in Iowa, provides an in-depth historical perspective on the stereotyping of African Americans and the general association in America of blacks with criminality. The roots of these stereotypes are address, as is the connection of crime in the black community to the historical inflictions of poverty, discrimination, and the lack of opportunity.

Finally, in a longer essay, Raphael Travis of Texas State University likewise explores the overrepresentation of blacks in the criminal justice system and among the American prison population. The disproportionate contact that African Americans have with criminal justice system is examined from a structural perspective. The essay is replete with statistics which highlight the disparity in the criminal justice system and explores the implications which follow.

## On Racial Profiling: Thorvald O. Dahle

While the term "racial profiling" can have a broader meaning, for the purposes of this essay it is defined as the targeting of racial minorities by members of the criminal justice system based substantially on racial appearances rather than actual evidence of wrong doing (Walker 2001). Race need not be the sole reason for taking action; it simply need only provide some illegitimate influence on the outcome of those decisions. Also, it may occur at different levels within the criminal justice system and not just by the police officer on the street.

Racial profiling has remained an area of considerable academic interest in the last two decades and likely will continue to be for the next several years with the support of new federal funding. On April 28, 2014, the Department of Justice released a statement from Attorney General Eric Holder outlining a $4.75 million project to gather data on issues of racial fairness in the criminal justice system. Research will be funded to study a number of areas, from stops and searches of persons to wrongful convictions. The purpose of the project is to curb racial bias in the criminal justice system in an effort to reduce the level of mistrust between law enforcement and minority communities. The attorney general said the project was spurred by a request from President Obama after the verdict in the Trayvon Martin case. Martin was a 17-year-old African American who was shot and killed by a neighborhood block watch captain named George Zimmerman in 2012.

Although academic research has been common on racial profiling, the level of public interest has not been so consistent. As is true with much of the public focus, it is driven by the coverage of significant events by the media. This is equally true with racial profiling. The Trayvon Martin case created substantial public interest in racial profiling as is made clear by the renewed public funding effort to study the issue. Interestingly, the renewed interest in racial profiling in this case is not driven by the direct action of the police, but by the shooting death of a black teen by a nonblack man. Of course, the primary source of conflict is driven by this racial difference and how it was suspected to have motivated the person pulling the trigger.

The decades leading up to the Trayvon Martin case show an inconsistent level of interest by media sources. A recent study of three large city newspapers shows coverage of racial profiling varied dramatically over a 25-year period (Archbold et al. 2013). The first appearance of the term "racial profiling" did not appear in any of the newspapers in the study until 1986. It was not until 1999 that coverage of racial profiling became noticeably more common, moving from just a handful of instances in 1998 to 88 stories in 1999. Reporting peaked the following year with 262 articles and began to fall in 2001 with 235 articles, finally falling back to pre-1998 levels with just one article in 2004.

Determining what drives media attention and resulting public interest is difficult. The 1991 case involving the police beating of Rodney King in Los Angeles did not drive a change in reporting in the newspapers in the study. Although a causal link cannot be drawn between the cases, the instances of police brutality and use of excessive force involving Abner Louima in 1997 and Amadou Diallo in 1999 may have contributed to the renewed interest in racial profiling at the end of the decade. Racial profiling also became a significant topic in the 2000 national presidential election given that when the topic was covered, it was most commonly in connection with the election coverage (Archbold et al. 2013).

The police executive or government official that denies racial profiling occurs in their jurisdiction does so at his or her own peril. A study by Barlow and Barlow (2002) responded to claims by the former governor of Wisconsin Tommy Thompson, the Milwaukee police chief, and the sheriff of Milwaukee County who all claimed racial profiling did not occur in their jurisdiction. The study surveyed African-American police officers for the city of Milwaukee in regards to their experiences with racial profiling. The results showed 69 percent had experienced racial profiling at some time during their life. Twenty-five percent of officers said it had also occurred during the last year, while they were employed as a police officer. While the vast majority of officers said they did not engage in racial profiling, 10 percent of the officers felt it was a necessary part of policing.

If racial profiling is seen as a legitimate tool for law enforcement, where does it come from? The existence of this belief suggests racial profiling may not be solely perpetuated by prejudice, but rather training and guidance by those in a position of authority. The drug war led to the widespread use of drug courier profiling and these profiles at times include the use of ethnicity or race in the profile. Kurlander (2000) specifically described the Florida Highway Patrol guidelines, which used ethnicity in profiling groups commonly attached to the drug trade. Supreme Court decisions may also have seemingly endorsed profiling to police officers by allowing the use of pretextual stops (*Whren v. United States* 1996). While the court emphasized selective enforcement of the law is unconstitutional, some officers may see this as a mixed message.

Research results suggest police officers believe racial profiling takes place (Barlow and Barlow 2002), and public opinion surveys suggest the general public believes it as well. A 2004 Gallup poll showed 53 percent of respondents believed the use of racial profiling by the police was widespread (Carlson 2004). Arrest statistics also seem to support the use of racial profiling as research showed 49 percent of black males had been arrested by age 23 compared with 38 percent of white males (Brame et al. 2014).

So why is it so hard to study racial profiling? One reason is that it is difficult to measure the motivation of a police officer in making a decision to take action. Black and Latino males between the ages of 14 and 24 made up 41.6 percent of stops by New York City police, while they only represented 4.7 percent of the population (New York Civil Liberties

Union 2012). While statistics like these suggest the matter of racial profiling is clear, the Rand Center on Quality Policing (Ridgeway 2007) studied the characteristics of these stops and found the racial differences were small when other factors were considered. They examined crime-suspect descriptions and the relationship with race and found black pedestrian stops were not disproportionate, but they were slightly more likely to be searched.

Place becomes a significant issue when assessing racial profiling. Rojek, Rosenfeld, and Decker (2012) found a racial disparity existed when looking at traffic stops in St. Louis, Missouri. However, this disparity was inconsistent when examining where the stops took place. Although overall black drivers were more likely to be searched by white officers than white drivers, white drivers were more likely to be searched in black neighborhoods. Meehan and Ponder (2002) referred to this as "out of place" policing as in their study they found that as black drivers went farther into white communities, they were more likely to be stopped. Novak and Chamlin (2012) discovered a similar result in Kansas City, Missouri where search rates were higher for white drivers in beats with a larger proportion of black residents.

What is clear is that more consistent data collection is needed to examine racial profiling, and lessons from previous research need to be considered in doing so. Lundman (2010) found that race data was more likely to be missing on traffic citations when the driver was from a zip code above average in minority residents. Further, other races and places need to be included in the examination. The racial profiling of Native Americans has also become more public with claims made in Utah and Arizona (Berry 2013; Sanchez 2010). Suggestions to address the issue have included ensuring that officers are more familiar with department policies and that better oversight is in place within agencies to identify those officers whose stop data is racially skewed (Ridgeway 2007). To ensure the criminal justice system is seen as fair and just, this type of analysis is needed at all levels to guarantee due process to all.

*Thorvald O. Dahle is a doctoral student and instructor in criminal justice at North Dakota State University, Fargo, North Dakota. His research interests concentrate primarily on policing, profiling, issues regarding ethics in law enforcement, race, gender, and criminal law and procedure. He is a coauthor on works published for the* Journal of Race and Justice *and* Journal of Interpersonal Violence. *He earned a master's degree in public and human service administration from Minnesota State University Moorhead in 1999. He spent 24 years in law enforcement including serving as a chief of police.*

## References

Archbold, C. A., T. O. Dahle, M. Fangman, E. Wentz, and M. Wood. 2013. Newspaper Accounts of Racial Profiling Accurate Portrayal or Perpetuation of Myth? *Race and Justice* 3(4): 300–320.

Barlow, D. E., and M. H. Barlow. 2002. Racial Profiling: A Survey of African American Police Officers. *Police Quarterly* 5(3): 334–358.

Berry, C. 2013. Boycott! Racial Profiling by Cops Angers Ute Indian Tribe. *Indian Country.* Retrieved May 21, 2014. http://indiancountrytodaymedianetwork.com/2013/09/02/racial-profiling-angers-ute-indian-tribe-leading-economic-boycott-151124.

Carlson, D. K. 2014. Racial Profiling Seen as Pervasive, Unjust. *Gallup Online.* Retrieved May 21, 2014. http://www.gallup.com/poll/12406/racial-profiling-seen-pervasive-unjust.aspx.

Kurlander, N. 2000. Software to Track Traffic Stop Data. *Law Enforcement Technology* 27(7): 148–153.

Lundman, R. J. 2010. Are Police-Reported Driving While Black Data a Valid Indicator of the Race and Ethnicity of the Traffic Law Violators Police Stop? A Negative Answer with Minor Qualifications. *Journal of Criminal Justice* 38(1): 77–87.

Meehan, Albert J., and Michael C. Ponder. 2002. Race and Place: The Ecology of Racial Profiling African American Motorists. *Justice Quarterly* 19: 399–430.

New York Civil Liberties Union online 2012. Retrieved May 21, 2014. http://www.nyclu.org/ news/new-nyclu-report-finds-nypd-stop-and-frisk-practices-ineffective-reveals-depth-of-racial-dispar.

Novak, K. J., and M. B. Chamlin. 2012. Racial Threat, Suspicion, and Police Behavior: The Impact of Race and Place in Traffic Enforcement. *Crime & Delinquency* 58: 275–300.

Ridgeway, G. 2007. *Analysis of Racial Disparities in the New York Police Department's Stop, Question, and Frisk Practices.* Rand Corporation Technical Report. http://www.rand.org/ pubs/technical_reports/TR534.html.

Rojek, J., R. Rosenfeld, and S. Decker. 2012. Policing Race: The Racial Stratification of Searches in Police Traffic Stops. *Criminology* 50(4): 993–1024.

Sanchez, A. N. 2010. Native American Suggests He Was Profiled By Arizona Police: "New Bill Targets People Of My Color." *Think Progress.* http://thinkprogress .org/security/2010/05/03/176035/native-american-immigration/.

United States Department of Justice news release. 2014, April 28. www.justice.gov/opa/pr/2014/April/14-ag-445.html.

Walker, S. 2001. Searching for the Denominator: Problems with Police Traffic Stop Data and an Early Warning System Solution. *Justice Research and Policy* 3: 63–96.

## Criminal Behavioral Profiling—A Critical Perspective: Penny R. Shtull

The use of criminal behavioral profiling by law enforcement agencies around the world has dramatically increased in the past two decades, and it has also gained considerable public attention. Profiling is often depicted in the media and on pop-ular television shows (e.g., *CSI*, *NCIS*, *Silence of the Lambs*, and *Mindhunters*) as the primary means by which sensationalistic crimes (particularly murders) are solved.

There are many types of violent crime profiling, and their names and varied methods are often mistakenly used inter-changeably, which can cause confusion. These names include, but are not limited to: criminal behavioral profiling, criminal investigative analysis, psychological profiling, behavioral evi-dence analysis, criminal investigation assessment, offender pro-filing, and crime scene analysis.

The most commonly known method of criminal profiling, criminal investigative analysis, has its origins in the early 1970s, when the FBI developed a Behavioral Science Unit (BSU) at the FBI Academy. The Unit in the 1970s and 1980s brought significant support to criminal profiling and the eventual pub-lication of the *Crime Classification Manual: A Standard System for Investigating and Classifying Violent Crimes*. The BSU is cur-rently named the Behavioral Research and Instruction Unit (BRIU) and is run under the direction of the National Center for the Analysis of Violent Crime (NCAVC).

In general, the purpose of criminal profiling is to provide law enforcement with a comprehensive description of a poten-tial offender. It is a psychology-related investigative tool used to identify the "personality traits, behavioral patterns, geographic habits, and demographic features of an offender based on char-acteristics of the crime" (Bartol and Bartol 2011, 294). The basic assumption of this type of profiling is that the offender's personality is apparent in the crime scene.

The FBI developed an organized/disorganized dichotomy profiling approach that classifies offenders' personalities based on certain details of the crime scene. Although it has been widely criticized by researchers, it is still the most popular profiling model used internationally. An organized offender is someone methodical who spends "vast amounts of time planning their murders," and is assumed to have "a preoccupation with and constant need for control" (Godwin 2008, 10). In contrast, the crimes of a disorganized offender may be impulsive and generally reflect "no forensic awareness," and "evidence of little or no preparation" (Godwin 2008, 12–13).

Most methods of criminal profiling involve either inductive or deductive reasoning, which are the logical structures profilers used to draw their conclusions. Inductive reasoning uses "criminological studies, the profiler's own experience, intuition, bias, stereotypes and generalizations" (Petherick 2014, 33) to make inferences about a current case. It is often based on the profiler's subjective biases. In contrast, deductive reasoning involves assessment of the current case's physical evidence. Profilers using this method must establish that all premises are true and valid before basing a conclusion on them. This method is best suited for determining offender characteristics, while inductive reasoning can be used for developing hypotheses (Petherick 2014).

Some crimes are more appropriate for profiling than others. Profiling is best suited for solving crimes in which crime scene patterns and the motive of the offender can be detected. These include but are not limited to sadistic sexual assaults, sexual homicide, postmortem cases of abuse and humiliation, motiveless fire settings, lust and mutilation murders, rape, occult and ritualistic crimes, child sexual abuse including pedophilia, bank robberies, and anonymous obscene communications (Holmes and Holmes 2009, 5).

Although many consider profiling a useful asset for law enforcement and it is widely used throughout the world, the little research that has been done to assess its reliability and effectiveness is not encouraging. Furthermore, profiling is often perceived to be an exact science (especially by profilers themselves), although in fact much of profiling is "guesswork based on hunches and anecdotal information accumulated through years of experience, and it is full of error and misinterpretation" (Bartol and Bartol 2011, 296). According to Turvey, profilers themselves are part of the problem. He describes them as "often poorly educated in the forensic and behavioral sciences" (2012, xv). Similarly, Bartol and Bartol contend that many profilers "rely on outdated personality theory and psychological principles, and are basically unfamiliar with the current research literature on profiling and human behavior in general" (2011, 298).

Despite these drawbacks, criminal profiling can be an important investigative tool and current research is focused on developing valid methodological approaches to profiling. Godwin asserts that profilers must "bring science into the picture . . . and start relying on hard research" in order to improve their work (Godwin 2008, 250).

Holmes and Holmes note that profiling is "an art, not a science" (2009, 12). They stress the importance of intuition, while also acknowledging that a profiler must draw from "relevant concepts in criminology, sociology, psychology, and psychiatry" (2009, 13). Perhaps, it is more accurate to describe profiling as an art that must be informed and strengthened by science. Its critics note that a more rigorous joining of the two can be an antidote to current problems with profiling. But whether designated an art, a science, or a blend of both, profiling alone rarely identifies a specific offender, no matter what is shown on television.

*Penny R. Shtull earned a PhD in criminal justice from John Jay College of Criminal Justice in New York City and is the associate dean of the College of Liberal Arts and a professor of criminal justice in the School of Justice Studies at Norwich University in Vermont. Dr. Shtull is an expert on violent crime and often appears in the news media and international radio, and most recently she was featured as the expert/criminologist on the A&E true crime documentary* The Killer Speaks. *Dr. Shtull is a past president of the Northeastern Association of Criminal Justice Sciences (NEACJS) and has consulted for various organizations and state agencies. She serves on many state and national boards and committees and is the recipient of numerous faculty and research awards. She is a former recipient of the Northeastern Association of Criminal Justice*

*Sciences Association's Founders Award in recognition of her service and significant and outstanding contributions to the association. Her most current research addresses the police response to mental health issues on campus.*

## References

Bartol, C. R., and A. M. Bartol. 2011. *Criminal Behavior: A Psychological Approach.* 9th ed. Upper Saddle River, NJ: Prentice Hall.

Godwin, G. M. 2008. *Hunting Serial Predators.* 2nd ed. Sudbury, MA: Jones and Bartlett Publishers, Inc.

Holmes, R. M., and S. T. Holmes. 2009. *Profiling Violent Crimes: An Investigative Tool.* 4th ed. Thousand Oaks, CA: Sage Publications.

Petherick, W. 2014. *Profiling and Serial Crime: Theoretical and Practical Issues.* 3rd ed. Waltham, MA: Anderson Publishing.

Turvey, B. 2012. *Criminal Profiling: An Introduction to Behavioral Evidence Analysis.* 4th ed. Oxford, England: Academic Press.

## Media Influence on Perceived Offender-Victim Relationship: Paige Heinrich

Media exposure can change the ways in which people view the world around them. "[T]he public generally has limited direct experience with crime and depends primarily on news media for information about crime" (Gruenewald, Pizarro, and Chermak 2009, 262). Due to this, it is crucial the type of information the media covers is accurate. This is often not the case, and several studies have shown that homicides that are least common are actually given more coverage than those homicides which are more common. The studies, however, suggest that coverage isn't solely based upon how common or uncommon a homicide is, but instead is based upon how the story could be scripted. It has been observed that the less common offender-victim race relationship of black-white crime is reported more by news media in comparison to the less common offender-victim gender relationship of female-male crime. In other words, the race/ethnicity of the offender dictates whether or not the media will cover the case (Gruenewald, Pizarro and Chermak 2009; Lundman 2003; Quillian and Pager 2010).

In a study done by Quillan and Pager (2010), it was stated that while there is a wide range of influences upon a person's perception of risk, the largest concern is that of race. The idea that more blacks tend be involved in criminal behavior exists for several reasons. It is thought that "during the last 50 years as a result of race-coded politics and politicization of crime, criminal justice policies and practices that have resulted in the disproportionate criminalization of Blacks, and racially biased depictions of crime in the media" (Pickett et al. 2012, 149).

Several studies conducted have compared the composition of a neighborhood and the perceived risk of victimization in that neighborhood. These studies indicate that both whites' and nonwhites' perceived risk of victimization increases when the composition of the neighborhood is mostly nonwhite (Chiricos, Hogan, and Gertz 1997; Pickett et al. 2012; Quillan and Pager 2001). It appears that "the mere presence of black males increasingly is identified with crime and the fear of crime in popular and political culture" (Chiricos, Hogan, and Gertz 1997, 107). This perceived notion has been found to be related to the stereotype that black males are more prone to violence and criminality. Therefore, more people are likely to be fearful of a neighborhood with more black males in it in comparison to surrounding neighborhoods (Pickett et al. 2012). However, some research argues that the racial composition of a neighborhood is actually a proxy to nonracial elements of the neighborhood, for example, poverty (Quillan and Pager 2001).

When exploring the research conducted about female offenders, it appears that very few significant studies have been completed. While there have been several studies about female homicides, it appears that "there are still inconsistencies between studies regarding the relevance of social structural and gender-specific theories of crimes" (Pizarro, DeJong, and McGarrell 2010, 52). From the standpoint of the victim, many would assume that women are more likely than man to be victims; however, this is untrue. This assumption appears to be connected to the amount of news coverage an offender-victim relationship such as male-female would obtain in comparison to a relationship of male-male (Gruenewald, Pizarro, and Chermak 2009; Lundman 2003).

In order to explain the differences between a male and a female offender, one should look at the culture in which these people exist. In American society, people have come to recognize certain traits as being "masculine" or "feminine" and people believe that males and females should act accordingly. Masculine traits are those such as aggressiveness, controlling personality, and risk-taking behavior; all of these things can be seen in the criminal world. Feminine traits on the other hand would appear not to be present in the criminal world. Such traits as docility, submissiveness, and vulnerability would tend to not fit into the criminal world (Britton 2000; Page 2008; Pizarro, DeJong, and McGarrell 2010; Vaske et al. 2011; West and Zimmerman 1987).

Historically, there seems to be a connection between people's notions of criminal offenders and their victims in regards to the race and gender of the two individuals. While race and gender are independent characteristics of a person, the two are commonly used as proxies when discussed in reference of offenders and victims. The perceived offender-victim relationship has several influencing factors. Media coverage appears to have the largest impact upon this perception.

*Paige Heinrich graduated in 2013 with her bachelor's degree from the College of Mount St. Joseph in Cincinnati, Ohio, with a dual degree in criminology and sociology. She is currently studying for her master's degree in Criminology at Marshall University in*

*Huntington, West Virginia. One day she hopes to pursue her PhD, but still undecided as to where she will attend.*

## References

Britton, D. M. 2000. Feminism in Criminology: Engendering the Outlaw. *The Annals of the American Academy* 571: 57–76.

Chiricos, T., M. Hogan, and M. Gertz. 1997. Racial Composition of Neighborhood and Fear of Crime. *Criminology* 35(1): 107–131.

Cross, C. P., and A. Campbell. 2011. Women's Aggression. *Aggression and Violent Behavior* 16: 390–398.

Gruenewald, J., J. Pizarro, and S. M. Chermak. 2009. Race, Gender, and the Newsworthiness of Homicide Incidents. *Journal of Criminal Justice* 37: 262–272.

Lundman, R. J. 2003. The Newsworthiness and Selection Bias in News about Murder: Comparative and Relative Effects of Novelty and Race and Gender Typifications on Newspaper Coverage of Homicide. *Sociological Forum* 18(3): 387–386.

Pager, A. D. 2008. Judging Women and Defining Crime: Police Officers' Attitudes toward Women and Rape. *Sociological Spectrum* 28: 389–411.

Pickett, J. T., T. Chiricos, K. M. Golden, and M. Gertz. 2012. Reconsidering the Relationship between Perceived Neighborhood Racial Composition and Whites' Perceptions of Victimization Risk: Do Racial Stereotypes Matter? *American Society of Criminology* 50(1): 145–186.

Pizarro, J. M., C. DeJong, and E. F. McGarrell. 2010. An Examination of the Covariates of Female Homicide Victimization and Offending. *Feminist Criminology* 5(1): 51–72.

Quillan, L., and D. Pager. 2001. Black Neighbors, Higher Crime? The Role of Racial Stereotypes in Evaluations of Neighborhood Crime. *American Journal of Sociology* 107(3): 717–767.

Quillian, L., and D. Pager. 2010. Estimating Risk: Stereotype Application and the Perceived Risk of Criminal Victimization. *Social Psychology* 73(1): 79–104.

Vaske, J., J. P. Wright, D. Boisvert, and K. M. Beaver. 2011. Gender, Genetic Risk, and Criminal Behavior. *Psychiatry Research* 185: 376–381.

West, C., and D. H. Zimmerman. 1987. Doing Gender. *Gender & Society* 1(2): 125–151.

## Going beyond "Flying While Arab"— Islamophobic Profiling in the Era of Homeland Security: Connie M. Koski

The events of September 11, 2001, have significantly impacted the United States in a number of ways. Many of these changes are particularly evident in analyses of the nation's collective views of Arab and Muslim Americans. More specifically, Arab and Muslim Americans immediately became the targets of profiling, violence, discrimination, and defamation. For instance, one analysis of major American newspaper stories noted over 640 incidents of bias and hate crimes against South Asians and Arab Americans in the seven days following September 11 (Cainkar 2002). In addition, the U.S. government quickly detained hundreds of Arabs and South Asians for several weeks without charges (Chandrasekhar 2003). The purpose of this essay is to provide a brief overview of the dynamics surrounding a variant of racial profiling that has become known as terror profiling; a practice that has emerged as one of the primary tools utilized by law enforcement in the War on Terror. This form of profiling has not only blurred the distinction between race and religion, but also generated a number of detrimental consequences for many Arab and Muslim Americans. Moreover, the effectiveness of terror profiling remains questionable in its ability to protect American from future attacks.

Before proceeding, it is first important to have a basic understanding of the American Arab and Muslim communities in the United States. Currently, there are over 3 million Americans of Middle Eastern Arabic descent living in post-9/11 America. Additionally, although the Muslim faith does represent the fastest growing portion of the Middle Eastern community worldwide, the majority of Arabs in America are actually Christian (Agguire and Turner 2010; Cainkar 2002). The geographic, cultural, religious, economic, and political diversity of Arabic immigrants residing in the United States is broad, yet many Americans' understanding of these individuals is limited. This situation becomes even more problematic when American citizens mistakenly associate persons of Arabic descent exclusively with religious terms such as "Islam" and "Muslim." Although the events of 9/11 were not the direct cause of this association, they served as the catalyst for terror profiling based upon pre-existing prejudice towards Arab Americans, regardless of their religious affiliations (Cainkar 2002). These practices can be attributed to two primary sources of origination, the first of which can be traced back to negative opinions which emerged following the 1967 Arab-Israeli Conflict. These negative opinions resulted in the "racialization" of religion (Chon and Arzt 2005; Elver 2012), whereby many Americans homogenized their anti-Arab sentiments with anti-Muslim suspiciousness and vilification (Agguire and Turner 2010; Elver 2012; Gottschalk and Greenberg 2008). The second can be traced to the historical racialization of religion by American law, dating back to World War II, when Shintoistic religious differences contributed to the association of Japanese American racial difference in the case of *Hirabayashi v. United States*, which justified the government's differential treatment of Japanese Americans "because a propensity to espionage and sabotage [could] be inferred from those differences" (Chon and Arzt 2005, 217). Similarly, many of the post-9/11 enforcement strategies surrounding counterterrorism surveillance and the profiling of suspected terrorists have been legally upheld in favor of national security concerns (Cole 2003). This "Islamophobia," or the "unfounded hostility toward Islam . . . [and the] practical consequences of such hostility [results] in unfair discrimination of Muslim individuals and communities" (Runnymede Trust 1997, 4).

Consequently, Islamophobic terror profiling has become particularly salient in the post-9/11 era as members of the Middle Eastern and Muslim American communities have frequently been stereotyped and targeted as the Muslim terrorist "other." Similar to racial profiling, terror profiling has been defined in a variety of ways (Onwudiwe 2005). For purposes of this discussion, terror profiling is defined as follows:

> In large populations of individuals . . . governments attempt to find the rare malfeasor [terrorists, for example] by assigning prior probabilities to individuals, in some manner estimating the chance that each is a malfeasor. Societal resources for secondary security screening are then concentrated against individuals with the largest priors. (Press 2009, 1716)

In the case of Arab and Muslim Americans, the connection between Islamophobia and terror profiling is not difficult to make in light of the religious and racial demographics of the 9/11 terrorists. This enforcement tactic has most typically been illustrated by incidents involving more frequent searches and arbitrary detention of Arab- or Muslim-appearing persons at airport and other border checkpoints, or outright removal of such people from domestic and international flights.

Notably, although a significant number of Americans disapproved of law enforcement practices involving the profiling of black and Hispanic motorists prior to 9/11 (Cainkar 2002; Newman and Brown 2009; Weitzer and Tuch 2006), opinion polls immediately following the attacks found "that a majority of Americans favored profiling of Arabs, including those who are American citizens, and subjecting them to special security checks before boarding planes" (Cainkar 2002, 23; see also Rudovsky 2007). During this time, the increased attention to the need for national security measures frequently outweighed civil rights concerns to the point that even Arab Americans felt terror profiling methods were justified (Coke 2003). In the years since 9/11, public opinion favoring the profiling of persons appearing to be of Arabic descent or of the Muslim faith at airports has only marginally dissipated (Gabbidon, Higgins, and Nelson 2012; Gabbidon et al. 2009; Johnson et al. 2011; Schildkraut 2009).

Most people would agree that the events of 9/11 invoked the need for vigilance in a new era of homeland security. The manner in which this should be carried out, however, is a matter of debate. For example, recent research indicates that "law enforcement officers were more likely to support the value of terrorist profiling and are more likely to be suspicious of a Middle Eastern male," whereas non-law-enforcement subjects were less likely to be suspicious of Middle Eastern males and less likely to support the usefulness of terror profiling (Newman and Brown 2009, 371). Furthermore, Islamophobic terror profiling has negatively impacted the Arab and Muslim American communities in a variety of ways; many of which are similar to those noted in African American and Latino American communities resulting from other forms of racial profiling. The unfortunate consequence of this has been the deterioration of trust and legitimacy in the police and significant alienation of those who are likely the most needed partners in the War on Terror in this country (Creating Law Enforcement Accountability & Responsibility Project, The Muslim Fund American Civil Liberties Coalition, and The Asian American Legal Defense and Education 2013).

It is unlikely that a resolution to civil rights/national security debate over Islamophobic terror profiling will occur anytime soon. However, recent events in New York City may be contributing to a shift in American terror profiling practices. The publication of a series of articles by the Associated Press in 2011 documented terror profiling practices by the NYPD which had gone far beyond the intrusiveness of the profiling of Arab and Muslim Americans at airports and other border crossings. These articles revealed the manner in which the NYPD's secret Demographics Unit, in conjunction with the CIA, employed tactics such as warrantless mapping, monitoring, and analysis of the daily lives of American Muslims throughout the city and in surrounding states (Apuzzo and Goldman 2011). Publication of these stories lead to an outcry from local officials, Islamic religious leaders, civil rights activists, and the general public regarding the marginalization and criminalization of large numbers of innocent Arab and Muslim American residents (Goldman and Apuzzo 2012a). Notably, the following year, Lt. Paul Galati, Chief of the NYPD Intelligence Division, admitted that during his six-year command, the Demographics Unit had not produced a single criminal or terrorist lead (Goldman and Apuzzo 2012b).

Evidence of inappropriate or ineffective uses of terror profiling strategies is not limited to the NYPD (see, e.g., American-Arab Anti-Discrimination Committee 2011). However, recent attempts to remedy these issues have emerged; the most notable of which includes the April 2014 expansion of the definition of racial profiling to include religion, national origin, gender, and sexual orientation by the U.S. Department of Justice. This move not only prohibits federal agents from considering these factors in their investigations but also mandates data collection on stops, searches, and arrests in an attempt to reduce bias and improve relations between law enforcement and minority communities (Apuzzo 2014; U.S. Department of Justice 2014). Although it remains unclear whether, or how, the new rules will be applied to national security investigations, civil rights advocacy groups like the ACLU and National Network for Arab American Communities remain hopeful that this change will provide a more efficient balance between civil rights and homeland security (Apuzzo 2014). While it is unlikely that this latest move by the Justice Department will put an end to Islamophobic terror profiling, it is arguably a positive step in the right direction. Only time will tell what its ultimate impact will be.

*Connie M. Koski received her PhD in criminology and criminal justice from the University of Nebraska at Omaha and is currently an assistant professor of criminology and criminal justice studies at Longwood University in Virginia. Dr. Koski is also a retired police officer from Michigan. Her primary research interests focus on neighborhood-level informal social control and collective efficacy, police-community relationships, qualitative methods, and teaching issues of race/ethnicity in criminal justice. Dr. Koski's work has been published in* Police Practice and Research: An International Journal, Journal of Criminal Justice Education, Journal of Criminal Justice, *and* The Criminologist.

## References

Agguire Jr., A., and J. H Turner. 2010. *American Ethnicity: The Dynamics and Consequences of Discrimination.* 7th ed. New York: McGraw-Hill.

American-Arab Anti-Discrimination Committee. 2011. *The 2010 ADC Legal Report: Legal Advocacy and Policy Review.* Retrieved from http://adc.org/fileadmin/ADC/Pdfs/2010_ADC_Legal_Report.pdf.

Apuzzo, M. 2014, January 15. U.S. to Expand Rules Limiting Use of Profiling by Federal Agents. *The New York Times.* Retrieved from http://www.nytimes.com/2014/01/16/us/politics/us-to-expand-rules-limiting-use-of-profiling-by-federal-agents.html?_r=0.

Apuzzo, M., and A. Goldman. 2011, August 23. With CIA Help, NYPD Moves Covertly in Muslim Areas. *Associated Press.* Retrieved from http://www.ap.org/Content/

AP-In-The-News/2011/With-CIA-help-NYPD-moves-covertly-in-Muslim-areas.

Cainkar, L. 2002. No Longer Invisible: Arab and Muslim Exclusion after September 11. *Middle East Report* 224: 22–29.

Chandrasekhar, C. A. 2003. Flying While Brown: Federal Civil Rights Remedies to Post-9/11 Airline Racial Profiling of South Asians. *Asian American Law Journal* 10(3): 215–252.

Chon, M., and D. E. Arzt. 2005. Walking While Muslim. *Law & Contemporary Problems* 68: 215–254.

Coke, T. E. 2003. Racial Profiling Post-9/11: Old Story, New Debate. In: C. Brown (Ed.), *Lost Liberties: Ashcroft and the Assault on Personal Freedom*. New York: The New Press, 91–111.

Cole, D. 2003. *Enemy Aliens: Double Standards and Constitutional Freedoms in the War on Terrorism*. New York: The New Press.

Creating Law Enforcement Accountability & Responsibility (CLEAR) Project, The Muslim Fund American Civil Liberties Coalition (MACLC), and The Asian American Legal Defense and Education (AALDEF). 2013. *Mapping Muslims: NYPD Spying and Its Impact on American Muslims*. Retrieved from http://www.law.cuny.edu/academics/clinics/immigration/clear/Mapping-Muslims.pdf.

Elver, H. 2012. Racializing Islam before and after 9/11: From Melting Pot to Islamophobia. *Transnational Law & Contemporary Problems* 21: 119–174.

Gabbidon, S. L., G. E. Higgins, and M. Nelson. 2012. Public Support for Racial Profiling in Airports: Results from a State-wide Poll. *Criminal Justice Policy Review* 23(2): 254–269.

Gabbidon, S. L., E. B. Penn, K. L. Jordan, and G. E. Higgins. 2009. The Influence of Race/Ethnicity on the Perceived Prevalence and Support for Racial Profiling at Airports. *Criminal Justice Policy Review* 20: 344–358.

Goldman, A., and M. Apuzzo. 2012a, March 9. NYPD Docs: "Focus" Scrutiny on Muslim Americans. *Associated Press.* Retrieved from http://www.ap.org/Content/AP-In-The-News/2012/focus-scrutiny-on-Muslim-Americans.

Goldman, A., and M. Apuzzo. 2012b, August 21. NYPD: Muslim Spying Led to No Leads, Terror Cases. *Associated Press.* Retrieved from http://www.ap.org/Content/AP-In-The-News/2012/NYPD-Muslim-spying-led-to-no-leads-terror-cases.

Gottschalk, P., and G. Greenberg. 2008. *Islamophobia: Making Muslims the Enemy.* Lanham, MD: Rowman & Littlefield Publishers, Inc.

Johnson, D., D. Brazier, K. Forrest, C. Ketelhut, D. Mason, and M. Mitchell. 2011. Attitudes Toward the Use of Racial/Ethnic Profiling to Prevent Crime and Terrorism. *Criminal Justice Policy Review* 22(4): 422–447.

Newman, D. W., and N. D. Brown. 2009. Historical Overview and Perceptions of Racial and Terrorist Profiling in an Era of Homeland Security. *Criminal Justice Policy Review* 20(3): 359–374.

Onwudiwe, I. D. 2005. Defining Terrorism, Racial Profiling and the Demonization of Arabs and Muslims in the USA. *Safer Communities* 4(2): 4–11.

Press, W. H. 2009. Strong Profiling is not Mathematically Optimal for Discovering Rare Malfeasors. *PNAS* 106(6): 1716–1719.

Rudovsky, D. 2007. Racial Profiling and the War on Terror. *University of Pennsylvania Law Review* 155: 173–185.

Runnymede Trust. 1997. *Islamophobia: A Challenge for Us All.* Retrieved from http://www.divshare.com/download/launch/9605806-94b.

Schildkraut, D. J. 2009. The Dynamics of Public Opinion on Ethnic Profiling after 9/11. *American Behavioral Scientist* 53: 61–79.

U.S. Department of Justice. 2014. *Attorney General Holder: Justice Dept. to Collect Data on Stops, Arrests as Part of Effort to Curb Racial Bias in Criminal Justice System.* Retrieved from http://www.justice.gov/opa/pr/2014/April/14-ag-445. html.

Weitzer, R., and S. A. Tuch. 2006. Perceptions of Racial Profiling: Race, Class, and Personal Experience. *Criminology* 40: 435–456.

## Profiling as a Positive Intervention for Managing People with Mental Illness in the Criminal Justice System: Pat Nelson

The term profiling has received a negative connotation due to specific practices carried out by law enforcement during proactive stops; however, the importance of profiling in the criminal justice system can lead to the solving of crimes, the application of appropriate interventions, and the fair application of punishment. Profiling can also be used to provide a positive intervention by the criminal justice system in identifying and managing people who have mental illness. This positive intervention helps build communities, and as noted by the European Commission (2005), an indicator of a community that balances human rights with public safety interests is a criminal justice system that can incorporate modern psychiatry, penal practice, public safety intervention, and mental health practices to serve mentally ill offenders (6).

Law enforcement agencies have been recognized in many communities as the only emergency response system that is available all the time, and as a result, law enforcement officers routinely encounter people who are in a state of mental health crisis (Reuland 2012). The state of mental health crisis may be the result of an overwhelming situation, or could be a result of a mental illness; however, this distinction is not made in current crisis intervention strategies. The strategies focus on identifying the cause of the crisis, defusing the crisis, and then stabilizing the situation, which may include hospitalization, arrest, or referrals depending on the assessment of the law enforcement officer on the scene. This growth in crisis intervention for law enforcement agencies has led to many successful and safe encounters between law enforcement officers and people in crisis, although there are still challenges due to the complexity and time-consuming nature of the interactions (Hendricks, McKean, and Hendricks 2010; Reuland 2012). While crisis intervention is a strategy for dealing with people in crisis, there is only very limited assessment, or profiling, about a person's mental health during contacts that may be considered routine, or simply criminal.

The arrest for a minor crime, an increase in calls for service to an address, or repeated probation violations are examples of behavior changes that could be indicators of a person who may be suffering from mental illness. However, due to the low level nature of the change in behavior or the lack of communication between different parts of the criminal justice system, there is very little chance of an assessment of the persons' mental health being completed, and early opportunities are lost for identification and intervention. The institutionalization of a brief mental health assessment in the criminal justice process could help realize these lost opportunities.

A challenge that the criminal justice system appears to face in creating a profiling system for general assessment of mental health is the lack of identified mental illness characteristics outside the crisis intervention system that does not stigmatize community members who are involved in the contact. This stigma has been recognized internationally, and has led to global mental health awareness campaigns, however, the persistence of myths about those who may be impacted by mental illness and the treatment for mental illness means that any profiling system would have to be general enough to allow for honest answers, yet specific enough to provide a reliable indication of the need for mental health services (Moore 2012). The assessment would also have to be easy to incorporate into current criminal justice activity at all levels.

A possible profile, or assessment, that could be expanded into general use is a version of the behavioral clues used to determine if a person is displaying suicidal behavior. The application of these general behavioral clues to the general population may provide an opportunity to provide positive mental health intervention. These behavioral clues, which could include verbal clues, behavioral clues, situational communications, and syndromatic communications, provide benchmarks of changes of thought and behavior in an individual (Russell and Beigel 1990), and this profiling can identify a change in the individual's normal behavior to abnormal behavior. Law enforcement officers learn during crisis intervention to determine if behavior is appropriate for the situation and if there are underlying factors that may be causing the crisis; this same type of thinking and communication can be applied in noncrisis situations as part of a mental health profile.

The profiling of mental health has already started in some communities that have veteran's courts and mental health courts, where the impact of post-traumatic stress disorder (PTSD) on a veteran's behavior and criminal actions has been identified, and the need for mental health intervention has been identified as an appropriate solution, instead of incarceration. There are also juvenile courts in the United States which have started a system of identifying juveniles who need mental health services before they have been charged with a crime based on profiles of behavior and communications from schools and parents. This proactive approach has been shown to reduce juvenile detention rates and also allows for the early identification for mental health treatment without arrest (Usher 2014). These two examples demonstrate how effective profiling, done in a general manner, and without stigma, can lead to the identification, intervention, and reintegration of community members who may be impacted by mental illness through the cooperation of the criminal justice system and the community.

*Pat Nelson is a native Minnesotan who has lived all over the state, spending the last 30 years in the Twin Cities metro region. Dr. Nelson joined the Department of Government at Minnesota State University Mankato in the Fall of 2011 teaching in the Law Enforcement program as an assistant professor. Dr. Nelson had 17 years of law enforcement experience with the Minneapolis (MN) Police Department as a patrol officer, investigator, SWAT negotiator, trainer, and patrol sergeant before retiring due to a work-related back injury in November 2013. Dr. Nelson is a member of numerous professional organizations at the state and national level in law enforcement and public administration. She holds a BS degree in law enforcement and a master's of public and nonprofit administration, and holds a PhD in public policy and administration with a dual focus on homeland security policy and coordination as well as terrorism, mediation, and peace. She has many areas of interest including crisis intervention, negotiations, women in policing, homeland security, terrorism, and preparing future law enforcement officers.*

## References

European Commission. 2005. *Placement and Treatment of Mentally Ill Offenders—Legislation and Practice in EU Member States: Final Report.* Mannheim, Germany: Central Institute of Mental Health.

Hendricks, J., J. McKean, and C. Hendricks. 2010. *Crisis Intervention: Contemporary Issues for On-site Interveners.* Springfield, IL: Charles C. Thomas Publishers.

Moore, R. 2012. Current Trends in Policing and the Mentally Ill in Europe: A Review of the Literature. *Police Practice and Research* 11(4): 42–53.

Reuland, M. 2012. Tailing the Police Response to People with Mental Illness to Community Characteristics in the USA. *Police Practice and Research* 11(4): 27–41.

Russell, H., and A. Beigel. 1990. *Understanding Human Behavior for Effective Police Work.* USA: Basic Books.

Usher, L. 2014. *Unlikely Allies in the Fight for Mental Health Services: Criminal Justice Leaders Speak Out.* National Alliance on Mental Illness. Retrieved from http://www .nami.org/Content/NavigationMenu/Top_Story/Unlikely_ Allies_in_the_Fight_for_Mental_Health_Services. htm.

## Negative Stereotypes, Discrimination, Poverty, and Anger—The Enduring Factors Leading to African Americans' Overrepresentation in Prison: Lauren Kientz Anderson

African Americans have been consistently overrepresented in the penal system of the United States because of discrimination and negative stereotypes, which have led to more frequent arrests and higher sentences, in addition to the crimes committed, because of the persistent effects of entrenched poverty in black communities.

In 2003, *The New York Times* reported that 12 percent of African American men ages 20 to 34 are in jail or prison (compared to 1.6 percent of similarly aged white men), the highest rate ever recorded. The U.S. Justice Department compiled this statistic and also reported that 28 percent of black men were imprisoned at some point in their lifetime. This has proven to be a hugely destabilizing force in black community life. It also means that a large percentage of black men cannot vote, because felons are stripped of the right to vote. There are several historical trends that led to this high rate. After European indentured servitude began to fade away, people of African descent became solely identified with slavery and bonded servitude. At this point in history, many colonies and states wrote laws specifically to control free black populations.

After the emancipation of slaves, different societies in the United States—from small towns to states to the federal government—felt that they had to continue to control black populations. They did this in part through new laws and in part through new associations of African Americans with criminality. This perception led to greater police attention to black communities and the willingness to incarcerate a black person who only vaguely fit the description of the perpetrator. In addition, blacks reacted to poverty and discrimination with a deep-seated anger that sometimes emerged as violence toward things and people physically close to them.

In the United States, there is a stereotypical association of African Americans with criminality. This was based in part on the fear of people of African descent that whites had. After Haitian slaves freed themselves through the Haitian Revolution in the late 1700s, U.S. white slave owners feared a similar rebellion and bloodbath. It was important to Euro-Americans to always control black behavior, and jail time became a primary way to do so. The media perpetuated the image of blacks as dangerous and criminal. For a long time after the Civil War, for example, newspapers would report on a crime and the suspected villain not by naming that person but by simply calling him or her "a negro" or giving the person's name, followed by "a negro." This implicated all African Americans in that single crime also stripped the individual of any identity but a racial one. Furthermore, almost all of the coverage of African Americans in mainstream newspapers was only about black people being charged with crimes. This gave white readers the perception that all black people were criminals or about to become criminals. This stereotypical association continues into the present, and recent scholarship has found "a direct relationship between the endorsement of negative black stereotypes and support for punitive criminal-justice measures" (Federico and Holmes 2005).

The relationship between African Americans and the police in many communities was one fraught with problems. Often blacks were only charged with a crime if it was against a white person. In addition, whites were rarely prosecuted for crimes that they committed against black people, including white men who raped black women or landowners that cheated their tenants or sharecroppers. This meant that black taxpayers did not have the same police protection as white taxpayers.

The perception that more African Americans were criminal got caught in a cycle: the perception led to more arrests, which then strengthened the perception, leading to more arrests, and so on. The idea that all African Americans were the same also meant that black men were arrested for crimes they did not commit because they loosely fit the "black and male" criteria being searched for. Sometimes if black men and white women were caught in a consensual love affair, the white woman would claim that the black man had forced her to avoid the social stigma of loving a black man or having sex out of wedlock (since it was illegal for blacks and whites to marry).

Furthermore, crowds of whites sometimes bypassed the legal system altogether, stole black people from their homes or their jail cells, and hung them from a tree or burned them at the stake. This is called lynching. Sometimes police attempted to stop this and sometimes they helped it occur. This usually happened before the black suspect had been given a fair trial and often because the black person had risen out of poverty and challenged the economic supremacy of the whites around him or her. Ida B. Wells Barnett was a major antilynching activist at the turn of the 20th century who first proved that most lynchings occurred for economic reasons, not the often cited reason of a black man raping a white woman. It was common for those at the lynching to take photographs of them beside the black person's dead body, to take pieces of the body for souvenirs, or to make postcards out of those photos and send them to friends and relatives in other parts of the country.

This difficult relationship with the police, including charges of police brutality, continued throughout the Jim Crow era into the civil rights movement of the 1950s and 1960s and afterward. The need for black men and women on the police force and a more just treatment of African American communities by the police was frequently raised during conversations about what actions were needed to improve black communities. A phrase popular within black communities was being pulled over by the police for DWB—Driving While Black. In other words, they are pulled over by police for no other reason that they are black and driving a car. Black leaders with the public ear have often commented that all black men know what it is like to be suspected by the police or have been stopped and interrogated by the police. This hyper-vigilance, coupled with stark inequalities and poverty, can create fierce anger.

The perception that people of African descent are criminals has outweighed the actual criminality of black communities and individuals throughout U.S. history. However, it is also true that some African Americans have committed crimes and some black communities have had high crime rates. One of the reasons for those crimes is the anger that journalist Eddy L. Harris described in his 1992 memoir: "Forgive me if I rant, but you cannot know how I have cried and despaired and nearly given myself over to the dark gods of bitterness and frustration. You cannot know, unless I now tell you, how the anger often wells up in me lately and I am driven to the edges of violence and hate and I want to insanely fight men bigger than myself and burn buildings down, set fire to their homes, their happiness, their way of life" (Harris 1997). Because Harris moved through a society that ignored his anger, he tried to repress it, "for it seems in my case to be especially unfounded, to make little sense. I was not born into slavery or into abject circumstances. Luckily for me and for those around me the gods in whose lap we sit saw fit that I should not be so cursed, for then surely I would have been a murderer, indeed a butcher" (Harris 1997).

This anger is compounded when it seems like there is no legal way to protect oneself and when poverty is entrenched. For example, in the late 1800s and early 1900s, white landowners constructed a system of sharecropping, which was better than slavery but created financial holes that black sharecroppers could never work their way out of. The sharecroppers had almost no one to turn to protect their legal rights. Sometimes, as in the case of Steve Greene in 1910, a black man went to the landowner's house to demand proper wages, a fight broke out, and the black man killed the white man. Whether or not it was in self-defense rarely became clear because it was very difficult for the black man to receive a fair trial in a culture that presumed his guilt.

Rather than attacking the source of their oppression, this anger has most often been directed at people and resources within reach. Another way to look at the same phenomenon is that most violent crime in impoverished neighborhoods occurred as a way to protect honor, family members, or assets in places that do not have a positive police presence. Most murdered black men, for instance, are killed by other black men. Throughout the 20th century, blacks tended to live in communities with a majority of African Americans. Before the civil rights movement, communities in the South were legally segregated, and in the North were segregated by practice. After the civil rights movement, it became legally possible for blacks to move into white neighborhoods, but remained practically difficult. In the latter half of the 20th century, whites left city centers in droves, frightened by the race riots in many American cities that followed the assassination of Martin Luther King Jr. in 1968. In addition, some middle-class blacks were able to move out of city centers into more upscale neighborhoods for the first time. This left behind single-class and single-race communities of the working class and the working poor. Studies have shown that mixed-income neighborhoods tend to have less crime, which began to prove true in inner cities around the country.

Urban density also created a higher crime rate as individuals lost some of the societal boundaries of small rural communities that had kept behavior in check, and also began to face persistent joblessness. A large migration of African Americans to urban centers in the North and South—known as the Great Migration—began during World War I. By the time World War II concluded, African Americans had become a primarily urban people, drawn by the promises of greater freedoms and jobs in factories. For a brief time, these communities flourished, though they always faced segregation, higher rents than other areas, and higher density.

Several factors came together in the late 20th century to challenge the health of all black city centers. Only a few decades after factories had beckoned blacks North, the processes of deindustrialization began to set in. Factories closed as corporations followed cheaper taxes to different parts of the country and then overseas. It became increasingly difficult for blacks to find good jobs, like those in General Motors' Michigan auto manufacturing plants that had raised a generation of African Americans into the middle class following World War II. For many young men, it seemed easier to live off of the underground economy than try to fit into the few resources of the legal one. When communities are entirely composed of the impoverished, with no opportunities for jobs, there is little for children to aspire to.

Before the Great Migration, many African Americans were trapped in the cycle of sharecropping and Jim Crow laws, which restricted how much they could learn and what kinds of jobs they could take. But the industries that brought African Americans to urban centers began to leave after the mid-20th century. Furthermore, without many layers of socioeconomic status, there were no small or large business owners to reinvest capital into their communities. After desegregation, many small black business owners lost their businesses because of the sudden surge in competition from white businesses and professionals that had more resources and often greater selection. That meant that there were fewer community resources to sponsor schools, cultural events, clubs, and other alternatives to crime.

Long-term poverty can create a persistent sense of despair and push families into repeated setbacks. Even so, it is important to note that while poverty creates circumstances in which it is understandable that some would turn to crime, the poor are no more or less apt to commit crimes than other socioeconomic groups. Many impoverished people strive every day to take care of their families, but struggle with poor health care, difficulty finding child care, difficulty raising children (as young people themselves), and fewer institutional resources. Research is beginning to show that it is not poverty itself, but all the structural problems that accompany poverty for many (but not all) poor people, that increases the likelihood of childhood delinquency.

One of the major substances distributed through the underground economy in the late 20th century, which decimated many black communities, was crack cocaine. People addicted to it were willing to do almost anything to get more. Neighborhoods of the working poor and working class, like Harlem in northern Manhattan, saw an influx of theft that made black homeowners afraid to leave their townhouses and apartments. At the same time, the way that the Ronald Reagan administration decided to deal with the influx of crack in the 1980s was to treat it like a war, with addicts and dealers as the enemy, rather than as someone with an affliction that could be treated. State legislatures across the country instituted mandatory sentencing laws that required everyone convicted of a law to be given the same sentence, no matter the circumstances. This took much of the power of discretion out of the hands of individual judges.

California and other states instituted a "three-strikes law" that required anyone convicted of three felonies to be given a life sentence. This swelled the prison population. Ethnic and racial tensions in some prisons created gang environments that required individual prisoners to choose a gang for protection and as a kind of family, while violence between gangs led to longer sentences. Gangs outside of prison created their own laws, and the introduction of guns to the streets created the possibility of drive-by killings and revenge killings.

One of the drug war's consequences was that the type of cocaine (smoked) used predominantly by African Americans required mandatory sentences that were longer than similar amounts of the cocaine used primarily by Euro-Americans (snorted or injected). Ironically, crack is an inferior form of cocaine containing many impurities. Thus, blacks ended up in jail for possessing smaller amounts of narcotics, and after serving jail time and having a felony on their record found it difficult to be employed. That made it hard to provide food and housing through any way but through the underground economy, opening an easy route back to their addiction. A jail sentence usually did not offer any help recovering other than cold turkey withdrawal. In 2001, California voters passed a ballot measure that mandated treatment rather than jail time for nonviolent drug offenders.

Throughout the country's history, African Americans have had a higher rate of imprisonment than other Americans. This can be traced to many factors. White people's fear that slaves would revolt and overturn their society, similar to what Haiti experienced, caused many white governments to set up stricter laws for black freedmen and women during the slave era and for freed blacks after the Civil War. Thus, there developed a persistent stereotype that African Americans were more criminal than other Americans. This meant that African Americans were more often suspected of a crime, and that one black person could be charged with a crime that another black person committed. When blacks began to urbanize in the first half of the 20th century, they found some greater freedoms but also continued discrimination and poverty. Feeling trapped and discriminated against led to a brewing anger among inner city dwellers that sometimes turned on the closest people to them—killing other African Americans and damaging local property.

The drug war begun in the 1980s dramatically increased the number of African Americans in jail. The greater proportion of African Americans in jail has become an even greater problem for our society in the last few decades. Knowing the historical trends that contribute to this problem will help us untangle some of the reasons for the preponderance of blacks incarcerated today.

*Lauren Kientz Anderson graduated from Michigan State University in 2010 with a PhD in African American intellectual history. Her dissertation explores the group of intellectuals and activists in W.E.B. Du Bois's shadow during the 1920s and 1930s, particularly how they educated themselves, how they lived through and challenged Jim Crow, and how they interacted with each other. She is pursuing post-doctoral studies at the University of Kentucky for 2010–2011 in the Office of the Dean of Arts and Sciences. She is special projects manager in that office and is facilitating three projects: a year-long focus on South Africa culminating in a celebration of Barbara Hogan and Ahmed Kathrada, development of the digital humanities and social sciences, and pursuit of interdisciplinarity throughout the campus.*

### References

Federico, C. M., and J. W. Holmes. 2005. Education and the Interface between Racial Perceptions and Criminal Justice Attitudes. *Political Psychology* 26(1): 47–75.

Harris, E. L. 1997. *South of Haunted Dreams: A Memoir.* New York: Holt.

### Epidemic Proportions: How Person and Environment Combine in the Overrepresentation of African Americans in the Criminal Justice System: Raphael Travis Jr.

Currently within state and federal prisons are 1,610,584 prisoners (Sabol, West, and Cooper 2010). California leads all states with 173,320 prisoners. Incarceration rates differ substantially by race/ethnicity, with African Americans being incarcerated at significantly higher rates that other groups, but even more so within certain age groups. For example, among individuals aged 30 to 34, the incarceration rate for all individuals is 3,328 per 100,000. However, as an example of overrepresentation and disparities by race/ethnicity, the rate of incarceration in 2008 was 1,793 for whites, 3,446 for Latinos, and 11,137 for African Americans (Sabol, West, and Cooper 2010).

Rates for women shared similar ethnicity-based disparities. Recidivism, or individuals returning to prison after being released, has not been tracked well at the national level, thus the most common rates cited come from the 2002 recidivism study from the Bureau of Justice Statistics. For prisoners released in 1994, 67.5 percent were rearrested within three years, an increase over the 62.5 percent found for those released in 1983 (Langan and Levin 2002). In 2008, parole violators accounted for 34.2 percent of all prison admissions, 36.2 percent of state admissions, and 8.2 percent of federal admissions (Sabol, West, and Cooper 2010). The magnitude of overrepresentation differs among states, but a net massive increase in incarceration for all U.S. residents has existed since the late 1970s due to several factors including legislative changes, reformed sentencing guidelines, changes in public opinion, and prison financing strategies (Golembeski and Fullilove 2005).

Disproportionate minority contact (DMC) with the criminal justice system, or the fact that racial and ethnic minorities are arrested, convicted, and sentenced at substantially greater rates than other groups, exists for both adults and juveniles. Racial and ethnic minorities in general, and African Americans in particular, have been overrepresented among the incarcerated and have been disproportionately impacted by this overrepresentation. While African Americans comprised 13 percent of the population, they accounted for 28 percent of arrests and 40 percent of prison inmates. Young African Americans are present in jail, in prison, on probation, on parole, or under other criminal justice supervision in staggering proportions. A bit of encouraging news is that the prisoner growth rate has been on decline since 2006 (Sabol, West, and Cooper 2010).

These statistics do not apply universally across all African Americans and instead tend to reflect the relationship between less-educated and underemployed African Americans and crime and incarceration (Western 2006). Similar challenges exist for less-educated and underemployed white and Latino populations, but the rate of incarceration is much higher for African Americans. Thus, education and employment appear to be at the core of persistent over-representation. However, the barriers to educational and employment success are linked to broader interrelated factors that limit the supports and opportunities available to African American youth; all are closely tied to the risk of involvement in the criminal justice system.

Again, overrepresentation of African Americans in the criminal justice system can be directly linked to a dynamic, ongoing person-environment relationship reinforced by (a) the roles of race/ethnicity in criminal justice decision making, and (b) available supports and opportunities critical to well-being and behavior.

First, evidence suggests that race and ethnicity are factors playing a role within pathways predicting negative criminal justice outcomes, including biases in public policy, arrest, adjudication, and sentencing. Second, structural/environmental factors have shaped the context that interacts with personal factors in determining criminal justice outcomes; in particular, punitive public policies, poorer educational opportunities, less employment opportunities, and heightened law enforcement surveillance. Third, for many African Americans, these factors—better described as external developmental assets—have been chronically weaker. This limits the ability to build upon personal strengths and increases chances of high-risk behavior. The results further entrench disparate criminal justice outcomes. Fourth, once involved in the criminal justice system, recidivism is likely. Insufficient prisoner reentry and transition resources coupled with the aforementioned asset deficiencies are obstacles to well-being and minimization of risky behaviors—conditions ripe for high recidivism.

The initial factor helping explain overrepresentation of African Americans is consistent documentation of the influence of race and ethnicity in varied pathways to negative criminal justice outcomes. Ethnic minorities, particularly African Americans and Latinos, continue to be more highly represented in the criminal justice system and are more likely to come from situations of social and economic disadvantage. However, aside from disadvantage, police officers, probation officers, and politicians have shown bias via racialized thinking and behaviors.

Biases in how ethnic minorities are viewed have shown the ability to directly influence decision making and ultimately unfavorable criminal justice outcomes. Studies have shown that the way decisions are made at all stages of the criminal justice system greatly increases the chance that those of low socioeconomic status and populations of color find themselves involved in the criminal justice system (Crow 2008). Despite federal intervention efforts since 1988 to reduce disproportionate minority contact with the criminal justice system, particularly among juveniles, efforts have failed to make statistically significant strides in reducing overrepresentation.

Thus, differences in incarceration patterns are a culmination of legislation, sentencing guidelines and tendencies, political leanings, and even unconscious decision making by criminal justice system stakeholders. Further, these influences help explain why declining crime rates after the peak of the early 1990s did little to stem the tide of incarceration.

Sentencing, grounded in unfair public policies, tends to be harsher for African Americans when compared to whites for the same offenses, including a higher chance of arrest for first-time offenders (Crow 2008). Particularly harsh disparities exist for drug offenses, due to mandatory sentencing guidelines but also when judicial discretion is possible. The U.S. Senate recently

passed S.1789, the Fair Sentencing Act of 2010, a bill addressing one of the most widely recognized sentencing disparities.
Penalties for two different forms of the same drug had a five-
year minimum sentence for distribution of 5 grams of crack
cocaine (more consistently linked to African Americans), but
to trigger the same sentence it would take 500 grams of powder
cocaine (more consistently linked to whites). This 100:1 sentencing disparity was not totally equalized by S.1789, but the
disparity was reduced to 18:1.

Keen and Jacobs (2009) examined incarceration rates and
race/ethnicity and found that broader political biases were
linked to differences in incarceration trends. States with high
support for Republican presidential candidates had the highest growth in disparate incarceration by race. Inherent in these
trends was that African American populations were considered a threat to the political and cultural landscape of certain
geographic areas. When African American populations were
below a certain level, incarceration disparities were clear. But
when population numbers rose above that threshold, the relationship did not continue. The assumption was that incarceration of African Americans helped reduce their perceived
threat. However, when the African American population
existed in larger numbers, they were sufficiently involved in
area decision making to avoid marginalization. This was an
example of a group-level process where race/ethnicity played
a role in sustaining influence, decision making, and political
and cultural advantage.

Among criminal justice system stakeholders, police officers
and probation officers have been shown to be influenced at
individual decision-making levels. Unlocking unconscious stereotypes had induced harsher punishments, greater attribution
of blame, and expected recidivism, regardless of conscious attitudes about race/ethnicity (Graham and Lowery 2004). Probation officers have been shown to support harsher sentencing
for African Americans than other individuals, but more recent research in one state showed an interaction between race/

ethnicity and prior record as a more robust predictor than either factor independently (Crow 2008).

The aforementioned dynamics showcase highly racialized pathways throughout the criminal justice systems at all levels, where African Americans are substantially vulnerable to disparate overrepresentation simply due to racial/ethnic status. These dynamics exist in partnership with other structural conditions to help shape person-environment relationships resulting in decreased supports and opportunities for young people and very high criminal justice representation.

Structural influences or developmental contexts also contribute to overrepresentation of African Americans in the criminal justice system. But these influences are not unidirectional, as these contexts help facilitate strengths present in African Americans. Person-context dynamics exist among interrelated developmental systems. For many African Americans, the result is that the community as a developmental context is no longer a supplier of sufficient resources or opportunity. Policy changes such as a shift toward more punitive criminal justice policies, away from education or rehabilitation, increased determinate sentencing, and harsher drug sentencing had real social impacts. Ineffective parole supervision has also been cited as an ineffective criminal justice policy (Aos, Miller, and Drake 2006)

Additional structural conditions exacerbated challenges for African Americans, including poverty, underemployment, insufficient education systems, and concentrated police activity/ hypersurveillance (Kubrin, Squires, and Steward 2007). These influence where criminals are likely to come from and where they are likely to return. In fact, Wacquant linked contemporary impoverished "ghetto" communities and prison as essentially the same oppressive, restrictive, and caste-maintaining entity for African Americans following in the legacy of slavery and the Jim Crow South (Wacquant 2000). Conflict theorists suggest that decision-makers perpetuate these dynamics to preserve the social order. Social disorganization theory suggests that a range of structural forces, not necessarily deliberate, combine in a web of disadvantage promoting excess vulnerability to arrest or re-arrest for African Americans. Further, the uniformity and rigidity of the prison experience is considered a source of institutionalization reinforced by residence in a high-risk geographic location/residence. Individuals are taken from (arrest) and returned to (reentry) these locations (Lynch 2006).

Several contemporary theoretical explanations are offered for why individuals recidivate that are not structural, including personal attributes and a lack of self-control not as amenable to change, and the lack of positive attachment to social groups, institutions, and supports (Clear 2005). Low-educated African Americans have very high risk of being incarcerated, including 52 percent of individuals aged 30 to 34. When unemployed or not in the labor force, more than two-thirds of African Americans are more likely to be engaged in illicit income generation, and thus increasing vulnerability to crime and incarceration due to high-risk behaviors (Mincy 2006).

These explanations differ in some regard, but share a common thread of interrelated person-context dynamics, a core element of developmental systems theory. Structural conditions inhibit available supports and opportunities and increase chances of high-risk behaviors or contact with the criminal justice system. The personal factors and the environmental contexts, together known as developmental assets, are the primary engine for well-being. If compromised, as is the case for many African Americans, disparities between a strong and weak asset profile can be profound, with increases in high-risk behaviors and decreases in well-being outcomes. These assets are examined in greater detail later in the chapter.

Developmental assets are critically important for African Americans because they are the supports and opportunities essential for safe, healthy, and productive functioning. Conversely, inhibited assets, particularly systematically inhibited/decreased assets, promote high-risk behaviors, decreased well-being, and limited engagement with positive contexts (Benson et al. 2006). Increased developmental assets and the ability to capitalize upon the strengths of African Americans allows resilience despite high risk from challenging environmental conditions or the residual impacts of racialized pathways within the criminal justice system (Toldson 2008).

In a study of the Search Institute's developmental assets across racial/ethnic groups, increased assets were associated with less risky behaviors and more positive outcomes, regardless of income status. Youth who engaged in none of 10 high-risk behavior patterns said they experienced about 23 assets, while youth participating in 5 or more risk behaviors reported 15 or fewer assets (Benson, et al. 2006). These assets comprise external (context) and internal (personal) assets. External assets include support, empowerment, boundaries and expectations, and constructive use of time. Internal (individual/person) assets include commitment to learning, positive values, social competencies, and positive identity. Several developmental asset frameworks exist, but one promoted by Richard Lerner and colleagues and supported in literature by the National Research Council comprise the "5 Cs" of positive youth development (PYD). External assets include connection, while internal assets are framed as competence, character, confidence, and caring.

Connection captures positive bidirectional bonds with family and friends—a sense of belonging (Gambone et al. 2004). These connections often contribute to how youth are cared for, accepted, and affirmed in life. The persistent value of connection exists across developmental settings, whether in the home, in school, or in the community. When individuals are incarcerated, there is a direct loss in meaningful connections. For children of incarcerated parents, a major phenomenon among African American families, similar loss ensues. Children of incarcerated parents face threats to important connections including positive mentorship and modeling by parents. Results of these impaired parent-child dynamics have included psychological instability and high-risk behavioral outcomes that increase vulnerability to later criminal justice involvement (Simmons 2000).

Competence within the "5 C" framework of PYD captures both academic and work competencies as well as productivity (Gambone et al. 2004). As outlined earlier, less-educated and underemployed individuals comprise the bulk of the incarcerated. Higher-educated individuals have significantly greater employment prospects, comparable to other groups, but lower-educated African Americans have substantially lower employment prospects than lower-educated whites or Latinos (Mincy 2006).

The current repertoire of environmental supports and opportunities challenges the building of competencies for African Americans. Further, educational opportunities for African Americans have been consistently poorer, including a greater chance of suspension or expulsion. Graduation prospects are vulnerable as is sufficient preparation for professional success within an economy heavily reliant on knowledge in contrast to physical skills. The developmental assets shown to be important for academically successful African Americans highlight obstacles present for African American youth raised within challenging environmental circumstances. Influential assets facilitating academic competence included mentorship, emotional well-being, father presence and education level, SES, future aspirations, and better nutrition (Toldson 2008).

Character captures respect for societal and cultural rules, standards, and behavior (Lerner, Lerner et al. 2005). The Gambone framework groups risk behavior/illegal activity together. Within a developmental assets framework, these assets are considered important for youth to be able to negotiate the challenges of life in a healthy and prosocial manner (Scales and Leffert 1999). Appropriate healthy and positive modeling from parents may be impaired. The corrosive influence of peer delinquency is also a risk that increases substantially with involvement in the criminal justice system. Assets are also interrelated and mutually reinforcing while reducing high-risk behaviors and promoting thriving. For example, highly competent youth have positive interactions with other youth, minimal association with delinquent peers, and less involvement with fighting or bullying (Toldson 2008).

Confidence is an internal sense of overall positive self-worth and self-efficacy; one's global self-regard, as opposed to domain-specific beliefs. Evidence shows that an individual's happiness about life is the strongest predictor of academic success, and that individuals aspiring to go to college were similarly successful (Toldson 2008). Finally, caring and empathy toward others is simply not stressed within criminal justice settings, where violence is rampant and integrated into the culture.

The unique social reality of African Americans, including excess vulnerability to involvement with the criminal justice system (one in three in lifetime), also includes ongoing threats to critical developmental constructs. There are systematic influences to the family, to schools, to neighborhoods, and to multiple levels of a young person's ecology. These influences pertain whether an individual is incarcerated, a family member of the incarcerated, or simply are part of a community with high representation in the criminal justice system. For far too many African Americans, as a result of their proximity to the criminal justice system, connections are often impaired, competency-building is threatened, the shaping of character is vulnerable to poor modeling, confidence is ripe for discouragement, and a culture of caring is not reinforced.

Involvement in the criminal justice system increases the likelihood of further involvement. Recidivism is high for all individuals, but particularly challenging for African Americans. Efforts to assist individuals reentering communities upon discharge are often fragmented and narrow in scope, causing problems for formerly incarcerated individuals and for families of the formerly incarcerated (especially developing children). One in 10 black youth have a father in prison (The Urban

Institute 2002). Employers are often resistant to hiring individuals with a criminal record (Holzer, Raphael, and Stoll 2003). The magnitude of this trend is compounded for African Americans, for whom it is often harder to gain employment than a white person with a criminal record. And many of the communities to which the formerly incarcerated return are economically depressed, and where employment is scarce. The net result is a continuous population of developmentally inhibited youth with unsustainable environmental assets. Resulting survival strategies are often high-risk behaviors, further complicating reentry efforts.

Existing disparities for African Americans are not the simple result of a disagreement among stakeholders or due to uncontrollable high-risk behaviors. Evidence highlights the interplay between personal factors and existing environmental contexts. This relationship is often shaped by public policy (e.g., crack cocaine disparities), racialized criminal justice decision making, and social conditions. This interplay influences well-being, behaviors, and ultimately ongoing contact with the criminal justice system.

Developmental assets offer promise for resilience and change when decision-makers increase the amount and quality of assets for individuals. For example, Harlem Children's Zone (HCZ) is a community-based organization pioneering an effort that works with a heavily African American community to serve children from birth through college in New York City. HCZ is an example of an intervention that focuses attention on person and context, acknowledging the critical role of education and employment opportunities, but also the foundation of critical developmental assets starting in the home. More importantly, HCZ emphasizes accountability within the context of a unique social reality vulnerable to insufficient developmental supports and opportunities for families. Incarceration rates have already begun to decline, despite still being woefully disparate. For these trends to continue, and more importantly for the ratio between African Americans and other groups to decline significantly, attention must be given to racialized pathways, structural conditions, and the developmental assets shown to be critical to well-being and behavior.

*Raphael Travis Jr., DrPh, LCSW, is an associate professor in the School of Social Work at Texas State University—San Marcos. He currently teaches both undergraduate and graduate students. Dr. Travis holds degrees from the University of Virginia, University of Michigan, and University of California at Los Angeles. His current research interests include positive youth development over the lifecourse, adolescent resilience, and youth participation in individual and community transformation. His work background blends mental health practice with public health issues.*

## References

Aos, S., M. Miller, and E. Drake. 2006. *Evidence-Based Adult Corrections Programs: What Works and What Does Not.* Olympia: Washington State Institute for Public Policy.

Benson, P., P. Scales, A. Sesma, K. Hong, and E. Roehlkepartain. 2006, November. Positive Youth Development So Far: Core Hypotheses and Their Implications for Policy and Practice. *Search Institute/Insights and Evidence* 3(1): 1–13.

Clear, T. R. 2005. Places Not Cases: Re-Thinking the Probation Focus. *Howard Journal of Criminal Justice* 44: 172–184.

Crow, M. S. 2008. The Complexities of Prior Record, Race, Ethnicity and Policy: Interactive Effects in Sentencing. *Criminal Justice Review* 33(4): 502–523.

Gambone, M. A., H. C. Yu, H. Lewis-Charp, C. L. Sipe, and J. Lacoe. 2004. *A Comparative Analysis of Community Youth Development Strategies.* College Park, MD: University of Maryland School of Public Policy/Center for Information and Research on Civic Learning and Engagement.

Golembeski, C., and R. Fullilove. 2005. Criminal (In)Justice in the City and Its Associated Health Consequences. *American Journal of Public Health* 95(10): 1701–1706.

Graham, S., and B. S. Lowery. 2004. Priming Unconscious Racial Stereotypes about Adolescent Offenders. *Law and Human Behavior* 28(5): 483–504.

Holzer, H. J., S. Raphael, and M. Stoll. 2003. *Employer Demand for Ex-Offenders: Recent Evidence from Los Angeles.* Unpublished manuscript.

Keen, B., and D. Jacobs. 2009. Racial Threat, Partisan Politics, and Racial Disparities in Prison Admissions: A Panel Analysis. *Criminology* 47(1): 209–238.

Kubrin, C. E., G. D. Squires, and E. A. Steward. 2007. Neighborhoods, Race, and Recidivism: The Community-Reoffending Nexus and Its Implications for African Americans. *Race Relations Abstracts* 32(1): 7–37.

Langan, P. A., and D. J. Levin. 2002. *Recidivism of Prisoners Released in 1994.* NCJ 193427. Washington, DC: Bureau of Justice Statistics.

Lerner, R. M., J. V. Lerner, J. B. Almerigi, C. Theokas, E. Phelps, and D. L. Bobek. 2005. Positive Youth Development, Participation in Community Youth Development Programs, and Community Contributions of Fifth-Grade Adolescents: Findings from the First Wave of the 4-H Study of Positive Youth Development. *Journal of Early Adolescence* 25(1): 17–71.

Lynch, J. P. 2006. Prisoner Reentry: Beyond Program Evaluation. *Criminology and Public Policy* 5(2): 401–412.

Mincy, R. B. 2006. *Black Males Left Behind.* Washington, DC: Urban Institute Press.

Sabol, W. J., H. C. West, and M. Cooper. 2010. *Prisoners in 2008.* NCJ 228417. Washington, DC: Bureau of Justice Statistics.

Scales, P., and N. Leffert. 1999. *A Fragile Foundation: The State of Developmental Assets among American Youth.* Minneapolis: Search Institute.

Simmons, C. W. 2000. *Children of Incarcerated Parents.* Sacramento, CA: Prepared at the Request of Assembly Member Kerry Mazzoni.

Toldson, I. 2008. *Breaking Barriers: Plotting the Path to Academic Success for School-Age African American Males.* Washington, DC: Congressional Black Caucus Foundation.

The Urban Institute. 2002. *The Public Health Dimensions of Prisoner Reentry: Addressing the Health Needs and Risks of Returning Prisoners and Their Families.* Los Angeles: A Focus on California National Reentry Roundtable Meeting.

Wacquant, L. 2000. The New Peculiar Institution. *Theoretical Criminology* 4(3): 377–389.

Western, B. 2006. *Punishment and Inequality in America.* New York: Russell Sage.

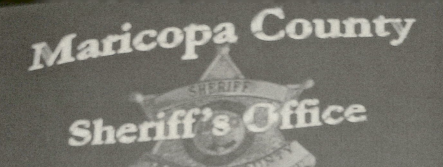

This chapter is organized into two main sections: personalities and organizations. In personalities portion of the chapter, readers are introduced to a sampling of individuals who directly or indirectly have played a significant role in relation to the issue of profiling. Few, if any, individuals of notoriety have focused their lives solely on the issue of profiling. Many people, however, have concerned themselves with the issue of profiling within the context of their broader life's work. Many of the individuals listed in this chapter have served in the larger cause of civil rights for groups traditionally discriminated against, and confronting the issue of profiling is simply a manifestation of the larger cause to which they are dedicated. Others listed in the following pages have served in law enforcement, politics, or in the judiciary—particularly the U.S. Supreme Court. These individuals, in their professional capacities, have been connected to the issue of profiling and have wielded influence in one way or another with regard to this issue. Still others listed were theorists or philosophers whose ideas, passed on through history, had and have an impact on the debate over profiling.

The following list of individuals should not be construed as complete or absolute. Countless others have weighed in on the

---

Maricopa County Sheriff Joe Arpaio seen at a 2013 press conference regarding a large drug bust. Arpaio's stance in favor of tougher immigration enforcement, in part due to the never-ending flow of drugs coming into Arizona from Mexico, has been likened to a form of racial profiling and has generated considerable controversy. (AP Photo/Ross D. Franklin) issue of profiling, and many have worked all their adult lives as proponents of equal treatment under the law while achieving justice. A cursory examination of the individuals listed here provides the reader with at least a start in compiling biographies of people who have influenced the debate over profiling along racial, gender, or other lines.

Following the list of individuals is a list of key organizations that contribute to the understanding of criminal justice profiling in various forms. Many people interested in criminal justice profiling find themselves unsure of where to turn to research the issue further. Fortunately, there are many government agencies and organizations that are available to serve as resources. In this chapter, a number of public and private organizations are presented to the reader. The purposes of these organizations are summarized as are the types of information one can receive from them. Information concerning how to contact these agencies and organizations is provided as well.

When researching an issue that is potentially controversial, as criminal profiling is, it is important to remember that many relevant organizations exist with a specific agenda in mind. This does not mean the information those organizations provide is invalid; but in some cases, the information may not be complete. As with most issues, people and organizations who advocate a particular position are inclined to emphasize information that supports their position. So, when conducting research using the organizations listed in the second part of this chapter, readers should be mindful that not all the information they receive is gospel. This caveat notwithstanding, the organizations listed can provide a wealth of information and support for those interested in the issue of profiling. In many cases, the organizations summarized below have a broader purpose than simply addressing or responding to the issue of profiling. Nonetheless, these organizations can serve as an invaluable source for becoming thoroughly familiar with profiling and its ramifications.

## Personalities

### Freda Adler (1933–)

Freda Adler is one of America's most well-known criminologists, past or present. Acclaim for her work and theories first emerged in 1975 when she published *Sisters in Crime*, which set out to explain female criminal behavior from a feminist perspective. This has come to be known as the liberation theory of criminology. Adler's work consistently rejected the notion that women commit crime or not because of biological or psychological determinants. Instead, Adler suggested that women commit crime in proportion to their decreasing oppression in society. Adler said that as women are increasingly liberated from society's traditional notions of womanhood, and thereby are free to pursue legitimate economic, social, and political advancement, so are they increasingly empowered and are in a position to pursue illegitimate gains in these same areas. According to Adler, women are no longer confined to the most menial of offenses; rather, they are capable of being world class in their criminality just as men can be. Today, Adler continues to be an influential member of academia as a proponent of feminist criminology.

### Joe Arpaio (1932–)

Joe Arpaio is the sheriff of Maricopa County, Arizona. The county seat is the City of Phoenix. He is currently in his sixth elected term as sheriff. Arpaio has been dubbed "America's Toughest Sheriff" because of his reputation for not coddling criminals and county inmates. In years past, he was most known for the tent cities that he erected to house the county's burgeoning inmate population. Inmates were denied "luxuries" common to other jails and had few amenities. More recently, though, Arpaio has been in the news as a legal combatant against the federal government and the federal judiciary over the issue of racial profiling. Unlike many other parts of the country where questions of profiling center on the relationship between the police and black citizens, the profiling allegations in Maricopa County relate to how the sheriff's department has dealt with Hispanics—both citizens and noncitizens. Arpaio has made many public statements in recent years in support of aggressive law enforcement tactics to address crime committed by illegal immigrants in Arizona. He was a vocal supporter of SB 1070, the Arizona law which permitted local law enforcement to enforcement immigration status violations at the state level. Key parts of that law were struck down by the U.S. Supreme Court in 2012. Arpaio has been very critical of the federal government for failing to secure the borders, particularly the Arizona border, and therefore creating a public safety hazard from the criminal element among illegal immigrants. In 2012, the U.S. Justice Department filed suit against Arpaio and the Maricopa County Sheriff's Department, after conducting a "pattern or practice" investigation of the department which resulted in findings that Arpaio condones and encourages racial profiling. The lawsuit, which is still working its way through federal court, comes on the heels of a class action civil rights lawsuit filed in 2007 (*Melendres v. Arpaio*) and concluded in 2013. The federal court found that the sheriff's department under Arpaio did in fact engage in unlawful discrimination through racial profiling. Federal District Judge Murry Snow ordered the sheriff's department to implement a number of reforms and appointed a monitor to ensure compliance. Arpaio has remained defiant and reportedly has ordered an investigation by his detectives to examine whether Judge Snow and the U.S. Justice Department colluded against the Maricopa County Sheriff's Department.

## Harry A. Blackmun (1908–1999)

Harry Blackmun was born in southern Illinois in 1908. His family moved to Minnesota, where he grew up. In fact, a childhood friend in grade school was the future chief justice Warren Burger. Blackmun attended Harvard University and received his BA in 1929. He went on to attend Harvard Law School, receiving his law degree in 1932. Blackmun returned to Minnesota upon graduation and set up a law practice that ran from 1933 to1959. He left his private practice to accept an appointment from President Dwight Eisenhower to the U.S. Eighth Circuit Court of Appeals. Blackmun served in that capacity until President Richard Nixon appointed him to the U.S. Supreme Court in1970, where he served for 24 years. He retired in 1994. Blackmun is most noted for his controversial authorship of the Court's opinion in *Roe v. Wade* in 1973. That decision took the privacy rights established in the case of *Griswold v. Connecticut* and extended them to establish a constitutional right to an abortion. In Blackmun's final year on the Court, he authored the majority opinion in *J.E.B. v. Alabama*. In that case, the Court ruled that gender, just as race, cannot be the basis for a prosecutor's decision to strike a potential juror through peremptory challenges.

## Julian Bond (1940–)

Julian Bond was born in Nashville, Tennessee, in 1940. He has lived a life dedicated toward advancing the cause of civil rights for oppressed and depressed economic and racial classes of people. As a college student at Morehouse College in Atlanta, Georgia, in the late 1950s, Bond worked as a student activist in the effort to bring about integration in Atlanta's cinemas, restaurants, and other public places. In 1965, Bond was elected to the Georgia House of Representatives. The Georgia House refused to seat him, however, because of his opposition to the Vietnam War. He was elected two more times before he finally was permitted to serve after the legislature was ordered by the Supreme Court to seat him. Bond served in the Georgia House, and then Senate, from 1965 until 1987. He sponsored dozens of bills relating to civil rights that eventually were passed into law in Georgia. While serving in the state legislature of Georgia, Bond also served the cause of civil rights as an official of the

Southern Poverty Law Center. In fact, he was appointed the center's first president upon its founding in 1971. For several years, Bond also served on the National Board of the National Association for the Advancement of Colored People (NAACP), which is the oldest and largest civil rights organization in the United States. In 1998, Bond became the NAACP National Board Chairman.

### Henry Brown (1836–1913)

Henry Brown was born in Massachusetts in 1836. He attended Yale University, graduating in 1856. Brown then pursued a legal education at Harvard and Yale law schools. He received his law degree in 1859. After law school, Brown moved to Michigan and served as a deputy U.S. marshal and as an assistant U.S. attorney in the Eastern District of Michigan. In 1868, Brown began his judicial career as a local judge in Detroit. In 1875, Brown was appointed as a federal district judge in the Eastern District of Michigan. He had served as a district judge for 14 years when President Benjamin Harrison nominated him to the Supreme Court in 1890. Brown served as a Supreme Court justice for 16 years and then retired. During those 16 years, Brown authored more than 450 majority opinions for the Court. One of those, however, stands out more than the others: *Plessy v. Ferguson* (1896), in which the Supreme Court upheld state-sanctioned race consciousness. In particular, the concept of "separate but equal" was found to be constitutional. This enabled southern and some northern states to lawfully continue the practice of segregation for decades until the landmark decision in *Brown v. Board of Education* in 1954.

### Warren E. Burger (1907–1995)

Warren Burger was born in 1907 in St. Paul, Minnesota. He grew up in Minnesota and attended the University of Minnesota as an undergraduate student from 1925 to 1927. Burger went on to attend the St. Paul College of Law (now known as the William Mitchell College of Law) in St. Paul. Upon being admitted to the Minnesota bar, Burger engaged in private practice for over 20 years. He also taught law on the side. In 1953, the Eisenhower administration hired Burger to serve as the assistant attorney general for the Civil Division in the U.S. Department of Justice.

In 1956, Burger was nominated and appointed to the U.S. Court of Appeals for the District of Columbia. In 1969, Burger was appointed by President Richard Nixon to the U.S. Supreme Court to replace outgoing Chief Justice Earl Warren. Burger was a strict constructionist in his judicial philosophy, and many conservatives had hopes that he would roll back some of the judicial activism seen in the previous decade. Although Burger was generally considered a conservative on the Court, he did not live up to the expectations of countering the more liberal tide on the bench. Many significant civil rights cases were heard during the Burger Court, which spanned the period from 1969 to 1986. During his tenure, Burger authored an opinion upholding the practice of forced busing as a part of desegregation. He also authored the opinion holding valid the subpoena that required Richard Nixon to give up his private tapes concerning Watergate. This led to Nixon's resignation in 1974.

## William J. Clinton (1946–)

William (Bill) Clinton was born William Jefferson Blythe III in Hope, Arkansas. His father died in a car accident three months before he was born. His mother married Roger Clinton when Bill was four years old, and Bill took his stepfather's last name. Clinton earned a bachelor's degree from Georgetown University with a major in international relations in 1968. He also attended Oxford University in England as a Rhodes Scholar and received a law degree from Yale University in 1973. Clinton served as governor of Arkansas from 1978 to 1980 and from

1982 to 1988. In1992, Clinton was elected president of the United States and was reelected in 1996.

The Clinton presidency, which ran from January 1993 until January 2001, is known for many things. One of the legacies of the Clinton years in the White House is the advancement of community policing in the United States. President Clinton established the Community Oriented Policing Service (COPS) office in the U.S. Department of Justice. Through this office, the federal government subsidized the hiring of tens of thousands of police officers around the country. To qualify for the subsidy, local departments would have to commit officers to community policing efforts. Additionally, the Clinton administration began the funding of dozens of regional community policing institutes around the country, the purpose of which was to support community policing efforts through training and technical advising. Still another legacy is the Clinton administration's stepped-up effort to confront illegal police actions through Department of Justice investigation and intervention. President Clinton set out to end the practice of racial profiling. He directed the Departments of Justice, Treasury, and Agriculture to collect data on race, ethnicity, and gender of individuals subject to stops by federal law enforcement. He also supported legislation encouraging states to collect the same data. During the Clinton years, several consent decrees were entered into between the U.S. Department of Justice and local police departments accused of racial profiling and other biased policing actions. President Clinton's positive relations with African Americans in the area of law enforcement and other areas caused many to dub him America's first black president. President Clinton also developed positive relations with the gay and lesbian community. He instituted a "don't ask, don't tell" policy in the military that resulted in the cessation of screening gays from military service. He also made dozens of appointments in his administration of openly gay or lesbian public officials. Finally, President Clinton sought to include sexual orientation among the categories covered by hate crime and employment discrimination legislation.

## Morris Dees (1936–)

Morris Dees is a civil rights attorney and activist in the United States. He is the cofounder of the Southern Poverty Law Center, which was started in 1971 with the goal of confronting discrimination through civil court action. Dees grew up in rural Alabama and witnessed the adverse effects of discrimination close-up. Through the Southern Poverty Law Center, Dees and his colleagues have pursued a strategy of suing organizations that engage in discrimination. Although most known for its efforts to combat racial discrimination, the Southern Poverty Law Center also fights discrimination along other protected lines, such as gender and sexual orientation.

Dees received wide acclaim for his efforts to go after the money and assets of domestic hate groups based on the unlawful actions of its member. Dees posited the legal theory that the organizations were liable for the damages their members caused while acting under their name. Most notably, Dees successfully sued the national Ku Klux Klan in 1981 for condoning the lynching of a black man. A $7 million judgment was awarded to the victim's mother and effectively bankrupted the Ku Klux Klan. Dees intended not only to help victims, but principally to put hate groups out of business. In 1991, a similar lawsuit resulted in a $6 million judgment against the Aryan Nations.

In recent years, Dees has received criticism from some who believed that the Southern Poverty Law Center had become too much about the aggrandizement of Morris Dees. Additionally, other critics pointed to a growing and evident liberal political bias of the Center. Indeed, the Center has published documents and training materials for law enforcement which attempt to link mainstream conservative groups, such as Evangelical Christians, the Family Research Council, and the Catholic Church with right-wing extremism and terrorism.

In 2014, the Federal Bureau of Investigation announced that it would no longer provide an Internet link to the Southern Poverty Law Center from the FBI's website. Although the FBI downplayed the disassociation with the Center, many pundits believed the FBI simply could no longer be closely identified as being in partnership with a patently partisan organization.

### John Douglas (1947–)

John Douglas is a name that has long been associated with criminal profiling—particularly behaviorally rooted profiling. As an FBI special agent and head of the FBI's Investigative Support Unit (also known as the Behavioral Science Unit), he pioneered the development of behavioral profiles as investigative tools and has used such profiles in investigating infamous crimes such as the Tylenol poisonings in Chicago, the Green River Killer in Washington State, a serial killer of children in Atlanta, and a serial killer of prostitutes in Alaska. He has also studied and profiled famous criminals such as Charles Manson, Richard Speck, John Wayne Gacy, David Berkowitz, and others. Although many outside of criminal justice circles have never heard of Douglas, most have heard of fictional characters for whom he or his criminal subjects have served as inspiration. Of particular fame are Thomas Harris's books and subsequent movies (including *Red Dragon* and *Silence of the Lambs*) featuring the character Scott Glenn, who was a nemesis of Hannibal Lecter.

### W.E.B. DuBois (1868–1963)

William Edward Burghardt DuBois was an African American who defied all stereotypes for the role of blacks in the late 19th and early-middle 20th centuries. He received a bachelor's degree from Fisk University and a PhD from Harvard. He served as a professor of classical languages at the University of Pennsylvania and as a professor of economics and history at Atlanta University. He was a founding member of the National Association for the Advancement of Colored People (NAACP). He wrote several books concerning the struggle of African Americans for equality, both before and after slavery. DuBois was also among the first civil rights leaders to address the issue of gender discrimination—particularly as applied against black women. The reputation of DuBois is that he genuinely desired equality for all people, regardless of race, religion, or gender.

### Franz Gall (1758–1828)

Franz Joseph Gall was born in Baden, Germany, in 1758. He studied medicine in Austria and became a well-known medical scientist. He is most remembered for his development of "phrenology," the attempted method of determining personality types and traits in individuals by examining the shape and size of their skulls. He believed that personality traits were localized in different modules of the brain and therefore more pronounced areas of one's brain would predict the talents one likely possessed. Likewise, skull depressions would reveal a person's negative behavioral tendencies, including potential criminality. Many ruling-class people in England during the 19th century embraced Gall's theories because they could be used to support the notion that colonial subjects and others in lower social classes were biologically inferior. His theories significantly influenced the early "science" of predicting criminality.

### Ruth Bader Ginsburg (1933–)

Ruth Bader Ginsburg was born in New York in 1933. She received her bachelor's degree from Harvard University and her law degree from Columbia University School of Law. She attended law school in the 1950s when women were not particularly welcome in the profession and a great deal of hostility toward female law students could be felt. In 1963, Ginsburg joined the faculty of Rutgers University School of Law. She eventually returned to Columbia University to join the law faculty there. As a law professor, Ginsburg became very active in feminist issues and used her standing in the legal profession to advance feminist causes. In 1971, she shepherded the Women's Rights Project of the American Civil Liberties Union (ACLU) and served as the general counsel for the ACLU from 1973 to 1980, all while serving as a tenured professor of law at Columbia. In that capacity, she had the opportunity to argue cases on behalf of women seeking the same suspect class/strict scrutiny that racial minorities had won in the courts. In 1980, Ginsburg was appointed as a federal appellate judge for the District of Columbia federal circuit. In 1993, President Clinton nominated her to the U.S. Supreme Court. She was confirmed and took her seat that year. She was President Clinton's first Supreme Court nominee. Justice Ginsburg has been a reliable vote on the Court for the cause of affirmative action and minority rights, be they members of a racial or ethnic minority, women, or members of the LGBT community.

### Herman Goldstein (1931–)

Herman Goldstein is the pioneer of the community policing movement. As far back as the 1970s, this University of Wisconsin professor began focusing his writing and research efforts toward developing a model of policing that emphasizes partnership between the police and the community and incorporates principles of empowerment and democracy within the policing structure. His model of police work permits officers to actually solve problems rather than simply react to them. Community policing has become a popular model for law enforcement in urban centers, especially where there exist high concentrations of ethnic or racial minorities. In many urban areas, police have historically been dimly viewed by the public for their heavy-handedness and perceived racism. Community policing seeks to change that perception by involving the community in the law enforcement and crime control process through partnership with the police. Although not perfect, the model has gone a long way to bridging the gulf between minority groups and the law enforcers serving them.

## John M. Harlan (1833–1911)

John Harlan was born the son of a lawyer in Boyle County, Kentucky. He graduated from Centre College in 1850 and studied law at Transylvania University. In 1853, Harlan was admitted to the bar in Kentucky and began practicing law. Although a southerner and a slaveholder, Harlan remained loyal to the Union during the Civil War. In fact, Harlan joined the Union army and served as an officer. In 1863, he resigned his army commission to serve as the attorney general for Kentucky. In 1877, President Rutherford B. Hayes nominated Harlan to the U.S. Supreme Court, where he served for 33 years. He was known as the "Great Dissenter" for his many often solitary dissents against the majority on the Court. One of his most worthy dissents was in the case of *Plessy v. Ferguson*, where Harlan demonstrated that he was ahead of his time. In that case, Harlan wrote that it was not proper under the Constitution for a government organization to know the race of people under its charge. In other words, Harlan believed that the government should not be race-neutral, but race-blind.

## Thomas Hobbes (1588–1679)

Thomas Hobbes was born in Wiltshire, England, in 1588. He lived a long and productive life, dying in 1679. Over his 90 years on Earth, he developed into one of the most influential political philosophers of all time. Hobbes believed and wrote that mankind, if left to its own devices in a state of nature, would exist in a very brutal, violent, and selfish way. Hobbes wrote that government is very important in that without it, social order would erode into savagery. He said that there exists a social contract in which individuals subordinate to the government a limited amount of their inherent freedom in exchange for government's protection and maintenance of order. Given that the natural state of mankind, according to Hobbes, was extremely brutal, his vision of government was fairly authoritative. Government was not to be given unlimited and everlasting authority, however. Should government fail in its obligation of protecting the people under its charge or in securing their individual liberties, then the contract would be broken and a different government could appropriately and morally be crafted to replace the old one. Hobbes's works were very influential upon colonists during the run-up to the American Revolution. Although Hobbes was certainly for individual freedom, he was also for a strong enough and effective enough government to overcome humankind's natural tendencies toward violence and mayhem. Therefore, with regard to criminal justice and profiling, one might conclude that Hobbes would encourage government to use whatever tools are reasonably necessary to ensure the public's safety from crime.

### J. Edgar Hoover (1895–1972)

John Edgar Hoover was born in Washington, D.C., in 1895. In 1917, he graduated with a law degree from George Washington University. Soon after, Hoover joined the U.S. Justice Department as a special agent. In 1917, the United States entered World War I. Concern over espionage was very high. Hoover quickly became recognized as an accomplished and skilled federal agent and was promoted to head the Enemy Aliens Registration Section. In 1919, he was promoted to the head of the General Intelligence Division within the Department of Justice. In 1921, Hoover joined the Bureau of Investigation as the deputy director. In 1924, at the age of 29, he became director of the bureau, which had over 400 special agents. In 1935, the Bureau of Investigation was renamed the Federal Bureau of Investigation (FBI) and was given expanded powers as the federal government's premiere law enforcement and domestic intelligence agency. By all accounts, Hoover ran a "tight ship" at the FBI. It was his FBI. He made great strides to professionalize the Bureau. He instituted background checks for all special agents, implemented rigorous training and physical fitness requirements, and created a national laboratory for the analysis of forensic evidence. Under Hoover, the FBI became a part of American popular culture in its fight with gangsters of the 1930s. The Bureau's most famous foe was John Dillinger, who was killed in a gun battle with FBI agents in Chicago. Hoover's FBI emerged as the lead agency to enforce civil rights laws in the 1960s and 1970s and had some success in prosecuting violent segregationists in the South when state and local law enforcements were unwilling to take action. Hoover was shrouded in controversy during his 48-year career with the Bureau. Many have speculated that Hoover kept secret files on potential political opponents. Those files presumably contained information that could be used to blackmail opponents into compliance with Hoover's wishes. In some cases, Hoover is alleged to have leveraged the sexual orientation and sexual practices of some opponents. Hoover remained the director of the FBI until his death in 1972.

## Jesse Jackson (1941–)

Jesse Louis Jackson Sr. was born in Greenville, South Carolina, in 1941. He grew up in South Carolina and earned a bachelor's degree from North Carolina A & T University in 1964. Jackson began studies at the Chicago Theological Seminary in Illinois, but dropped out owing to his heavy involvement in the civil rights movement. He eventually returned to seminary to receive his Master of Divinity degree in 2000. Jackson became a civil rights activist in 1960 when he led sit-ins to desegregate local public facilities in South Carolina and elsewhere. In 1965, he began working full-time for the Southern Christian Leadership Conference and for Martin Luther King Jr. In 1971, Jackson founded Operation PUSH (People United to Serve Humanity) in Chicago. The goal of PUSH was to empower people of color to overcome economic disadvantage. In 1984,

Jackson founded the National Rainbow Coalition in Washington, D.C. The Rainbow Coalition was created to advocate social justice and change public policy to that end. In 1996, Jackson's two organizations merged into the Rainbow/PUSH Coalition. Jackson is one of the more controversial figures in the civil rights movement. He has been an outspoken critic of law enforcement and the criminal justice system, conservative politicians, conservative religious groups and denominations, and others. He ran for president of the United States in 1984 and 1988 as an unabashed liberal. He has also inserted himself many times into international crises; in doing so, he has negotiated the release of hostages and prisoners of war from hostile foreign countries. He has also been an ardent supporter of labor unions worldwide. His political activities have won him support from some and criticism from others. More recently, Jackson regained the spotlight in the wake of the Travyon Martin killing by George Zimmerman. He has continued to be a frequent guest on television and radio shows.

## Martin Luther King Jr. (1929–1968)

Perhaps the most famous and well-regarded American civil rights leader in the nation's history is Martin Luther King Jr., who was born in 1929 in Atlanta, Georgia. King grew up in Atlanta and eventually attended and graduated from Morehouse College with a bachelor's degree in sociology. He went on to earn a divinity degree from Crozer Theological Seminary in Pennsylvania in 1951 and a PhD in theology from Boston University in1955. King, like so many African American civil rights champions of his day, began his adult life in the ministry. He was ordained as a Baptist minister and served as a pastor in Alabama before returning to Georgia as the director of the Southern Christian Leadership Conference in 1959. King was very passionate for the cause of civil rights. He was responsible for organizing the Montgomery bus boycott in 1955 and 1956 to protest segregation on the bus. He was jailed dozens of times for his involvement in nonviolent civil disobedience. He was greatly influenced by Gandhi's own example of nonviolence to influence change. King aggressively sought the help of the federal government in enforcing the right of blacks to register and vote. His efforts, and others, created the impetus for a variety of sweeping civil rights laws. In 1963, King organized and led the March on Washington, where he gave his famous "I have a dream" speech. That speech remains an anthem of the ideal for race relations in the United States. In 1964, King was awarded the Nobel Peace Prize for his efforts to bring justice and equality to the American South and urban North. In 1968, Martin Luther King Jr. visited the city of Memphis for the purpose of leading a protest march in support of striking garbage workers. While standing on the balcony of his hotel room on April 4, 1968, King was shot dead by James Earl Ray. Ray pleaded guilty to the assassination and was sentenced to 99 years in prison, where he died. Since 1994, the third Monday in January each year is a national holiday dedicated in King's honor.

### Rodney King (1965–2012)

Rodney King was born in Sacramento, California, in 1965. He has become one the most visible symbols of police violence against African Americans in today's society. On March 3, 1991, Rodney King was involved in a high-speed pursuit. King had a significant criminal history. He had been convicted of beating his wife. He was on parole for robbery of a convenience store and assault, and he was intoxicated. Consequently, he fled in his vehicle when a California Highway Patrol officer attempted to stop him on a Los Angeles freeway. During the pursuit, the Los Angeles Police Department became involved to assist the highway patrol. When King finally pulled over and exited his vehicle, four Los Angeles police officers used their batons to subdue him. The baton blows were caught on tape by a bystander and made it to the television news. The officers involved in the beating were eventually charged by the Los

Angeles district attorney for assault and police misconduct. On April 29, 1992, a jury found the officers not guilty of criminal wrongdoing. The black and Hispanic communities in Los Angeles were outraged at the verdict, and a riot broke out in the south central part of the city. Many storefronts and homes were set on fire and burned to the ground. Damage totaled $16 billion. More importantly, 52 people were killed in the riots and 3,000 people were injured. Rodney King, already famous from the videotaped beating, solidified his status as an icon when he asked on national television his famous question "Can't we all just get along?" The same four police officers were retried for civil rights violations in federal court. Two of the four were found not guilty; the remaining two—Lawrence Powell and Stacey Koon—were found guilty and sentenced to federal prison. In 1994, the city of Los Angeles agreed to pay King $3.8 million in damages. King continued to have run-ins with the law after fading from the spotlight. He was arrested multiple times for offenses such as domestic assault, drug use, and driving while under the influence of drugs. King died in 2012 after being found by his fiancé at the bottom of his swimming pool. Although the cause of death was accidental drowning, drugs found in his system, including cocaine and PCP, were determined to be a contributing factor to drowning.

### John Lewis (1940–)

John Lewis was born in rural Alabama in 1940. He attended segregated schools during his elementary and secondary education. He went on to earn a bachelor's degree in religion from Fisk University and a divinity degree from the American Baptist Theological Seminary in Nashville. John Lewis began his long civil rights advocacy career as a freedom rider in the South in the early1960s. He frequently participated in civil disobedience in order to protest the segregation policies throughout the South. He was recognized at an early age as a leader in the civil rights movement. In fact, at age 23, he helped organize and spoke at the March on Washington in 1963. Lewis was intimately involved in the "Freedom Summer" of 1964 in Mississippi. He led hundreds of marchers across the Edmund Pettus Bridge in Selma, Alabama. That particular march was notoriously confronted by state troopers—an event that came to be known as "Bloody Sunday." Lewis was no stranger to police contacts. He was arrested over 40 times for his acts of nonviolent civil disobedience. Lewis served as an activist for 20 more years until he was elected to the U.S. Congress in 1986 by the citizens of Atlanta, Georgia. He has been a leader among the congressional Democrats and has worked very hard to achieve fairness and equity for minorities in the United States, especially within the context of the criminal justice system.

### Cesare Lombroso (1835–1909)

Cesare Lombroso was a 19th-century Italian criminologist who believed that there existed a relationship between the physical characteristics and features of people and criminal behavior. It is from Lombroso that we have taken the stereotypical notions of "beady eyes" or a "slack jaw" serving as an indicator of criminality. Lombroso was influenced in the development of his theories by Charles Darwin's theory of evolution and Franz Gall's theories of phrenology. Lombroso's theories were popular in Europe and parts of South America into the 20th century. Criminological theories that focused on social and environmental causes of crime eventually replaced biological and genetic determinants, however, as the mainstream hypotheses concerning crime's origins.

### Thurgood Marshall (1908–1993)

Thurgood Marshall was born in Baltimore, Maryland, in 1908. He attended Lincoln University as an undergraduate, receiving a BA in 1930. He then studied law at Howard University, a predominantly black university in Washington, D.C. He received a law degree in 1933. After practicing law in Maryland for a couple of years, Marshall became the legal director for the National Association for the Advancement of Colored People (NAACP). He served in that capacity from 1940 to 1961. During that time, Marshall litigated many significant civil rights cases. The most famous civil rights case he successfully litigated was *Brown v. Board of Education* in 1954. In that case, Marshall argued persuasively before the U.S. Supreme Court that racial segregation in public schools was unconstitutional. The Supreme Court agreed and ended the idea of "separate but equal," previously established in the case of *Plessy v. Ferguson.* In 1961, Marshall was appointed by President John F. Kennedy to serve as a judge on the U.S. Court of Appeals for the Second Circuit. In 1965, Marshall became the solicitor general of the United States under President Johnson. The solicitor general is the chief trial lawyer for the U.S. government and has the responsibility of representing the United States before the Supreme Court. In 1967, Johnson nominated Marshall to become the first black justice of the Supreme Court. By the time he took office, he had successfully argued nearly 30 cases before the court on which he now sat. As a Supreme Court justice, Marshall was considered a staunch liberal. He opposed the death penalty because he believed it to be inherently "cruel and unusual" and applied in a discriminatory fashion, both of which would be violations of the Constitution.

### Kweisi Mfume (1948–)

Kweisi Mfume was born of Frizzell Gray in 1948 in Baltimore, Maryland. He grew up in that city and became active in politics and the civil rights movement. He attended and graduated from Morgan State University, serving as the editor of the college paper and as the president of the Black Student Union on campus. He eventually earned a master's degree in international studies at Johns Hopkins University. In 1979, Mfume was elected to the Baltimore City Council. He served as a council member until 1986, when he was elected to the

U.S. House of Representatives. As a congressman, he worked very hard on civil rights legislation. This included legislation relating to affirmative action, protection of Americans with disabilities, reforming financial institutions, reforming the equal employment opportunity laws, and tightening up gun control. Mfume served as chair of the Congressional Black Caucus and as such gained national attention as a spokesperson for issues affecting African Americans. In 1996, Mfume left the Congress to become president of the National Association for the Advancement of Colored People (NAACP). In that capacity, he has continued to champion affirmative action and other civil rights issues, including the elimination of brutality and discrimination inflicted by the criminal justice system on minorities.

## Rosa Parks (1913–2005)

Rosa Parks is an icon in the American civil rights movement. An African American woman born and raised in Alabama, she dared as a 42-year-old adult to challenge the absurdity that was segregation in her home state. On December 1, 1955, while riding home from work on a city bus in Montgomery, Alabama, she was ordered by the driver to give up her seat to a white man. She was further told to move from the front of the bus to the back of the bus, where blacks were permitted to sit. She refused to comply, which resulted in her arrest. This high-profile incident resulted in a boycott of the Montgomery city buses. Blacks all across town, led by Martin Luther King Jr., simply refused to give patronage to a transportation system that treated them as second-class citizens. Instead, they walked or helped each other with rides. The boycott lasted over a year. Eventually, the U.S. Supreme Court ruled that segregation in public transportation was unconstitutional. The civil rights activism that started with her refusal to move to the back of the bus gave rise to the Civil Rights Act of 1964 and the Voting Rights Act of 1965. After this incident, Parks began to work full-time on the cause of civil rights. Eventually, due to threats and harassment, Parks and her family left Alabama and moved to Detroit, Michigan, where she remained the rest of her life. She died of natural causes at the age of 92 in 2005.

### Lewis Powell (1907–1998)

Lewis Powell was born in Virginia in 1907. He also grew up there. In 1929, Powell graduated with a bachelor's degree from Washington and Lee. He remained there to study law, receiving his degree in 1931. Powell went on to receive a master's degree in law from Harvard University in 1932. Powell practiced law in Virginia from 1933 to 1971, with the exception of four years' service as an officer with the U.S. Army Air Corps from 1942 to 1946. In 1972, Powell was appointed from private practice to the U.S. Supreme Court by President Richard Nixon. During his 15 years on the Court, Powell was considered a moderate and frequently served as a swing vote. Notably, Powell authored the Court's opinion in the case of *Batson v. Kentucky*. This 1986 case resulted in the prohibition of prosecutors' use of the peremptory challenge to eliminate potential jurors from sitting on a case because of their race. Powell retired in 1987.

### William H. Rehnquist (1924–2005)

William H. Rehnquist was born in Milwaukee, Wisconsin, in1924. Before he could enter college, World War II broke out. Rehnquist enlisted in the U.S. Army Air Corps and served in North Africa. After the war, Rehnquist attended Stanford University, using funds from the GI Bill. He received a bachelor's and a master's degrees in political science. He then went to obtain a second master's degree, this time in government, from Harvard University. In 1950, he returned to Stanford University to attend law school and graduated number one in his class. After law school, Rehnquist practiced law in Arizona and became active in the Republican Party. In 1971, President Richard Nixon appointed him to the U.S. Supreme

Court. Rehnquist served on the Court as an outspoken, if often solitary, conservative. His dissenting opinions on several cases demonstrated a restrictive view concerning the breadth of the Fourteenth Amendment vis-à-vis nonracial matters. In 1986, President Reagan nominated him to replace the retiring Warren Burger as the chief justice of the U.S. Supreme Court. The Senate confirmed the nomination, and Rehnquist served as chief justice until his death in 2005. Rehnquist authored or contributed to many significant court opinions. Notably, Rehnquist authored the Court's opinion in *Sokolow*, which upheld the use of objectively constructed profiles to identify possible drug couriers at airports.

## Janet Reno (1938–)

Janet Reno became America's first female U.S. attorney general when she was appointed to that post by President Clinton in 1993. She served in that capacity until 2000. Reno was born in Miami in 1938. She grew up in the Miami area and graduated from high school there. In 1956, she enrolled at Cornell University in New York State. In 1960, she was accepted into Harvard Law School. She was one of 16 women in a class of 500 students. In 1963, she received her law degree and returned to Florida. Prior to becoming the U.S. attorney general, Reno served as a Dade County assistant state's attorney, as a staff member for the Florida legislature, and as the Dade County state's attorney. She helped establish the Miami Drug Court, which served as an alternative to the traditional criminal justice adjudication and punishment process for nonviolent drug offenders. As the U.S. Attorney General, Janet Reno set a course for the Justice Department to aggressively enforce civil rights laws, thereby ensuring equal opportunity for all. In particular, her Justice Department entered into several consent decrees with local police agencies, which required those agencies to adhere to predetermined practices and policies in order to avoid federal litigation.

### Jean-Jacques Rousseau (1712–1778)

Jean-Jacques Rousseau was born in Geneva, Switzerland, in 1712. He lived there until the age of 16, when he moved to Paris. He remained in France until his death in 1778. Rousseau is considered perhaps the most influential philosopher to emerge from the Enlightenment. In Rousseau's earlier works, he wrote that people were basically good and noble but became corrupted and were made unhappy by the influence of a corrupt society upon them. He believed that the social customs of his time, particularly among the aristocracy, were artificial and should be rejected. Rousseau emphasized the notion that people are born free and should be afforded equality within society. Among his later works was his most important publication: *The Social Contract.* In this work, Rousseau reiterated much of what Thomas Hobbes said about the need for government—namely, that it exists to secure personal freedom and keep what would otherwise be a violent, disorderly society in check. Rousseau, however, emphasized the notions of equality, at the expense of majority will, and challenged the right to hold private property. Rousseau's work is considered to have laid the groundwork for the emergence of socialism and communism—particularly given his defense of "Everyman" against society elites who own all the property and hold all the power. Although one cannot be certain, his writings suggest that he would hold disdain for the practice of profiling when done so on the basis of race, religion, or other classifications. Rousseau would likely find profiling to be a tool of the ruling class for keeping elitist social order in place.

### Margaret Sanger (1879–1966)

Margaret Sanger is considered a chief pioneer of feminism in the United States. She was born as Margaret Higgins in 1879 to an Irish American, devoutly Catholic family in Coming, New York.

Her mother died at the age of 50 after bearing 11 children. Higgins believed that her mother's chronic condition of pregnancy contributed to her relatively early death. This belief helped shape Higgins's views of the pitfalls of "traditional" living for women and contributed to the development of her feminist philosophy. Margaret Higgins attended Claverack College in 1896 and then entered a nursing training program at White Plains Hospital in 1900. In 1902, she married William Sanger, with whom she had three children. Margaret Sanger became an early advocate for women's health issues and the use of birth control. In 1912, she began to publish newspaper columns related to sex education. She actively promoted the ideas of anarchist Emma Goldman and saw birth control as a way to secure freedom from the economic shackles that a family creates. In 1914, Sanger divorced her husband and carried on a sexually liberated life consisting of several affairs. Sanger's driving issue throughout her adult life centered on the right of women to use birth control. In fact, Sanger was the founder of the Planned Parenthood Federation of America. In 1965, her lifelong battle culminated in the U.S. Supreme Court's decision of *Griswold v. Connecticut*, in which a right to privacy and the use of birth control was deemed to be contained in the Constitution. This court decision decriminalized laws in several states that had restricted the use of birth control methods. Sanger was not an uncontroversial figure even by modern standards. She was directly allied with anarchists and socialists of her day. She was a believer in eugenics, which involves the attempt to produce biologically superior humans by socially controlling reproduction—an idea also popularized in Nazi Germany. Even so, Sanger was undeniably a stalwart of early efforts at women's liberation and decriminalization of matters pertaining to women's health.

### Antonin Scalia (1936–)

Antonin Scalia was born in Trenton, New Jersey, in 1936. Scalia is considered, even by his critics, to be one of the sharpest justices academically in Supreme Court history. His father was a college professor, and the love for all things intellectual was passed on to him. Scalia received his bachelor's degree in history from Georgetown University. After graduating from Georgetown summa cum laude as valedictorian, he went on to Harvard Law School. There, he served as the Law Review editor and graduated magna cum laude in 1960. After practicing law from 1961 to 1967, Scalia joined the faculty of the University of Virginia's Law School. He served there until 1974 and then again as a law professor at the University of Chicago from 1977 to 1982. He served as assistant attorney general during the Ford administration from 1974 to 1977. In 1982, he was appointed by President Reagan to the Federal Court of Appeals for Washington, D.C. There, Scalia established a record of judicial restraint and strict constructionism (i.e., belief that government's authorities are only those expressly granted to it in the U.S. Constitution). In 1986, Reagan nominated Scalia to the Supreme Court at the same time William Rehnquist was nominated to become chief justice. Scalia was confirmed unanimously. Scalia is widely known by admirers and critics as the Supreme Court's most conservative justice. His written opinions have demonstrated a belief in states' rights to regulate things such as abortion or consensual sexual relations. He has also challenged the permissibility of programs such as affirmative action that are race conscious. Scalia wrote the opinion of the court in *Whren v. U.S.*

### Al Sharpton (1954–)

Alfred Sharpton was born in Brooklyn, New York, in 1954. Sharpton is widely known as a television commentator, minister, civil rights activist, and presidential candidate. His career has centered on civil rights issues and has included regular confrontations with the criminal justice system when he has perceived abuses or injustices against minorities to have occurred. Sharpton entered politics in 1978 when he ran for a New York state senate seat. He was not elected and so continued his political activism. In 1986, Sharpton gained prominence nationally by organizing demonstrations after an African American man was killed by several whites in the Howard Beach neighborhood of New York City. A couple of years later, Sharpton became an adviser for Tawana Brawley, who claimed to have been sexually assaulted by a group of white people. Sharpton lost considerable credibility in the public eye by defending Brawley, as her claims later turned out to be a hoax. Sharpton also gained national attention when he led protests in 1989 following the shooting death of a black youth named Yosuf Hawkins by whites in Bensonhurst, another New York City neighborhood. More recently, Sharpton has organized demonstrations after the sexual assault of Haitian immigrant Abner Louima by police officers in 1997 and the police shooting of Amadou Diallo, an unarmed Ghanaian immigrant in 1999. In addition to Sharpton's failed campaign in 1978, he unsuccessfully ran for New York City mayor in 1997 and for the U.S. Senate in 1992 and 1994. Sharpton also ran as a candidate for President of the United States in 2003–2004. In recent years, Sharpton has attempted to resurrect his credibility as a mainstream pundit. He has regularly appeared on Fox and CNN news programs. Since 2011, Sharpton has hosted his own news commentary program on MSNBC called *PoliticsNation*.

## Roger Taney (1777–1864)

Roger Taney was born in Calvert County, Maryland, in 1777. He graduated from Dickinson College in 1795. After studying law on his own, he was admitted to the Maryland bar in 1799. That year, he was also elected to the Maryland House of Delegates, where he served one term. In 1821, he entered into private practice but remained active in politics and political campaigns. In 1831, Taney was appointed as U.S. attorney general by President Andrew Jackson. Five years later, Taney was nominated to be the chief justice of the Supreme Court to replace John Marshall.

Taney significantly contributed to the Court's early development. He has primarily come to be known, however, for the notorious decision of *Dred Scott v. Sandford* (1857). The Court's opinion in that case, which Taney delivered, officially declared that blacks were not "people" for the purposes of the Constitution and were indeed inferior beings. That decision damaged the credibility of the Court in the minds of many people at that time. Taney served on the Supreme Court until his death in 1864.

## August Vollmer (1876–1955)

August Vollmer is often referred to as the father of modern policing. By all accounts, Vollmer was in many ways ahead of his time. He served as the town marshal, and then police chief, for Berkeley, California, from 1905 to 1932. During his tenure there, he instituted many innovations. He collaborated with the University of California at Berkeley to develop a police training program for his officers. He required all of his officers to be formally trained in criminology and the social and physical sciences. He also developed a code of ethics for his department, which, among other things, eliminated the acceptance of gratuities or favors.

Other innovations of his and his department included being first to hire a female police officer; first to use automobiles and motorcycles for patrol; first to use crystal radios for dispatched communications; first to rely on scientific investigative techniques (e.g., analysis of blood, fibers, and soil); and among the first to require new recruits to pass psychological screenings and intelligence tests. In 1936, Vollmer published a book entitled *The Police and Modern Society* in which he explained his vision for the emerging profession of law enforcement. Vollmer was an advocate for advancing the goal of impartial police work. Many departments today that still have difficulties navigating through issues of community relations and relations with minority groups would still find Vollmer to be innovative.

## Earl Warren (1891–1974)

Earl Warren was born in Los Angeles in 1891. He grew up in Bakersfield, California, and attended the University of California at Berkeley. He received his bachelor's degree from that institution in 1912 and his juris doctor degree from there in 1914. He worked in private practice in the San Francisco Bay area for three years before entering the U.S. Army as a lieutenant in 1917. His early career in civilian government included several terms as Alameda County's (Oakland, California) district attorney. Serving as a prosecutor proved to be a good career to come from when entering politics. Warren, a moderate to liberal Republican, was elected governor of California three successive times: in1942, 1946, and 1950. In 1948, Warren ran unsuccessfully as the vice presidential candidate for Thomas Dewey, who narrowly lost to Harry Truman. In 1953, President Dwight Eisenhower appointed Warren as the chief justice for the U.S. Supreme Court. President Eisenhower would later call the appointment of Warren, as well as his appointment of William Brennan, among the biggest mistakes he ever made. Warren proved to be very liberal and judicially active on the Supreme Court. It was during his tenure as chief justice that the Bill of Rights was incorporated into the Fourteenth Amendment through one case after another, thereby requiring state and local authorities to abide by the provisions of the Fourth, Fifth, Sixth, and Eighth Amendments in particular. The Warren Court also oversaw the end of legal segregation and a host of other civil rights advances. Despite being a liberal, Warren wrote the opinion of the Court in *Terry v. Ohio*, in which the conviction of armed, would-be robbers was upheld after a police officer patted them down for weapons without a warrant.

## Ida B. Wells (1862–1931)

Ida B. Wells is also known as Ida B. Wells-Barnett and was born into a Mississippi slave family in 1862. Wells learned to read as a child owing to the emphasis her parents placed on hard work and education. She went on to receive her college training at Fisk University. In 1884, Wells was traveling on a train and was forcibly removed from first class and placed into the "Jim Crow" car (a blacks-only car), despite having paid for a first class ticket. Wells sued the railroad company over this incident and won the case. The Tennessee Supreme Court reversed, however, in favor of the railroad. She then dedicated her life to confronting racial injustice and bigotry. She did this primarily through writing and giving speeches. One injustice Wells frequently decried was the substandard facilities and supplies for black school children as compared to white children in the same school districts. Wells was also touched by violence against blacks. Three of her friends in Memphis, Tennessee, were killed by whites, and she herself was threatened with death for continuing to write about segregation. She eventually moved to Chicago and wrote several pieces on lynchings and mob rule in the South. In Chicago, Wells worked aggressively for equality for blacks and equality for women. Wells became a very influential civil rights leader in Chicago and wielded that influence until her death in 1931.

## Byron White (1917–2002)

Byron White was born in Colorado in 1917. He grew up there and attended the University of Colorado. He played football, basketball, and baseball for the university, earning 10 varsity letters. He was also an outstanding student and won the Rhodes Scholarship to Oxford University in England in 1939. From 1942 to 1946, White served as a naval intelligence officer. Once World War II ended and he was released from active duty, he attended Yale Law School. Amazingly, while at Yale, he played professional football for the Detroit Lions on the weekends. After graduating from law school, White clerked for U.S. Supreme Court justice Fred Vinson and then returned to Colorado to practice law. He was in private practice in Colorado for 14 years before being selected to serve as deputy attorney general in Robert Kennedy's Justice Department. Less than a year later, in 1962, White was selected by President John F. Kennedy to take a seat on the U.S. Supreme Court. White developed a reputation on the court as a moderate. His views may have been more liberal than moderate, but compared to the overall tenor of the truly liberal Warren Court, it didn't take much judicial restraint to be considered a moderate. White authored a couple of court opinions directly impacting the issue of profiling. In 1975, he authored the Court's opinion in *Taylor v. Louisiana*, in which the systematic exclusion of women from potential jury duty was ruled unconstitutional. He also authored the opinion of the Court in *Delaware v. Prouse*, in which a police officer's stop of a motorist without an objective basis for the stop was ruled unconstitutional.

### Christine Todd Whitman (1947–)

Christine Todd Whitman is well known in political circles for a variety of accomplishments. Most recently, she served as the head of the U.S. Environmental Protection Agency under President George W. Bush. She first gained wide, national notoriety, however, when she was elected governor of New Jersey in 1993, defeating incumbent Jim Florio. Whitman was considered a moderate to liberal Republican by national party standards. She was not as conservative as the national Republican Party on many social issues such as abortion. She believed sincerely in the need to cut taxes, however, as the number-one priority in putting an overall budget together. Whitman cut state income taxes by 30 percent in just two years, something for which she remains well known in New Jersey to this day. Whitman did not shy away from controversy in the criminal justice arena either. As governor, Whitman aggressively sought to end racial profiling in her state—particularly as practiced by the state police. The New Jersey State Police had been regularly accused by civil rights groups of targeting blacks for traffic stops. In 1999, that accusation gained some footing when the New Jersey attorney general concluded the same thing. Whitman, who had been a long-time supporter of law enforcement, then became very loud and visible in her opposition to racial profiling—even to the point of angering many police officers and troopers. Her crusade against profiling hit a bump in the road in 2000 when a 1996 photo of Whitman surfaced, showing her frisking a black male, spread-eagled against the wall, with a state trooper by her side. She was smiling in the picture, seemingly enjoying the encounter. Whitman was in the situation in the first place because she was engaged in a ride-along with that particular trooper. It turned out the subject, who had been stopped for acting "suspiciously," had no weapons or contraband in his possession and was not eventually arrested. Whitman received considerable criticism for her participation in this apparent act of racial profiling. Despite this public relations setback, Whitman's reforms that she forced upon the state police and the antiprofiling legislation she pushed through the legislature have remained.

## James Q. Wilson (1931–2012)

James Q. Wilson was one of the premier criminal justice and public policy scholars of modern times. He attended the University of Redlands in southern California, graduating with a bachelor's degree in 1952. He then went on to earn a master's degree and PhD at the University of Chicago in 1957 and 1959, respectively. Wilson served on numerous commissions concerning crime and criminal justice. He also published several books on crime, law enforcement, and other social issues. He is best known for his "broken windows" theory of crime, which he introduced with criminologist George Kelling in 1982. That theory hypothesizes that ignoring public and social order matters, such as prostitution, abandoned buildings, and small-time drug dealers, sends the message that "crime and the criminal element are welcome here." Instead, police should address those quality-of-life and social order issues. In doing so, more serious crime will be rooted out or will not emerge in those areas to begin with. The application of the broken windows theory has been varied over the years. Some departments have embraced the theory as a reason for community policing, which is a model of law enforcement geared toward solving problems—including social order problems. Others have embraced Broken Windows as a justification for aggressive policing strategies—that is, aggressively arresting minor offenders in hopes of uncovering or preventing more serious criminal conduct. The latter response has typically been received poorly by communities of color in urban areas. Wilson died at the age of 80 in 2012 after battling leukemia.

### O. W. Wilson (1900–1972)

O. W. Wilson was one of the most significant police reformers of the 20th century. A protégé of August Vollmer in Berkeley, California (see Vollmer entry), Wilson went on to influence police professionalism greatly in his own right. Wilson served as a scholar of police studies and as a police administrator over his long career. He served as the police chief for Fullerton, California; Wichita, Kansas; and Chicago. He also served as the first dean of the School of Criminology at the University of California, Berkeley. Wilson is well known for having implemented a professional style of policing everywhere he served as chief. His leadership style is reflected in the well-known text he published in 1950 entitled *Police Administration*. In that book, Wilson argued for the true bureaucratic model of organization for police departments, including strict adherence to rules and regulations, a clear and hierarchical chain of command, division of responsibilities, and impartiality in providing service. His book also outlined principles for building relations with the public. Wilson also is noted for having refined the practice of preventative patrol, that is, fielding roving police officers in squad cars in an effort to deter crime through presence or to intercept crime in the act. He believed that aggressively policing a neighborhood or city could in fact reduce crime. This model of policing continues to be common today but is generally considered to be at odds with community policing.

## Organizations and Agencies

### Private Organizations

### American Civil Liberties Union

125 Broad Street, 18th Floor
New York, NY 10004
http://www.aclu.org

The American Civil Liberties Union (ACLU) is a nonprofit organization founded in 1920. The purpose of the ACLU is to defend civil liberties—particularly those granted under the U.S. Constitution's Bill of Rights. It was originally founded in response to the widespread jailing of foreign-born political radicals in the early part of the 20th century as the United States geared up for and then fought World War I. The ACLU advances its agenda through dissemination of information and through legal action. Common issues of importance to the ACLU include immigrant rights, women in prison, police misconduct, and religious liberties (usually seeking the removal of religion from the public square). Information concerning these issues, and on the ACLU's national "Campaign against Racial Profiling" specifically, can be accessed through the ACLU website. The website also links to ACLU press releases, legal briefs, and legislation around the United States.

### American Civil Rights Institute

P.O. Box 188350
Sacramento, CA 95818
http://www.acri.org

The American Civil Rights Institute exists for the purpose of educating the public about race and gender preferences. The Institute publishes summaries of cases relating to the issue of preferences on its website. Further, the website contains links to pertinent legislation, legal briefs, speeches, and a full bibliography of suggested reading materials. The institute monitors the implementation of legislation and legal decisions concerning race and gender neutrality and then works to educate public officials and private citizens on the issue.

## Americans for Effective Law Enforcement

P.O. Box 75401
Chicago, IL 60675
http://www.aele.org

Americans for Effective Law Enforcement (AELE) was formed in 1966. It created a legal research center in 1973. AELE is a research-driven educational organization. Its primary mission is to disseminate legal information through seminars, other training, use of the legal center, and through the Web. AELE maintains information concerning law enforcement practice, including the use of profiling. AELE also maintains information concerning jails and prisoner rights issues.

## Amnesty International

1 Easton Street
London
WC1X 0DW, UK
http://www.amnesty.org

Amnesty International is the premiere privately funded global organization concerned with human rights issues. Amnesty International conducts investigations of alleged abuses around the world. It has chapters located in dozens of countries around the world. From the website, a researcher can access reports relating to abuses in the United States and abroad. Frequently, the abuses tie directly to the military and criminal justice authorities of a given country. Amnesty International is a leading opponent of the death penalty. It also fights inhumane treatment of the incarcerated. Reports and other documents concerning racism, sexism, and homophobia are also available through the website.

## The Cato Institute

1000 Massachusetts Avenue NW
Washington, DC 20001
http://www.cato.org

The Cato Institute is a think tank whose purpose is to promote public policies consistent with the traditional American principles of limited government, individual liberty, free markets, and peace. The Cato Institute pursues this goal through involvement in public presentations and debates, conducting research, publishing, and through maintaining its website. Although often considered a conservative organization, the Cato Institute is actually libertarian and a good resource for information concerning the dangers of excessive police authority and actions. A search of the website will link to several documents concerning profiling.

## Center for Constitutional Rights

666 Broadway, 7th Floor
New York, NY 10012
http:///www.ccrjustice.org

The Center for Constitutional Rights uses litigation and advocacy to advance the law in a direction it views as positive, to empower poor communities and communities of color, and to guarantee the rights of people with few legal resources. The center also seeks to train constitutional and human rights attorneys and to foster a broad movement for constitutional and human rights. Through the center and through its website, much information is available concerning constitutional rights generally and profiling specifically.

## Center for Equal Opportunity

7700 Leesburg Pike Suite 231
Falls Church, VA 22043
http://www.ceousa.org

The Center for Equal Opportunity is a nonprofit organization established out of devotion to a truly color-blind society in which equal opportunity and racial harmony can reign. The organization maintains an extensive website for the research to peruse. The site offers an "in the news" section with current stories relating to equal opportunity. The organization has a significant section relating to immigration issues as well as issues concerning disparate impact between the races.

## Commission on the Accreditation of Law Enforcement Agencies

13575 Heathcote Boulevard, Suite 320
Gainesville, VA 20155
http://www.calea.org

The Commission on the Accreditation of Law Enforcement Agencies (CALEA) was founded in 1979. It is an organization dedicated to the standardization of professional police practice. CALEA does this by assessing police agencies seeking accreditation against a list of standards. Many of the standards are measured by whether a police agency has adopted certain policies supported by CALEA. Although CALEA officially finds profiling generally to be a potentially useful tool in law enforcement, it requires of its member organizations the maintaining of strict policies governing them in the use of profiling—particularly making law enforcement decisions based solely on race, ethnicity, religion, gender, and sexual orientation. The CALEA website offers its model policy concerning profiling for any viewer who wishes to read it.

## Congressional Black Caucus Foundation

1720 Massachusetts Avenue NW
Washington, DC 20036
http://www.cbcfinc.org/

The Congressional Black Caucus Foundation was established in1976. It was set up for the purpose of broadening the influence of African Americans in the public policy and legal arenas. The foundation's website is an excellent source of information concerning public policies, research, and education in the many areas of importance to the African American community.

Through the foundation website, a researcher can access audio/video materials and publications relating to bias and discrimination in the criminal justice system, among other topics.

## Drug Policy Alliance

131 West 33rd St., 15th Floor
New York, NY 10001
http://www.drugpolicy.org

This organization's purpose is to primarily focus on drug laws and policies in the United States. The Drug Policy Alliance seeks to reform the drug laws so as to deemphasize the use of punitive criminal justice measures. Key issues for the alliance include sentencing reform, police conduct, and profiling. The alliance publishes position papers on a variety of topics. Additionally, the website serves as a portal to an online library, from which documents can be viewed concerning the effect of drugs and drug laws on different communities, including racial minorities, women, and homosexuals.

## Drug Reform Coordination Network

P.O. Box 9853
Washington, DC 20016
http://www.stopthedrugwar.org

The Drug Reform Coordination Network is an organization that seeks to reform U.S. drug laws through decriminalization. The organization's website is very thorough, with links to attorney general opinions, research data, and commercial documents relating to drug use and drug crimes. The site permits users to access a citizen's guide to police encounters and also offers information concerning profiling within the context of drug enforcement.

## EthnicMajority.com

655 13th Street, Suite 303
Oakland, CA 95612
http://www.ethnicmajority.com

EthnicMajority.com is a privately funded organization committed to exposing discrimination against minorities in various walks of life. The group is funded by an organization called Diverse Strategies. EthnicMajority.com emphasizes minority issues in the workplace, politics, the criminal justice system, housing, and other areas. The organization website, which is the group's primary product, provides several links and publications of relevance to profiling.

## Human Rights Watch

350 Fifth Avenue, 34th Floor
New York, NY 10118
http://www. hrw.org

The purpose of Human Rights Watch is to advocate on behalf of victims of human rights abuses. The organization investigates various types of abuses and discrimination. It then presents its findings to governmental bodies to encourage them to respect human rights laws that are implicated in their findings. Human Rights Watch also seeks to increase public support for ending various human rights abuses in the United States and around the world. Key issues of interest for this organization include prisoner rights, the rights of immigrants and refugees, and women's rights.

## International Association of Chiefs of Police

44 Canal Center Plaza, Suite 200
Alexandria, VA 22314
http://www.iacp.org

The International Association of Chiefs of Police (IACP) was founded in 1893 for the purposes of advancing police professionalism through modern (at the time) administrative practices and reform, increased use of technology to fight crime, improving training and education among the police ranks, and fostering high ethical standards in policing. The IACP provides a vast array of resources to those interested in researching police practices. It offers police professionals model policies for their departments, including policies concerning the use of profiling. The IACP publishes one of the leading police trade journals available—*Police Chief.* Archived articles from past issues of *Police Chief* can be accessed through the website. Additionally, many links are available to other sites and documents concerning police/community encounters and the issue of profiling as a tool for law enforcement.

## International Association of Directors of Law Enforcement Standards and Training

1330 N Manship Pl.
Meridian, ID 83642
http://www.iadlest.org

The International Association of Directors of Law Enforcement Standards and Training (IADLEST) is an organization made up of the various state agencies that guide the standards for police training and practice. These agencies generally are responsible for certifying police officers in a given state and revoking that certification or license when officers engage in serious misconduct. The IADLEST website provides users links to relevant law enforcement organizations in every state. The site also provides model policies for standards and training boards to use, as well as police agencies. Among the model policies are ones that relate to profiling and traffic stops.

## International Association of Forensic Criminologists

(formerly the Academy of Behavioral Profiling)
P.O. Box 2175
Sitka, AK 99835
http://www.profiling.org

The International Association of Forensic Criminologists is a professional association whose mission is to advance the application of evidence-based criminological theory and criminal profiling techniques within the criminal justice system. The emphasis with this organization is to improve the science behind using offender behavior to predict and solve crimes. The association recognizes that race, gender, sexual orientation, and other such classifications are not sufficient criteria by themselves to build a profile. The association publishes a journal that is available to members.

## John M. Ashbrook Center for Public Affairs

401 College Avenue
Ashland, OH 44805
http://www.ashbrook.org

The Ashbrook Center for Public Affairs is housed by Ashland University. The purpose of the center is to conduct research and promote discussion of the principles and practices of U.S. constitutional government and politics. The center emphasizes the scholarly defense of individual liberty, limited government, and civil morality—all of which together make up America's "democratic way of life." The Ashbrook Center website offers users a search engine through which one can access well over 100 documents relating to profiling.

## Leadership Conference on Civil Rights

1629 K Street NW, 10th Floor
Washington, DC 20006
http://www.civilrights.org

The Leadership Conference on Civil Rights is a socially concerned, issue-oriented organization that attempts to promote civil rights agenda through education. Resources available through the conference include audio resources, videos, and publications. The website is intended to serve as an online "nerve center" for people struggling against discrimination of all types and for the public at large to gain a better understanding of the nation's need for social and economic justice. The website offers users links to a variety of other relevant sites and organizations, including sites related to profiling.

## National Association for the Advancement of Colored People

4805 Mt. Hope Drive
Baltimore, MD 21215
http://www.naacp.org

The National Association for the Advancement of Colored People (NAACP) is a long-standing civil rights organization specifically founded to promote equality and justice among the races and to advance opportunities to succeed for minorities—particularly African Americans. The organization was founded in 1909 by Ida Wells-Barnett, W.E.B. DuBois, and others. The purpose of the organization then was to fight segregation and violence perpetrated against black Americans. Today, the organization continues to be among the premiere civil rights organizations in the United States, representing itself as standing for civil and political liberty. The NAACP maintains volumes of resources governing a wide variety of topics concerning justice and equality. Although headquartered in Baltimore, the organization has chapters in every major urban center in the country. The website presents a wealth of resources concerning civil rights matters, including racial profiling. The site also links to many other sources of information.

## National Organization of Black Law Enforcement Executives

4609 Pinecrest Office Park Drive, Suite F
Alexandria, VA 22312
http://www.noblenatl.org

The National Organization of Black Law Enforcement Executives (NOBLE) was founded in 1976 for the purpose of confronting the issue of high crime in urban, low-income areas. Today, NOBLE sets out to work closely with urban communities to create greater cooperation with the criminal justice system so as to have a favorable impact on crime and violence. The organization also seeks to create a unified front of African American law enforcement executives in order to affect public policy, further opportunities for minorities in policing, and disseminate information, training, and consultation where needed. NOBLE emphasizes the need for law enforcement officers to be respectful of all citizens they deal with and for police personnel and organizations to be accountable to the public. The NOBLE website provides a section on "areas of concern," which then link to several documents and publications on biased policing.

## National Sheriffs' Association

1450 Duke Street
Alexandria, VA 22314
http://www.sheriffs.org

The National Sheriffs' Association (NSA) is a nonprofit organization founded to advance professionalism and best practices in criminal justice, including both law enforcement and corrections. The NSA focuses on the unique role that sheriffs' departments have in that they serve law enforcement and correctional (through their jail operations) purposes at the same time. The NSA sponsors training around the country to modernize and improve criminal justice practice. The organization also helps local sheriffs' departments to secure grant funding for hot issues of the day (e.g., antiterrorism, dealing with methamphetamine labs, etc.). The NSA website, like the IACP site, offers useful information to those researching the relationship between the criminal justice system and minority communities.

## October 22 National Day of Protest to Stop Police Brutality, Repression and the Criminalization of a Generation

P.O. Box 2627
New York, NY 10009
http://www.october22.org

The October 22 National Day of Protest to Stop Police Brutality, Repression and the Criminalization of a Generation (NDP) was organized in 1995. Its name refers, in part, to the date on which the organization was formed. As the website notes, the NDP was initiated by a diverse coalition of organizations and individuals that came together out of a concern that the resistance against police brutality needed to take place at a national level. Every October 22, the NDP organizes a day of protest in several cities across the nation against police misconduct. These protests sometimes involve civil disobedience. The NDP website offers a variety of resources concerning the fight against police brutality. The perspective of the organization is radically left but nevertheless can serve as a useful resource site.

## Police Complaint Center

113 South Monroe St.
Tallahassee, FL 32301
http://www.policeabuse.com

The Police Complaint Center (PCC) serves as a clearinghouse for information concerning police misconduct—especially unlawful profiling. The PCC invites victims of police abuse from around the country to report their experiences to the center, which then publishes the alleged abuses online. The PCC works to document the extent of police misconduct in the United States so that public policy may be affected. The PCC assists citizens in filing formal complaints against law enforcement and ensures that those complaints are given fair hearing without falling through the cracks. The PCC website publishes several pieces of information concerning racial profiling and other dubious police activities.

## Police Executive Research Forum

1120 Connecticut Avenue NW, Suite 930
Washington, DC 20036
http://www.policeforum.org

The Police Executive Research Forum (PERF) describes itself as an organization made up of progressive police executives around the United States. The mission of PERF is to advance professionalism and best practices in policing and to help foster good public policy relating to law enforcement issues. PERF maintains an excellent website with an entire online library available to users. A whole section linked to the website deals with the issue of profiling.

Most of the information concerns racial and ethnic profiling; however, there are items of information that relate to profiling along other lines, for example, gender, sexual orientation, religion, and so on. PERF sponsors many studies and publications. PERF also partners with the U.S. Department of Justice (DOJ). The PERF website links to several DOJ publications.

## Police Foundation

1201 Connecticut Avenue NW
Washington, DC 20036
http://www.policefoundation.org

The Police Foundation is a nonprofit organization founded in1970. The foundation is committed to improving the ability of police officers to perform their duties, which cover a wide variety of police practice. The foundation works closely with police organizations around the country to conduct pragmatic and useful research concerning the best practices in policing. Additionally, the Police Foundation produces several practitioner-oriented publications to improve policing. The Police Foundation website maintains a whole section dedicated to community policing. Additionally, the website links to current and proposed legislation relating to police practices such as profiling.

## Public Agenda

6 East 39th Street
New York, NY 10016
http://www.publicagenda.org

Public Agenda is a nonprofit, nonpartisan organization created to address a wide range of policy issues through its research and citizen education programs. Issues the organization regularly confronts include health care, schools, national security matters, acquired immunodeficiency syndrome (AIDS), crime, the environment, and economics. By accessing its website and following the links to the organization's online library, articles on race, immigration, and other related issues can be viewed.

## Rainbow/PUSH Coalition

930 E. 50th Street
Chicago, IL 60615
http://www.rainbowpush.org

Rainbow/PUSH is a progressive organization founded by Jesse Jackson. The mission of Rainbow/PUSH is to fight for social change and social justice. The organization fields several speakers to events around the country. Many of the speeches can be read online. Additionally, the organization's website offers press releases, commentaries, and a weekly newsletter. A search of the documents online will yield several resources concerning profiling—particularly racial profiling.

## Robina Institute of Criminal Law and Criminal Justice

229 19th Avenue South
Mondale Hall 311
Minneapolis, MN 55455
http://www.robinainstitute.org

The Robina Institute is a public policy and research arm of the University of Minnesota Law School. Its purpose is to facilitate research in criminal justice policy areas, including sentencing and law enforcement reform, and to build partnerships with practitioners. The website contains links to many publications and posted lecture videos relating to race and disparities in the criminal justice system.

## Southern Poverty Law Center

400 Washington Avenue
Montgomery, AL 36104
http://www.splcenter.org

The Southern Poverty Law Center was founded in 1971 as a small civil rights law firm in the racially tense South. The organization in recent years has come to be known for its aggressive battles against white supremacist organizations on behalf of victims of hate crimes. Law enforcement agencies frequently utilize the center's thorough tracking of hate groups. The center publishes an e-newsletter that contains articles and commentary on the center's work. The center does engage in advocacy relating to the criminal justice system. The Southern Poverty Law Center is an ardent foe of the death penalty and the uneven sentencing patterns of minorities.

## Federal Government Agencies

## U.S. Department of Justice

http://www.usdoj.gov

Easily, the most useful Internet site for the study of police practices generally and profiling specifically is the website maintained by the U.S. Department of Justice (DOJ). There are literally dozens of DOJ agencies with their own websites that can be accessed through the main DOJ website address. The DOJ is the lead federal entity responsible for setting law enforcement practice standards in the United States, gauging the extent of crime in the United States, researching the merits of particular police practices, and researching the extent of police misconduct. Additionally, the DOJ investigates and adjudicates criminal and civil action against law enforcers and their parent organizations when misconduct is alleged. Some of the many websites of interest to those researching biases in the criminal justice system are listed in the following. A seemingly unlimited number of links and publications relating to profiling and police/community relations are available through these sites. Even so, they represent only a partial list.

Bureau of Justice Assistance: http://www.bja.gov

Bureau of Justice Statistics: http://www.bjs.gov

Bureau of Prisons: http://www.bop.gov

Civil Rights Division: http://www.usdoj.gov/crt

Community Oriented Policing Services: http://www.cops .usdoj.gov

Community Relations Service: http://www.usdoj.gov/crs

Federal Bureau of Investigation: http://www.fbi.gov

National Criminal Justice Reference Service: http://www .ncjrs.gov

National Institute of Justice: http://www.nij.gov

Office of Legislative Affairs: http://www.usdoj.gov/ola

## U.S. Department of Homeland Security

http://www.dhs.gov

While the Department of Justice is the first stop among federal agency websites to collect information on profiling, it certainly shouldn't be one's only stop. The Department of Homeland Security has a number of publications and resources for citizens and for the law enforcement community relating to racial and other forms of profiling. This makes sense given that the department is home to several key law enforcement bureaus where profiling is implicated, including the Bureau of Immigration and Customs Enforcement, the Bureau of Customs and Border Protection, the Secret Service, and the Transportation Security Administration, which is responsible for screening airline passengers and houses the Federal Air Marshal Service. Specific components within the Department of Homeland Security, all of which have publications relating to profiling and offender profiles, can be found by using the search feature at the websites listed in the following:

Bureau of Customs and Border Protection: http://www.cbp .gov

Bureau of Immigration and Customs Enforcement: http:// www.ice.gov

Federal Protective Service: http://www.dhs.gov/federal-protective-service

Secret Service: http://www.secretservice.gov

Transportation and Security Administration: http://www .tsa.gov

## U.S. Department of State

http://www.state.gov

The U.S. Department of State represents the United States to the world. Consequently, the State Department is the chief agency in the federal government to advocate America's values to other countries, including values concerning fair and equitable treatment in the criminal justice system. From the State Department website, one can navigate to several documents and other sites concerning prosecution and punishment of criminals and dissidents. Interestingly, the State Department website also maintains a section specifically on profiling. From the section, one can link to a variety of government documents, legislation, and opinion on the matter.

### State Government Agencies

It is safe to say that criminal justice practice is a major public policy issue in every state of the union. Many states are presently confronting the issues of discrimination in policing, prosecution, and punishment. Other states have confronted such issues in the past. Still others are exploring these types of issues tangentially while dealing with other criminal justice matters.

The best way to ascertain what a particular state is doing or saying about the issue of criminal justice profiling is to go directly to a state's website and do a search. Commonly, the attorney general's office and the Department of Corrections for any given state are good places to start. When accessing a state website, there will always be a link to the various state agencies, to include the attorney general and the Corrections Department. Other potentially useful sites in the state's executive branch of government include the Department of Public Safety (or a state's equivalent), the state police or highway patrol, and the state's Peace Officer Standards and Training Board.

Also accessible from a state's website are the legislative and judicial branches. By accessing the state legislature, a researcher will be able to conduct a search for proposed legislation concerning profiling. One could also search for existing statutes as well as studies and working papers commissioned and drafted at the behest of the legislature as a part of the public policy process.

Likewise, by accessing the judicial branch a researcher would be able to search court cases at the state and local level that relate to or involve the issue of profiling, either directly or indirectly. What's more, the judicial branch websites may include studies or policies concerning sentencing practices and guidelines.

As can be seen in the following, most state website addresses follow a simple pattern—http://www.state.??.us, where the "??" is simply the mail code for the state. So for Minnesota, the state website is http://www.state.mn.us. The website for each state follows:

Alabama: http://www.alabama.gov
Alaska: http://www.state.ak.us or http://www.alaska.gov
Arkansas: http://www.state.ar.us or http://www.arkansas.gov
California: http://www.state.ca.us or http://www.ca.gov
Colorado: http://www.state.co.us or http://www.colorado.gov
Connecticut: http://www.state.ct.us or http://www.ct.gov

Delaware: http://www.state.de.us or http://www.delaware
.gov

District of Columbia: http://www.dc.gov

Florida: http://www.state.fl.us or http://www.MyFlorida
.com

Georgia: http:// www.state.ga.us or http://www.georgia.gov

Hawaii: http://www.state.hi.us or http://www.hawaii.gov

Idaho: http://www.state.id.us or http://www.idaho.gov

Illinois: http://www.state.il.us or http://www.illinois.gov

Indiana: http://www.state.in.us or http://www.in.gov

Iowa: http://state.ia.us or http://www.iowa.gov

Kansas: http://www.state.ks.us or http://www.kansas.gov

Kentucky: http://www.kentucky.gov

Louisiana: http://www.state.la.us or http://www.louisiana
.gov

Maine: http://www.state.me.us or http://www.maine.gov

Maryland: http://www.maryland.gov

Massachusetts: http://www.mass.gov

Michigan: http://www.michigan.gov

Minnesota: http://www.state.mn.us or http://www.mn.gov

Mississippi: http://www.state.ms.us or http://www.missis
sippi.gov

Missouri: http://www.state.mo.us or http://www.missouri
.gov

Montana: http://www.state.mt.us or http://www.mt.gov

Nebraska: http://www.state.ne.us or http://www.nebraska
.gov

Nevada: http://www.nv.gov

New Hampshire: http://www.state.nh.us or http://www
.nh.gov

New Jersey: http://www.state.nj.us or http://www.nj.gov

New Mexico: http://www.state.nm.us or http://www.new mexico.gov

New York: http://www.state.ny.us or http://www.ny.gov

North Carolina: http://www.nc.gov

North Dakota: http://www.state.nd.us or www.nd.gov

Ohio: http://www.state.oh.us or http://www.ohio.gov

Oklahoma: http://www.state.ok.us or http://www.ok.gov

Oregon: http://www.oregon.gov

Pennsylvania: http://www.state.pa.us or http://www.pa.gov

Rhode Island: http://www.state.ri.us

South Carolina: http://www.sc.gov

South Dakota: http://www.state.sd.us or http://www.sd.gov

Tennessee: http://www.state.tn.us or http://www.tennessee.gov

Texas: http://www.texas.gov

Utah: http://www.utah.gov

Vermont: http://www.vermont.gov

Virginia: http://www.virginia.gov

Washington: http://www.wa.gov

West Virginia: http://www.wv.gov

Wisconsin: http://www.wisconsin.gov

Wyoming: http://www.wyo.gov

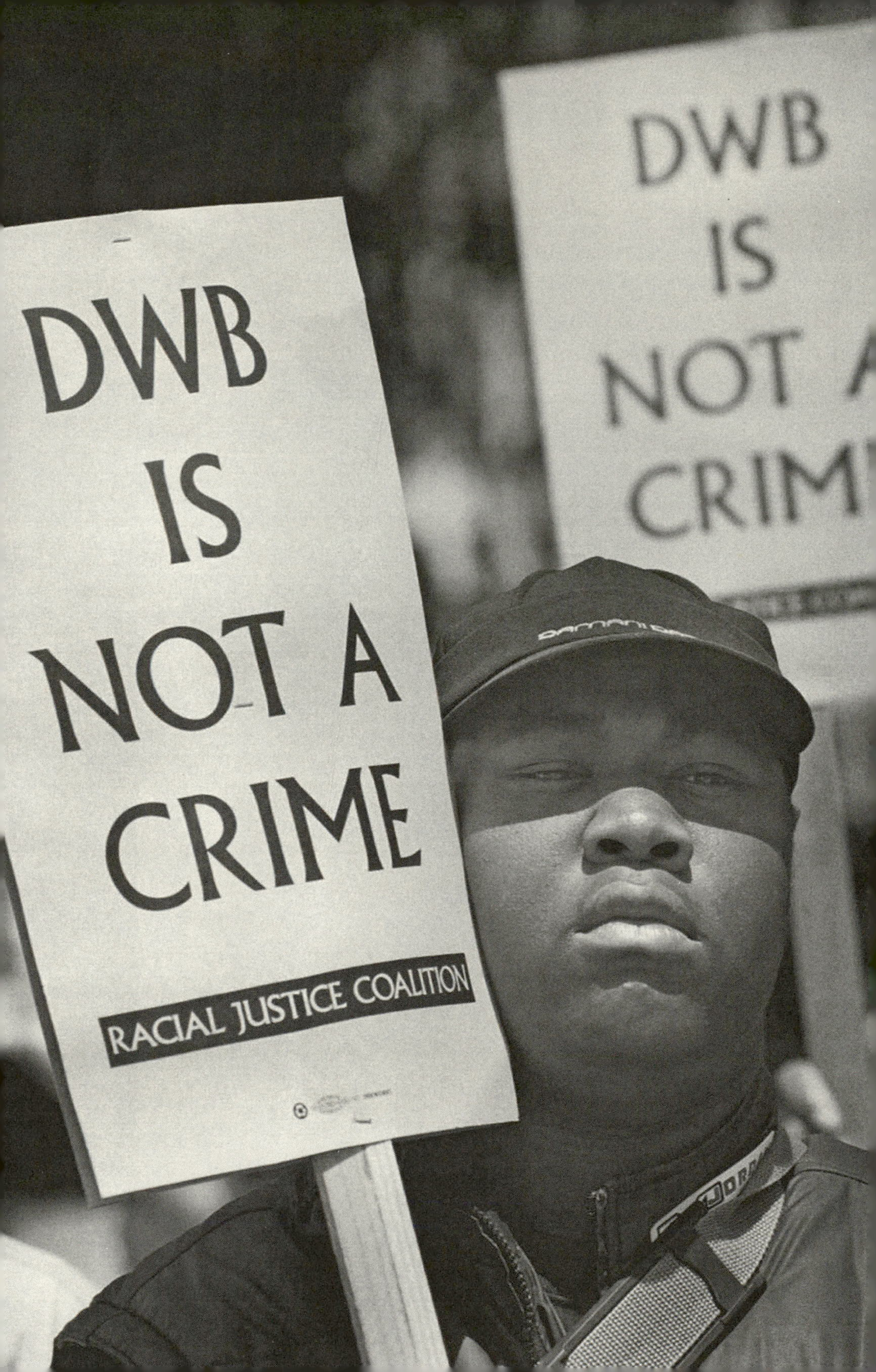
DWB
IS
NOT A
CRIME
RACIAL JUSTICE COALITION
DWB
IS
NOT A
CRIM

In this chapter, readers have an opportunity to peruse profiling-related documents originating from all three branches of the federal government, as well as from other sources. These documents collectively are rich with information, analysis, argument, and statistical data. Specifically, in the first section of the chapter, readers will find brief summaries of key reports, factsheets, and recent federal legislation relating to criminal justice profiling. In the second section of the chapter, readers will have an opportunity to review written Supreme Court decisions which directly relate to profiling and ancillary practices in the American criminal justice system. Additionally, summaries of the cases are provided as a means of introduction. The documents and court decisions in this chapter, coupled with the scholarly material highlighted in the next chapter, provide an excellent foundation for researching the issue of criminal justice profiling further.

## Government Documents

The documents summarized in the following are listed in alphabetical order by title. Brief summaries along with current Internet links to the documents are provided. Readers should note that if for some reason a link address is no longer active

Protesters assemble in 2000 at California's State Capitol in Sacramento to register support for SB1389, a proposed law that would have required law enforcement officers to collect data about the race of motorists on traffic stops and the outcome of those stops. (AP Photo/Steve Yeater)

when trying to pull a document up, simply searching the title of the document through an Internet search engine will reveal the most current web address for the document.

## Civil Rights Complaints in U.S. District Court: 1990–2006

http://www.bjs.gov/content/pub/pdf/crcusdc06.pdf

This Bureau of Justice Statistics report, written in 2008 by Tracey Kyckelhahn and Thomas Cohen, tracks the trends in federal civil rights lawsuits for over a decade and a half. These lawsuits include those filed by the federal government, as well as those brought by private parties. Among federal lawsuits are those targeting discriminatory criminal justice practices. Indeed, according to the report, 9 out of 10 civil rights lawsuits involve a private party suing another private party. Among other trends, the data in the report reflect the fact that civil rights lawsuits climbed in numbers steadily throughout the 1990s, stabilized in the early 2000s, and then dropped precipitously from 2003 to 2006. Further, civil rights cases as a percentage of the total federal civil case load have been declining since 2003.

## Confronting Discrimination in the Post-9/11 Era: Challenges and Opportunities Ten Years Later

http://www.justice.gov/crt/publications/post911/post911 summit_report_2012–04.pdf

This document is a report produced by the U.S. Department of Justice Civil Rights Division in 2011. The report was a culmination of a Post-9/11 civil rights summit which was held at the George Washington University School of Law in October of that year. The report recounts the Justice Department's role in the aftermath of the 9/11 attacks, including responding to hate crimes which emerged as a backlash response. The report also highlighted a survey of Muslim Americans regarding their attitudes toward the social climate in the United

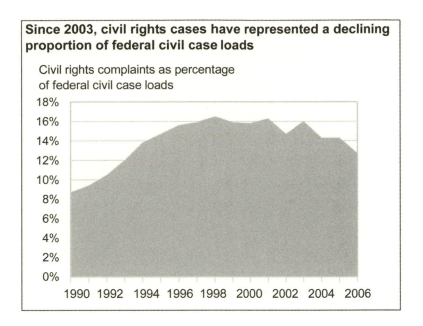

Since 2003, civil rights cases have represented a declining proportion of federal civil case loads

Civil rights complaints as percentage of federal civil case loads

Figure 5.1

States, discrimination, and the war against terrorism. Finally, the report identifies challenges and opportunities in the future regarding the protection of civil rights and civil liberties in Post-9/11 America.

## Contacts between the Police and the Public, 2008

http://www.bjs.gov/content/pub/pdf/cpp08.pdf

This document is a report produced by the Bureau of Justice Statistics in 2011 and was written by government statisticians Christine Eith and Matthew Durose. The report contains a tabulation and analysis of police contacts with members of the public in 2008. The information for the report was collected through the Police-Public Contact Survey, which is administered every three years as a supplement to the annually administered National Crime Victimization Survey. Consequently,

**Table 5.1  Number of U.S. residents age 16 or older who had contact with police, by demographic characteristics and reason for contact, 2002 and 2008**

| Demographic characteristic | Driver during traffic stop | | | | Resident reported crime/problem to police | | | |
| | Number (in thousands) | | Difference in contacts, 2002–2008 | | Number (in thousands) | | Difference in contacts, 2002–2008 | |
| | 2002 | 2008 | Number (in thousands) | Percent change | 2002 | 2008 | Number (in thousands) | Percent change |
|---|---|---|---|---|---|---|---|---|
| Total | 16,783 | 17,663 | 880 | 5.2 | 11,960 | 8,345 | –3,615 | –30.2 |
| Sex | | | | | | | | |
| Male | 10,210 | 10,330 | 119 | 1.2 | 5,232 | 3,665 | –1,567 | –29.9 |
| Female | 6,573 | 7,333 | 760 | 11.6 | 6,727 | 4,679 | –2,048 | –30.4 |
| Race/Hispanic origin | | | | | | | | |
| White[a] | 12,842 | 12,933 | 91 | 0.7 | 9,202 | 6,379 | –2,823 | –30.7 |
| Black/African American[a] | 1,852 | 1,845 | –8 | –0.4 | 1,347 | 713 | –634 | –47.1 |
| Hispanic/ Latino | 1,596 | 2,038 | 442 | 27.7 | 1,072 | 837 | –234 | –21.9 |
| Other[a,b] | 493 | 710 | 217 | 44.0 | 339 | 314 | –25 | –7.4 |
| Two or more races[a] | ~ | 137 | ~ | ~ | ~ | 102 | ~ | ~ |

(Continued)

**Table 5.1** *(Continued)*

| Demographic characteristic | Driver during traffic stop | | | | Resident reported crime/problem to police | | | |
|---|---|---|---|---|---|---|---|---|
| | Number (in thousands) | | Difference in contacts, 2002–2008 | | Number (in thousands) | | Difference in contacts, 2002–2008 | |
| | 2002 | 2008 | Number (in thousands) | Percent change | 2002 | 2008 | Number (in thousands) | Percent change |
| Age | | | | | | | | |
| 16–17 | 487 | 331 | −156 | −32.1 | 292 | 182 | −110 | −37.6 |
| 18–24 | 3,874 | 3,547 | −327 | −8.5 | 1,449 | 1,122 | −327 | −22.6 |
| 25–34 | 3,765 | 4,122 | 357 | 9.5 | 2,466 | 1,597 | −869 | −35.2 |
| 35–44 | 3,714 | 3,620 | −94 | −2.5 | 3,050 | 1,665 | −1,385 | −45.4 |
| 45–54 | 2,712 | 3,042 | 330 | 12.2 | 2,457 | 1,792 | −665 | −27.1 |
| 55–64 | 1,459 | 1,978 | 520 | 35.6 | 1,142 | 1,209 | 68 | 5.9 |
| 65 or older | 773 | 1,024 | 251 | 32.5 | 1,104 | 777 | −327 | −29.6 |

*Note:* Data are based on residents whose most recent contact with police in 2002 or 2008 occurred as the result of being a driver in a traffic stop or reporting a crime or problem.

~Not applicable. The 2002 PPCS did not separately identify persons of two or more races.

[a]Excludes persons of Hispanic origin.

[b]Includes American Indians, Alaska Natives, Asians, Native Hawaiians, and other Pacific Islanders.

the data are collected from the "public" side of police-public encounters. The report summarizes by age, race, and gender those who had contacts with the police in 2008 and what was the nature and outcome of those contacts.

The report also contrasts the 2008 data with data collected in earlier surveys to highlight emerging trends. For example, in the following table, traffic stops grew significantly as a percentage of all police contacts with the public between 2002 and 2008, even while the total number of contacts declined during that period.

Table 5.2   Reason for contact among U.S. residents age 16 or older who had contact with police, 2002, 2005, and 2008

| Reason for most recent contact | 2002 | 2005 | 2008 |
|---|---|---|---|
| Total | 100% | 100% | 100% |
| Traffic-related contacts | 52.8% | 56.4% | 59.2% |
| Driver during traffic stop | 37.1 | 41.0 | 44.1 |
| Passenger during traffic stop | 2.7 | 2.8 | 2.9 |
| Traffic accident | 13.0 | 12.5 | 12.2 |
| Other contacts | 47.3% | 43.6% | 40.8% |
| Resident reported crime/ problem to police | 26.4 | 23.7 | 20.9 |
| Police provided assistance or service | 7.2 | 6.2 | 6.3 |
| Poice investigating crime | 5.8 | 5.6 | 5.6 |
| Police suspected resident of wrongdoing | 2.6 | 2.8 | 2.5 |
| Other reason* | 5.3 | 5.3 | 5.5 |
| Number of residents with police contact (in thousands) | 45,279 | 43,658 | 40,015 |

Note: Data are based on the resident's most recent contact with police in 2002, 2005, and 2008. See appendix table 2 for standard errors. Detail may not sum to total because of rounding.
*Includes a small percentage of cases in which the reason for contact was unknown.

### Correctional Populations in the United States, 2012

http://www.bjs.gov/content/pub/pdf/cpus12.pdf

This report published by the Bureau of Justice Statistics in 2013, authored by Lauren Glaze and Erinn Herberman, explores the characteristics of the incarcerated and supervised criminal population in the United States at the local, state, and federal levels. The report provides an excellent overview of correctional trends over time, comparing the 2012 data with data collected in previous years. Among other findings, readers will see that prisoner populations have grown in jails, and state and federal prisons, since 2000. In 2012, nearly 7 million offenders were either incarcerated or under the supervision of an adult correctional system.

Despite the growth in raw numbers of those being supervised in one way or another by the correctional system, there are slightly fewer offenders, per capita, under the supervision of the correction system. The following table shows an overall decline in the rate of correctional supervision from 2000 to 2012.

Although this particular report, unlike others highlighted in this chapter, does not discuss the racial makeup of offenders in the correctional system, it provides solid trend-lines to observe in American corrections and gives greater context to other reports which do explicitly address racial imbalances in the correctional system.

### End Racial Profiling Act of 2013

https://www.govtrack.us/congress/bills/113/s1038/text

This proposed legislation, the text of which is accessible through the Library of Congress, would ban profiling on the basis of race, ethnicity, national origin, or religion. Various iterations of this legislation have been introduced in both houses of Congress for the past several years. The proposed law would permit complainants to sue police agencies, police supervisors, and officers who engage in profiling. What is

**Table 5.3 Estimated number of persons supervised by adult correctional systems, by correctional status, 2000, 2005, 2010–2012**

| Year | Total correctional population[a] | Community supervision | | | Incarcerated[b] | | |
|---|---|---|---|---|---|---|---|
| | | Total[a,c] | Probation | Parole | Total | Jail[d] | Prison[e] |
| 2000 | 6,461,000 | 4,565,100 | 3,839,500 | 725,500 | 1,938,500 | 621,100 | 1,317,300 |
| 2005 | 7,050,400 | 4,946,800 | 4,162,500 | 784,400 | 2,195,000 | 747,500 | 1,447,400 |
| 2010 | 7,079,500 | 4,887,900 | 4,055,500 | 840,700 | 2,270,100 | 748,700 | 1,521,400 |
| 2011 | 6,978,500 | 4,814,200 | 3,971,300 | 853,900 | 2,240,600 | 735,600 | 1,505,000 |
| 2012 | 6,937,600 | 4,781,300 | 3,942,800 | 851,200 | 2,228,400 | 744,500 | 1,483,900 |
| Average annual percent change, 2000–2011 | 0.7% | 0.5% | 0.3% | 1.5% | 1.3% | 1.5% | 1.2% |
| Percent change, 2011–2012[f] | −0.7% | −0.8% | −1.0% | −0.1% | −0.5% | 1.2% | −1.4% |

*Note:* Estimates were rounded to the nearest 100 and may not be comparable to previously published BJS reports due to updated information or rounding. Totals include estimates for nonresponding jurisdictions. See *Methodology*. Total community supervision, probation, parole, and prison custody estimates are for December 31; jail population estimates are for the last weekday in June.

*(Continued)*

**Table 5.3** *(Continued)*

| Year | Total correctional population[a] | Community supervision | | | Incarcerated[b] | | |
|---|---|---|---|---|---|---|---|
| | | Total[a,c] | Probation | Parole | Total | Jail[d] | Prison[e] |

[a]Estimates were adjusted to account for some offenders with multiple correctional statuses. See *Methodology*.

[b]Includes local jail inmates and prisoners held in the custody of state or federal prisons or privately operated facilities.

[c]Includes some offenders held in a prison or jail but who remained under the jurisdiction of a probation or parole agency.

[d]Totals are estimates based on the Annual Survey of Jails, except the total for 2005, which is a complete enumeration based on the Census of Jails Inmates. See appendix table 5 for standard errors and *Methodology*.

[e]Includes prisoners held in the custody of state or federal prisons or privately operated facilities. The custody prison population is not comparable to the jurisdiction prison population, which is BJS's official measure of the prison population. See text box on page 2 for a discussion of the differences between the two prison populations.

[f]See *Methodology* for information on the methods used to calculate annual change within each correctional population and the total correctional population.

*Sources:* Bureau of Justice Statistics, Annual Probation Survey, Annual Parole Survey, Annual Survey of Jails, Census of Jail Inmates, and National Prisoner Statistics Program, 2000, 2005, and 2010–2012.

**Table 5.4  U.S. adult residents supervised by adult correctional systems, 2000–2012**

| Year | Total population supervised by adult correctional systems[a] | | Community supervision population | | Incarcerated population[b] | |
|---|---|---|---|---|---|---|
| | Number supervised per 100,000 U.S. adult residents[c] | U.S. adult residents under correctional supervision— | Number on probation or parole per 100,000 U.S. adult residents[c] | U.S. adult residents on probation or parole— | Number incarcerated in prison or jail per 100,000 incarcerated in prison U.S. adult residents[c] | U.S. adult residents incarcerated in prison or jail— |
| 2000 | 3,060 | 1 in 33 | 2,160 | 1 in 46 | 920 | 1 in 109 |
| 2001 | 3,080 | 1 in 32 | 2,180 | 1 in 46 | 920 | 1 in 109 |
| 2002 | 3,120 | 1 in 32 | 2,200 | 1 in 45 | 940 | 1 in 106 |
| 2003 | 3,150 | 1 in 32 | 2,220 | 1 in 45 | 950 | 1 in 105 |
| 2004 | 3,170 | 1 in 32 | 2,230 | 1 in 45 | 970 | 1 in 103 |
| 2005 | 3,160 | 1 in 32 | 2,210 | 1 in 45 | 980 | 1 in 102 |
| 2006 | 3,190 | 1 in 31 | 2,230 | 1 in 45 | 1,000 | 1 in 100 |
| 2007 | 3,210 | 1 in 31 | 2,240 | 1 in 45 | 1,000 | 1 in 100 |
| 2008 | 3,160 | 1 in 32 | 2,200 | 1 in 45 | 1,000 | 1 in 100 |
| 2009 | 3,090 | 1 in 32 | 2,150 | 1 in 47 | 980 | 1 in 102 |
| 2010 | 2,990 | 1 in 33 | 2,070 | 1 in 48 | 960 | 1 in 104 |

(Continued)

Table 5.4 (Continued)

| | Total population supervised by adult correctional systems[a] | | Community supervision population | | Incarcerated population[b] | |
|---|---|---|---|---|---|---|
| Year | Number supervised per 100,000 U.S. adult residents[c] | U.S. adult residents under correctional supervision— | Number on probation or parole per 100,000 U.S. adult residents[c] | U.S. adult residents on probation or parole— | Number incarcerated in prison or jail per 100,000 incarcerated in prison U.S. adult residents[c] | U.S. adult residents incarcerated in prison or jail— |
| 2011 | 2,920 | 1 in 34 | 2,010 | 1 in 50 | 940 | 1 in 107 |
| 2012 | 2,870 | 1 in 35 | 1,980 | 1 in 50 | 920 | 1 in 108 |

*Note:* Rates were estimated to the nearest 10. Estimates may not be comparable to previously published BJS reports due to updated information or rounding.

[a]Includes offenders in the community under the authority of probation or parole agencies and those held in the custody of state or federal prisons or local jails.

[b]Includes inmates held in the custody of state or federal prisons, local jails, or privately operated facilities.

[c]Rates were computed using the U.S. adult resident population estimates from the U.S. Census Bureau for January 1 of the following year.

*Sources:* Adult correctional population estimates are based on the Bureau of Justice Statistics' Annual Probation Survey, Annual Parole Survey, Annual Survey of Jails, Census of Jails, and National Prisoner Statistics Program, 2000–2012. The adult resident population estimates are based on the U.S. Census Bureau's National Intercensal Estimates, 2000–2011, and unpublished adult resident population estimates on January 1, 2012, and January 1, 2013.

remarkable about the law is that it would define the existence of a disparate impact in enforcement, even from routine police activities such as traffic stops, as prima facie evidence of violation of the law. Critics note that this would significantly discourage even reasonable enforcement activities in minority areas because the disparate impact of the results, even without malicious intent on the part of the officers, would pose for the officers a significant liability risk. The proposed law also provides grant funding to support best practices research in policing and to set up monitoring systems to prevent profiling.

### Guidelines Regarding the Use of Race by Federal Law Enforcement Agencies

http://www.justice.gov/crt/about/spl/documents/guidance_on_race.pdf

This U.S. Department of Justice document was created in 2003 under the administration of President George Bush. At the time these guidelines were generated, President Bush claimed that they, once and for all, end the use of racial profiling by federal law enforcement agencies. Indeed, the guidelines generally bar the use of racial profiling. However, the guidelines have been criticized, especially in recent years, because of a loophole for national security investigations. In other words, the guidelines do permit the profiling of race, ethnicity, national origin, and religion in the interest of national security and the war against terrorism. In the immediate aftermath of the 9/11 attacks, most believed that this national security loophole was appropriate and prudent. However, in recent years, the criticisms have grown louder. President Barak Obama and Attorney General Eric Holder have both condemned the guidelines, and yet they have remained in effect through the first six years of the Obama presidency. In early 2014, Eric Holder announced that the guidelines would be changing to bar racial profiling by federal law enforcement under all circumstances. However, as of midway through 2014, new guidelines have not yet been implemented and the 2003 guidelines remain in effect.

## Immigration Offenders in the Federal Justice System, 2010

http://www.bjs.gov/content/pub/pdf/iofjs10.pdf

Much of the profiling debate, at least in the southwestern portion of the United States, is intimately connected to the discussion of illegal immigration and the securing of America's borders. In this 2013 Bureau of Justice Statistics report authored by BJS statistician Mark Motivans, data regarding immigrant criminality are analyzed and collated. The report is comprehensive in that it delves into immigrant offender intersections with law enforcement, prosecutors, the court system, and the federal correctional system. The most common charges for immigrant offenders and the common dispositions of the case are but a few of many different variables which this report highlights. The report also highlights the areas where the influx of illegal immigration is most concentrated. As one can see from the following map, Arizona's Tucson Sector led the nation in 2010 in Border Patrol apprehensions.

This provides some context for the dispute between the State of Arizona and the federal government regarding the securing of Arizona's southern border.

## Police Behavior during Traffic and Street Stops, 2011

http://www.bjs.gov/content/pub/pdf/pbtss11.pdf

Bureau of Justice Statistics statisticians Lynn Langton and Matthew Durose wrote this very informative 2013 report about police behavior during traffic stops. The data for the report come from the Police-Public Contact survey administered as a supplement to the 2011 National Crime Victimization Survey. The report covers some similar ground as the 2008 *Contact between the Police and the Public* report highlighted earlier. However, this present report offers greater detail regarding the conduct of the police during the police-public encounters. Variables reflecting conduct and attitudes are examined for association with the races of those whom the police encountered.

**Apprehensions by Border Patrol sector and criminal immigration suspects arrested in U.S. district courts on the southwest border, 2010**

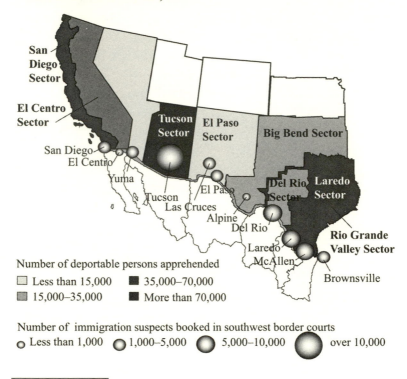

Figure 5.2

Interestingly, most motorists stopped by the police reported that the police behaved properly during their encounters. This includes 89 percent of white motorists and 83 percent of black motorists, as shown in the following table.

### Prisoners in 2011

http://www.bjs.gov/content/pub/pdf/p11.pdf

Ann Carson and William Sabol authored this 2012 report for the Bureau of Justice Statistics which examines the demographic and offender characteristics of prisoners in the

**Table 5.5  Involuntary contact with police among persons age 16 or older, by demographic characteristics and type of contact, 2011**

| Demographic characteristics | Street stops[a] | | | | Traffic stops[b] | | |
| --- | --- | --- | --- | --- | --- | --- | --- |
| | Percent of all persons | Percent of stopped persons | | Percent of all drivers[c] | Percent of stopped drivers | | |
| | | Total | Police behaved properly[d] | | Total | Police behaved properly[d] | |
| Total | 0.6 | 100 | 70.7 | 10.2 | 100 | 88.2 | |
| Sex | | | | | | | |
| Male | 0.8 | 67.5 | 69.8 | 11.9 | 58.8 | 86.9 | |
| Female | 0.4 | 32.5 | 72.7 | 8.4 | 41.2 | 89.9 | |
| Race/Hispanic origin | | | | | | | |
| White[e] | 0.6 | 65.2 | 77.6 | 9.8 | 69.3 | 89.4 | |
| Black/African American[e] | 0.6 | 12.4 | 37.7! | 12.8 | 12.6 | 82.7 | |
| Hispanic/Latino | 0.7 | 15.3 | 62.9 | 10.4 | 12.2 | 86.5 | |
| American Indian/Alaska Native[e] | 0.5! | 0.6! | 100! | 15.0 | 0.6 | 74.2 | |
| Asian/Native Hawaiian/ other Pacific Islander[e] | 0.4! | 3.6! | 85.0! | 9.4 | 4.0 | 89.5 | |
| Two or more races[e] | 1.8! | 3.1! | 76.6! | 13.4 | 1.3 | 94.8 | |
| Age | | | | | | | |
| 16–17 | 1.5 | 8.5 | 67.4 | 9.0 | 1.8 | 92.3 | |

(Continued)

**Table 5.5** *(Continued)*

| Demographic characteristics | Street stops[a] | | | Traffic stops[b] | | |
|---|---|---|---|---|---|---|
| | Percent of stopped persons | | | Percent of stopped drivers | | |
| | Percent of all persons | Total | Police behaved properly[d] | Percent of all drivers[c] | Total | Police behaved properly[d] |
| 18–24 | 1.6 | 31.7 | 72.1 | 17.8 | 19.5 | 85.1 |
| 25–34 | 0.9 | 27.1 | 64.4 | 12.7 | 22.4 | 88.1 |
| 35–44 | 0.4 | 10.6 | 81.6 | 11.3 | 19.8 | 87.9 |
| 45–54 | 0.4 | 10.9 | 79.7 | 9.4 | 17.9 | 88.7 |
| 55–64 | 0.2 | 5.5 | 62.2! | 7.1 | 11.4 | 89.7 |
| 65 or older | 0.2 | 5.7 | 68.8! | 4.8 | 7.2 | 92.3 |

*Note:* See appendix table 2 for estimates of the U.S. population and driving population age 16 or older and appendix table 3 for standard errors.

! Interpret with caution. Estimate based on 10 or fewer sample cases or the coefficient of variation is greater than 50%.

[a]Includes persons stopped by police during the past 12 months for whom the most recent contact involved being stopped by police on the street or in public, but not in a moving motor vehicle.

[b]Includes persons stopped by police during the past 12 months for whom the most recent contact was as a driver in a traffic stop.

[c]Percents based on the driving population age 16 or older, which includes PPCS respondents who reported driving a few times a year or more or were the driver in traffic stop.

[d]Denominator includes approximately 2% of respondents who did not know or did not report whether police behaved properly.

[e]Excludes persons of Hispanic or Latino origin.

*Source:* Bureau of Justice Statistics, National Crime Victimization Survey, Police–Public Contact Survey, 2011.

United State using data acquired in 2011. The report explains the prison system in the United States and provides the numbers of prisoners in each state. The crimes for which offenders were sentenced are cross-tabulated with the offenders' gender and race.

Other findings include the fact that between 6.6 percent and 7.5 percent of all black males ages 25 to 39 were in prison in 2011 as compared to less than 3 percent of Hispanic males in the same age group. Among prisoners 18 or 19 years of age, black males were imprisoned at nine times the rate of white males. These and many other measures in the report support the notion that blacks, and to a lesser degree Hispanics, are differentially treated by the criminal justice system. However, the data provided in the report also support the notion that blacks and Hispanics committing serious criminal offenses are far greater rates than whites, and so an overrepresentation of minorities in prison might be expected.

### Probation and Parole in the United States, 2011

http://www.bjs.gov/content/pub/pdf/ppus11.pdf

This Bureau of Justice Statistics report produced by Laura Maruschak and Erika Parks is similarly organized as the aforementioned *Prisoners in 2011* report, except that this report is focused on community-based corrections rather than incarcerative corrections. The report first explains the difference between probation and parole, with the former being a sentence to be served in the community in lieu of jail or prison time, and later an opportunity to finish one's prison sentence in the community after already serving some time behind bars. The data in the report indicate that there has been a decline in the numbers of offenders placed on probation.

In fact, in 2011, the number of probationers dropped below 4 million for the first time since 2002. Likewise, the number of prisoners entering parole is down as well. The racial composition of probationers and parolees is also addressed, as is the nature of the offenses.

**Table 5.6 Estimated number of sentenced prisoners under state jurisdiction, by offense, sex, race, and Hispanic origin, December 31, 2010**

| Offense | All in mates | Male | Female | White[a] | Black[a] | Hispanic |
|---|---|---|---|---|---|---|
| Total | 1,362,028 | 1,268,974 | 93,054 | 468,528 | 518,763 | 289,429 |
| Violent | 725,000 | 689,000 | 34,100 | 231,800 | 286,400 | 164,200 |
| Murder[b] | 166,700 | 157,000 | 9,400 | 47,200 | 70,100 | 38,900 |
| Manslaughter | 21,500 | 18,800 | 2,700 | 8,600 | 7,800 | 3,300 |
| Rape | 70,200 | 67,900 | 700 | 32,500 | 22,200 | 8,600 |
| Other sexual assault | 90,600 | 89,100 | 1,300 | 44,100 | 17,200 | 26,200 |
| Robbery | 185,800 | 178,000 | 8,300 | 40,400 | 96,600 | 38,000 |
| Assault | 146,800 | 137,700 | 8,500 | 44,300 | 57,200 | 38,500 |
| Other violent | 43,400 | 40,500 | 3,200 | 14,900 | 15,400 | 10,700 |
| Property | 249,500 | 223,100 | 26,900 | 110,800 | 76,300 | 41,900 |
| Burglary | 130,000 | 123,900 | 6,500 | 54,400 | 43,000 | 22,600 |
| Larceny | 45,900 | 38,500 | 7,900 | 20,500 | 14,600 | 6,700 |
| Motor vehicle theft | 15,000 | 13,600 | 1,000 | 6,000 | 3,100 | 5,700 |
| Fraud | 30,800 | 21,800 | 9,000 | 15,900 | 8,400 | 2,800 |
| Other property | 27,700 | 25,300 | 2,400 | 14,000 | 7,200 | 4,000 |
| Drug[c] | 237,000 | 215,600 | 23,400 | 69,500 | 105,600 | 47,800 |
| Public-order[d] | 142,500 | 134,100 | 7,800 | 53,100 | 47,800 | 34,400 |
| Other/ unspecified[e] | 7,900 | 7,100 | 900 | 3,300 | 2,700 | 1,200 |

*Note:* Counts based on state prisoners with a sentence of more than 1 year. Detail may not add to total due to rounding and missing offense data. See *Methodology* for estimation method.
[a]Excludes persons of Hispanic or Latino origin and persons of two or more races.
[b]Includes non-negligent manslaughter.
[c]Includes trafficking, possession, and other drug offenses.
[d]Includes weapons, drunk driving, court offenses, commercialized vice, morals and decency offenses, liquor law violations, and other public-order offenses.
[e]Includes juvenile offenses and other unspecified offense categories.
*Sources:* Bureau of Justice Statistics, National Prisoner Statistics Program and National Corrections Reporting Program, 2010.

## Adults on probation at year-end, 1980–2011

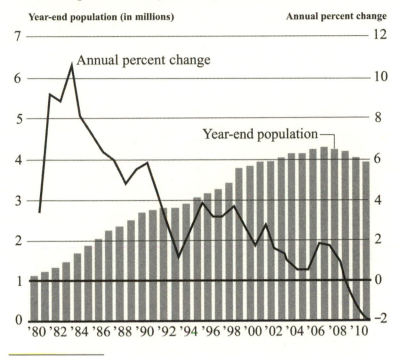

Figure 5.3

## Protecting Civil Rights: A Leadership Guide for State, Local, and Tribal Law Enforcement

http://www.cops.usdoj.gov/files/ric/Publications/e06064100
.pdf

This publication was prepared by the International Association of Chiefs of Police (IACP) in 2006 and made available to the U.S. Department of Justice, Office of Community Oriented Policing Services for dissemination. The publication was produced as a result of grant funding to the IACP from the Department of Justice. Although it is being highlighted here as a document, it could have just as properly been highlighted in Chapter 6 as a book; the document is nearly 280 pages long and consists of eight chapters. This publication is intended to be a resource for law enforcement administrators. Guidance is offered in several areas, including: navigating federal pattern and practice investigations, managing the use of force, outreach to the community, managing the complaint process, protecting civil rights, and addressing biased policing in the department, to name a few.

## Protecting the Rights of Lesbian, Gay, Bisexual, Transgender, and Intersex Individuals

http://www.justice.gov/crt/publications/lgbtibrochure.pdf

This document is a brief factsheet produced by the Civil Rights Division of the U.S. Department of Justice regarding the division's efforts to protect the civil rights of lesbians, gays, bisexuals, and transgendered and intersex individuals. Although not limited to the context of the criminal justice system, the factsheet does provide information to affected persons about the division's desire to protect individuals from biased policing and from constitutional abuses committed within correctional institutions. The factsheet also provides information about federal hate crimes investigative and prosecutorial authority under the *Matthew Shepard and James Byrd, Jr. Hate Crimes Prevention Act*.

## Protecting Women's Rights

http://www.justice.gov/crt/publications/wmnrights.pdf

As with the LGBTI factsheet introduced above, this document is also a factsheet produced by the U.S. Department of Justice Civil Rights Division. The purpose of this factsheet is to outline how the division is able to ensure that civil rights are not denied to anyone on the basis of gender. One section of the document is devoted to police misconduct and gender-biased policing. The document highlights the division's recent "pattern or practice" investigation of the New Orleans Police Department. Among its many findings in that investigation, the division found that police investigative reports were "replete with stereotypical assumptions and judgments about sex crimes and victims of sex crimes, including misguided commentary about the victims' perceived credibility, sexual history, or delay in contacting the police."

## Racial Profiling: Legal and Constitutional Issues

Jody Feder, Congressional Research Service, 2012 http://fas .org/sgp/crs/misc/RL31130.pdf

The Congressional Research Service (CRS) is a good resource on virtually any domestic public policy matter. The CRS regularly generates reports and documents to aid members of Congress, their staff, and the public in understanding various public policy issues. This document, written by Jody Feder, a CRS attorney, highlights racial profiling's attendant legal issues. The publication explains the Fourth and Fourteenth Amendments and their relationship to profiling. Feder also explains how various federal statutes are implicated in the discussion of profiling, including 42 USC 1983 actions and the federal sanctions and remedies under the Violent Crime Control and Law Enforcement Act of 1994.

## Racial Profiling Factsheet

http://www.justice.gov/opa/pr/2003/June/racial_profiling_ fact_sheet.pdf

This six-page-long factsheet, first published by the U.S. Department of Justice in 2003, defines racial profiling and summarizes the controversial aspects of it. The factsheet explains the distinction between legitimate and illegitimate uses of race and ethnicity when identifying criminal suspects.

## Key Supreme Court Cases

In this portion of the chapter, six selected U.S. Supreme Court cases related in some way to the issue of profiling have been highlighted. Four of the cases relate to profiling by race at different intervals of the criminal justice process; one case relates to gender profiling, and finally one case relates to the permissibility of criminal profiling generally. Excerpts of the important and historic opinions for each case are reprinted in the pages that follow. Despite the wealth of information and the gist of the court's logic in each excerpted opinion, readers are encouraged to obtain and read these opinions in their entirety. Supreme Court decisions are full of important information. In its opinions, the Supreme Court explains its logic for its decisions in light of judicial history. Prior cases that relate to each decision are cited. The reliance on precedence (i.e., previously decided cases) is known as stare decisis. In reading the excerpts that follow, you will see that the Supreme Court, in overturning or upholding a particular law or practice, heavily relies on what it has said in the past. Each case is preceded by a brief summary of the issues in the case and the Court's opinion. The opinions reprinted in the following represent the majority opinion of the Court in each case. Not included are the concurring or dissenting opinions. With the name of any party contained in the case heading, or with the case number, one may download majority and dissenting opinions of the U.S. Supreme Court by accessing its website at http://www.supremecourt.gov or by going to http://www .findlaw.com.

## Documents

### *Korematsu v. United States*, 323 U.S. 214 (1944)

*Korematsu was a U.S. citizen of Japanese descent during World War II. On December 8, 1941, the United States declared war on Japan, Germany, and Italy. In February 1942, President Franklin Roosevelt issued an executive order authorizing the creation of military zones that persons of Japanese descent could not enter. The motive behind the order was to prevent sabotage by people loyal to the Empire of Japan. By March, the entire West Coast of the United States to a depth of about 40 miles inland was designated as such a military zone. Eventually, about 112,000 persons of Japanese descent were involuntarily relocated from the West Coast to war relocation camps run by the military. Korematsu was prosecuted for remaining in a prohibited area when relocation was ordered.*

*This case is significant for profiling in that it involves the single most egregious and massive act of racial profiling that ever occurred in this country—the mass internment of Japanese Americans solely on the basis of their race. In this case, the Supreme Court upheld the conviction of Korematsu for remaining in a prohibited area— namely, his home. Indeed, the mass evacuation of all Japanese Americans from the West Coast was deemed constitutional. The Court did, however, declare that the involuntary internment of Japanese Americans whose loyalty to the United States was established was unconstitutional. It ordered that such people be immediately and unconditionally released, as they posed no threat of sabotage.*

JUSTICE BLACK delivered the opinion of the Court.

The petitioner, an American citizen of Japanese descent, was convicted in a federal district court for remaining in San Leandro, California, a "Military Area", contrary to Civilian Exclusion Order No. 34 of the Commanding General of the Western Command, U.S. Army, which directed that after May 9, 1942, all persons of Japanese ancestry should be excluded from that area. No question was raised as to petitioner's loyalty to the United States. The Circuit Court of Appeals affirmed, and the importance of the constitutional question involved caused us to grant certiorari.

It should be noted, to begin with, that all legal restrictions which curtail the civil rights of a single racial group are immediately suspect. That is not to say that all such restrictions are unconstitutional. It is to say that courts must subject them to the most rigid scrutiny. Pressing public necessity may sometimes justify the existence of such restrictions; racial antagonism never can. In the instant case prosecution of the petitioner was begun by information charging violation of an

Act of Congress, of March 21, 1942, 56 Stat. 173, 18 U.S.C.A. 97a, which provides that:

> . . . whoever shall enter, remain in, leave, or commit any act in any military area or military zone prescribed, under the authority of an Executive order of the President, by the Secretary of War, or by any military commander designated by the Secretary of War, contrary to the restrictions applicable to any such area or zone or contrary to the order of the Secretary of War or any such military commander, shall, if it appears that he knew or should have known of the existence and extent of the restrictions or order and that his act was in violation thereof, be guilty of a misdemeanor and upon conviction shall be liable to a fine of not to exceed $5,000 or to imprisonment for not more than one year, or both, for each offense. . . .

One of the series of orders and proclamations, a curfew order, which like the exclusion order here was promulgated pursuant to Executive Order 9066, subjected all persons of Japanese ancestry in prescribed West Coast military areas to remain in their residences from 8 p.m. to 6 a.m. As is the case with the exclusion order here, that prior curfew order was designed as a "protection against espionage and against sabotage." In Kiyoshi Hirabayashi v. United States, 320 U.S. 81, 63 S.Ct. 1375, we sustained a conviction obtained for violation of the curfew order. The Hirabayashi conviction and this one thus rest on the same 1942 Congressional Act and the same basic executive and military orders, all of which orders were aimed at the twin dangers of espionage and sabotage.

The 1942 Act was attacked in the Hirabayashi case as an unconstitutional delegation of power; it was contended that the curfew order and other orders on which it rested were beyond the war powers of the Congress, the military authorities and of the President, as Commander in Chief of the Army; and finally that to apply the curfew order against none but citizens of Japanese ancestry amounted to a constitutionally prohibited discrimination solely on account of race. To these questions, we gave the serious consideration which their importance justified. We upheld the curfew order as an exercise of the power of the government to take steps necessary to prevent espionage and sabotage in an area threatened by Japanese attack.

In the light of the principles we announced in the Hirabayashi case, we are unable to conclude that it was beyond the war power of Congress and the Executive to exclude those of Japanese ancestry from the West Coast war area at the time they did. True, exclusion from the area in which one's home is located is a far greater deprivation than constant confinement to the home from 8 P.M. to 6 A.M. Nothing short of apprehension by the proper military authorities of the gravest imminent danger to the public safety can constitutionally justify either. But exclusion from a threatened area, no less than curfew, has a definite and close relationship to the prevention of espionage and sabotage. The military authorities, charged with the primary responsibility of defending our shores, concluded that curfew provided inadequate protection and ordered exclusion. They did so, as pointed out in our Hirabayashi opinion, in accordance with Congressional authority to the military to say who should, and who should not, remain in the threatened areas. . . .

[In this case as with] curfew, exclusion of those of Japanese origin was deemed necessary because of the presence of an unascertained number of disloyal members of the group, most of whom we have no doubt were loyal to this country. It was because we could not reject the finding of the military authorities that it was impossible to bring about an immediate segregation of the disloyal from the loyal that we sustained the validity of the curfew order as applying to the whole group. In the instant case, temporary exclusion of the entire group was rested by the military on the same ground. The judgment that exclusion of the whole group was for the same reason, a military imperative answers the contention that the exclusion was in the nature of group punishment based on antagonism to those of Japanese origin. That there were members of the group who retained loyalties to Japan has been confirmed by investigations made subsequent to the exclusion. Approximately five thousand American citizens of Japanese ancestry refused to swear unqualified allegiance to the United States and to renounce allegiance to the Japanese Emperor, and several thousand evacuees requested repatriation to Japan.

We uphold the exclusion order as of the time it was made and when the petitioner violated it. . . . In doing so, we are not unmindful of the hardships imposed by it upon a large group of American citizens. . . . But hardships are part of war, and war is an aggregation of hardships. All citizens alike, both in and out of uniform, feel the impact of war in greater or lesser measure. Citizenship has its responsibilities as well as its privileges, and in time of war the burden is always heavier. Compulsory exclusion of large groups of citizens from their homes, except under circumstances of direst emergency and peril, is inconsistent with our basic governmental institutions. But when under conditions of modern warfare our shores are threatened by hostile forces, the power to protect must be commensurate with the threatened danger. . . .

It is said that we are dealing here with the case of imprisonment of a citizen in a concentration camp solely because of his ancestry, without evidence or inquiry concerning his loyalty and good disposition towards the United States. Our task would be simple, our duty clear, were this a case involving the imprisonment of a loyal citizen in a concentration camp because of racial prejudice. Regardless of the true nature of the assembly and relocation centers—and we deem it unjustifiable to call them concentration camps with all the ugly connotations that term implies—we are dealing specifically with nothing but an exclusion order. To cast this case into outlines of racial prejudice, without reference to the real military dangers which were presented, merely confuses the issue. Korematsu was not excluded from the Military Area because of hostility to him or his race. He was excluded because we are at war with the Japanese Empire, because the properly constituted military authorities feared an invasion of our West Coast and felt constrained to take proper security measures, because they decided that the military urgency of the situation demanded that all citizens of Japanese ancestry be segregated from the West Coast temporarily, and finally, because Congress, reposing its confidence in this time of war in our military leaders—as inevitably it must—determined that they should have the power to do just this. There was evidence of disloyalty on the part of some, the military authorities considered that the need for action was great, and time was short. We cannot—by availing ourselves of the calm perspective of hindsight—now say that at that time these actions were unjustified.

Affirmed.

### *Hoyt v. Florida,* 368 U.S. 57 (1961)

*Much of the profiling debate relates to race and ethnicity. In this case, however, the debate revolves around gender. Although for over 100 years the Supreme Court had held that the systematic exclusion of a particular race from a jury was unconstitutional, there had never been the same logic extended to gender. In the present case, Gwendolyn Hoyt was convicted by an all-male jury of killing her husband. Under Florida law at the time, male citizens were automatically subject to jury duty, whereas females had to register an interest in serving on juries. In other words, women had to actively seek eligibility for jury duty. This resulted in very few women actually being listed among eligible jurors. In Hoyt's view, this amounted to the systematic exclusion of women from jury duty based on their gender.*

*This case was one of several in the 1950s and 1960s that sought to overturn so-called Jane Crow laws, that is, laws that made women essentially second-class citizens. In this case and others, the Supreme Court refused to adopt the idea that gender was a suspect class similar to race and therefore required a strict scrutiny*

*test for any laws implicating gender. Eventually, federal and state
equal rights legislation would accomplish what the Supreme Court
would not do in this and other cases.*

MR. JUSTICE HARLAN delivered the opinion of the
Court.

Appellant, a woman, has been convicted in Hillsborough
County, Florida, of second degree murder of her husband. On
this appeal under 28 U.S.C. 1257 (2) from the Florida Supreme
Court's affirmance of the judgment of conviction, 119 So.2d
691, we noted probable jurisdiction, 364 U.S. 930, to consider
appellant's claim that her trial before an all-male jury violated
rights assured by the Fourteenth Amendment. The claim is that
such jury was the product of a state jury statute which works an
unconstitutional exclusion of women from jury service.

The jury law primarily in question is Fla. Stat., 1959, 40.01 (1).
This Act, which requires that grand and petit jurors be taken
from "male and female" citizens of the State possessed of certain qualifications, contains the following proviso:

> provided, however, that the name of no female person
> shall be taken for jury service unless said person has
> registered with the clerk of the circuit court her desire to
> be placed on the jury list.

Showing that since the enactment of the statute only a minimal number of women have so registered, appellant challenges
the constitutionality of the statute both on its face and as applied in this case. For reasons now to follow we decide that
both contentions must be rejected.

At the core of appellant's argument is the claim that the nature of the crime of which she was convicted peculiarly demanded the inclusion of persons of her own sex on the jury.
She was charged with killing her husband by assaulting him
with a baseball bat. An information was filed against her under
Fla. Stat., 1959, 782.04, which punishes as murder in the

second degree "any act imminently dangerous to another, and evincing a depraved mind regardless of human life, although without any premeditated design to effect the death of any particular individual.

. . ." As described by the Florida Supreme Court, the
affair occurred in the context of a marital upheaval involving,
among other things, the suspected infidelity of appellant's husband,
and culminating in the husband's final rejection of his
wife's efforts at reconciliation. It is claimed, in substance, that
women jurors would have been more understanding or compassionate
than men in assessing the quality of appellant's act. . . .

Of course, these premises misconceive the scope of the right to an impartially selected jury assured by the Fourteenth Amendment. That right does not entitle one accused of crime to a jury tailored to the circumstances of the particular case, whether relating to the sex or other condition of the defendant, or to the nature of the charges to be tried. It requires only that the jury be indiscriminately drawn from among those eligible in the community for jury service, untrammeled by any arbitrary and systematic exclusions. . . .

Several observations should initially be made. We of course recognize that the Fourteenth Amendment reaches not only arbitrary class exclusions from jury service based on race or color, but also all other exclusions which "single out" any class of persons "for different treatment not based on some reasonable classification". . . .

Manifestly, Florida's 40.01 (1) does not purport to exclude women from state jury service. Rather, the statute "gives to women the privilege to serve but does not impose service as a duty." Fay v. New York, supra, at 277. It accords women an absolute exemption from jury service unless they expressly waive that privilege. This is not to say, however, that what in form may be only an exemption of a particular class of persons can in no circumstances be regarded as an exclusion of that class. Where, as here, an exemption of a class in the community is asserted to be in substance an exclusionary device, the relevant inquiry is whether the exemption itself is based on some reasonable classification and whether the manner in which it is exercisable rests on some rational foundation.

In the selection of jurors Florida has differentiated between men and women in two respects. It has given women an absolute exemption from jury duty based solely on their sex, no similar exemption obtaining as to men. And it has provided for its effectuation in a manner less onerous than that governing exemptions exercisable by men: women are not to be put on the jury list unless they have voluntarily registered for such service; men, on the other hand, even if entitled to an exemption, are to be included on the list unless they have filed a written claim of exemption as provided by law.

In neither respect can we conclude that Florida's statute is not "based on some reasonable classification," and that it is thus infected with unconstitutionality. Despite the enlightened emancipation of women from the restrictions and protections of bygone years, and their entry into many parts of community life formerly considered to be reserved to men, woman is still regarded as the center of home and family life. We cannot say that it is constitutionally impermissible for a State, acting in pursuit of the general welfare, to conclude that a woman should be relieved from the civic duty of jury service unless she herself determines that such service is consistent with her own special responsibilities. . . .

Appellant argues that whatever may have been the design of this Florida enactment, the statute in practical operation results in an exclusion of women from jury service, because women, like men, can be expected to be available for jury service only under compulsion. In this connection she points out that by

1957, when this trial took place, only some 220 women out of approximately 46,000 registered female voters in Hillsborough County—constituting about 40 per cent of the total voting population of that county—had volunteered for jury duty since the limitation of jury service to males, see Hall v. Florida, 136 Fla. 644. 662–665, 187 So. 392, 400–401, was removed by 40.01 (1) in 1949. Fla. Laws 1949. c. 25,126.

This argument, however, is surely beside the point. Given the reasonableness of the classification involved in 40.01 (1), the relative paucity of women jurors does not carry the constitutional consequence appellant would have it bear. "Circumstances or chance may well dictate that no persons in a certain class will serve on a particular jury or during some particular period." Hernandez v. Texas, supra, at 482.

> We cannot hold this statute as written offensive to the Fourteenth Amendment.
> Appellant's attack on the statute as applied in this case fares no better.

In the year here relevant Fla. Stat., 1955, 40.10 in conjunction with 40.02 required the jury commissioners, with the aid of the local circuit court judges and clerk, to compile annually a jury list of 10,000 inhabitants qualified to be jurors. In 1957 the existing Hillsborough County list had become exhausted to the extent of some 3,000 jurors. The new list was constructed by taking over from the old list the remaining some 7,000 jurors, including 10 women, and adding some 3,000 new male jurors to build up the list to the requisite 10,000. At the time some 220 women had registered for jury duty in this county, including those taken over from the earlier list. . . .

This case in no way resembles those involving race or color in which the circumstances shown were found by this Court to compel a conclusion of purposeful discriminatory exclusions from jury service . . . There is present here neither the unfortunate atmosphere of ethnic or racial prejudices which underlay the situations depicted in those cases, nor the long course of discriminatory administrative practice which the statistical showing in each of them evinced.

In the circumstances here depicted, it indeed "taxes our credulity," Hernandez v. Texas, supra, at 482, to attribute to these administrative officials a deliberate design to exclude the very class whose eligibility for jury service the state legislature, after many years of contrary policy, had declared only a few years before. It is sufficiently evident from the record that the presence on the jury list of no more than ten or twelve women in the earlier years, and the failure to add in 1957 more women to those already on the list, are attributable not to any discriminatory motive, but to a purpose to put on the list only those women who might be expected to be qualified for service if actually called. Nor is there the slightest suggestion that the list was the product of any plan to place on it only women of a particular economic or other community or organizational group.

Finally, the disproportion of women to men on the list independently carries no constitutional significance. In the administration of the jury laws proportional class representation is not a constitutionally required factor. . . .

Finding no substantial evidence whatever in this record that Florida has arbitrarily undertaken to exclude women from jury service, a showing which it was incumbent on appellant to make, we must sustain the judgment of the Supreme Court of Florida.

Affirmed.


### *Delaware v. Prouse*, 440 U.S. 648 (1979)

*Leading up to this case in 1979, it had been common practice in police work to conduct motor vehicle stops without any specific violation. In such cases, the stop would still have to be brief absent the emergence of evidence of a crime. But the stop itself was considered within the purview of legitimate proactive police work. If an officer thought something looked funny with a particular vehicle or occupant, then on the officer's hunch, he or she could stop the vehicle and investigate. In the present case, a police officer pulled over a vehicle because, in the officer's words, the officer wasn't doing anything else, had no calls waiting, and thought he would check the identification and registration.*

*This practice of pulling over vehicles solely at the discretion of the officer, even when no observed violation existed, certainly had its critics. However noble it was for police officers to be proactive in their fight against crime, the practice litigated in Delaware v. Prouse certainly lent itself to abuse—particularly against individuals who matched whatever personal profiles officers held regarding likely offenders. For many officers, such profiles included young adult males of color. Hence, this case was particularly important for criminal profiling in that the*

*Supreme Court here first noted that random stops of vehicles simply to "check things out" without articulable suspicion of criminal activity are unconstitutional. Neither the whim of the officer, nor the mere status of driving one's vehicle on a public road, would qualify as a legitimate basis for pulling a vehicle over.*

*The logic the Supreme Court followed in this case sets up the Whren decision nearly two decades later, in which the Court emphasized the fact that an officer must have reasonable suspicion of a violation to pull over a vehicle and that reasonable suspicion is the only element that matters with regard to the legality of a stop.*

MR. JUSTICE WHITE delivered the opinion of the Court.

The question is whether it is an unreasonable seizure under the Fourth and Fourteenth Amendments to stop an automobile, being driven on a public highway, for the purpose of checking the driving license of the operator and the registration of the car, where there is neither probable cause to believe nor reasonable suspicion that the car is being driven contrary to the laws governing the operation of motor vehicles or that either the car or any of its occupants is subject to seizure or detention in connection with the violation of any other applicable law.

At 7:20 P.M. on November 30, 1976, a New Castle County, Del., patrolman in a police cruiser stopped the automobile occupied by respondent. The patrolman smelled marihuana smoke as he was walking toward the stopped vehicle, and he seized marihuana in plain view on the car floor. Respondent was subsequently indicted for illegal possession of a controlled substance. At a hearing on respondent's motion to suppress the marihuana seized as a result of the stop, the patrolman testified that prior to stopping the vehicle he had observed neither traffic or equipment violations nor any suspicious activity, and that he made the stop only in order to check the driver's license and registration. The patrolman was not acting pursuant to any standards, guidelines, or procedures pertaining to document spot checks, promulgated by either his department or the State Attorney General. Characterizing the stop as "routine," the patrolman explained, "I saw the car in the area and wasn't answering any complaints, so I decided to pull them off." The trial court granted the motion to suppress, finding the stop and detention to have been wholly capricious and therefore violative of the Fourth Amendment.

The Delaware Supreme Court affirmed, noting first that "[t]he issue of the legal validity of systematic, roadblock-type stops of a number of vehicles for license and vehicle registration check is not now before the Court." . . . The court held that "a random stop of a motorist in the absence of specific articulable facts which justify the stop by indicating a reasonable suspicion that a violation of the law has occurred is constitutionally impermissible and violative of the Fourth and Fourteenth Amendments to the United States Constitution." . . .

The Fourth and Fourteenth Amendments are implicated in this case because stopping an automobile and detaining its occupants constitute a "seizure" within the meaning of those Amendments, even though the purpose of the stop is limited and the resulting detention quite brief. . . . The essential purpose of the proscriptions in the Fourth Amendment is to impose a standard of "reasonableness" upon the exercise of discretion by government officials, including law enforcement agents, in order "'to safeguard the privacy and security of individuals against arbitrary invasions. . . .'" Thus, the permissibility of a particular law enforcement practice is judged by balancing its intrusion on the individual's Fourth Amendment interests against its promotion of legitimate governmental interests. Implemented in this manner, the reasonableness standard usually requires, at a minimum, that the facts upon which an intrusion is based be capable of measurement against "an objective standard," whether this be probable cause or a less stringent test. In those situations in which the balance of interests precludes insistence upon "some quantum of individualized suspicion," other safeguards are generally relied upon to assure that the individual's reasonable expectation of privacy is not "subject to the discretion of the official in the field." . . .

In this case, however, the State of Delaware urges that patrol officers be subject to no constraints in deciding which automobiles shall be stopped for a license and registration check because the State's interest in discretionary spot checks as a means of ensuring the safety of its roadways outweighs the resulting intrusion on the privacy and security of the persons detained. . . .

The question remains, however, whether in the service of these important ends [particularly, safety on the state roadways] the discretionary spot check is a sufficiently productive mechanism to justify the intrusion upon Fourth Amendment interests which such stops entail. On the record before us, that question must be answered in the negative. Given the alternative mechanisms available, both those in use and those that might be adopted, we are unconvinced that the incremental contribution to highway safety of the random spot check justifies the practice under the Fourth Amendment.

The marginal contribution to roadway safety possibly resulting from a system of spot checks cannot justify subjecting every occupant of every vehicle on the roads to a seizure—limited in magnitude compared to other intrusions but nonetheless constitutionally cognizable—at the unbridled discretion of law enforcement officials. To insist neither upon an appropriate factual basis for suspicion directed at a particular automobile nor upon some other substantial and objective standard or rule to govern the exercise of discretion "would invite intrusions upon constitutionally guaranteed rights based on nothing more substantial than inarticulate hunches . . ."

An individual operating or traveling in an automobile does not lose all reasonable expectation of privacy simply because the automobile and its use are subject to government regulation. Automobile travel is a basic, pervasive, and often necessary mode of transportation to and from one's home, workplace, and leisure activities. Many people spend more hours each day traveling in cars than walking on the streets. Undoubtedly, many find a greater sense of security and privacy in traveling in an automobile than they do in exposing themselves by pedestrian or other modes of travel. Were the individual subject to unfettered governmental intrusion every time he entered an automobile, the security guaranteed by the Fourth Amendment would be seriously circumscribed. As Terry v. Ohio, supra, recognized, people are not shorn of all Fourth Amendment protection when they step from their homes onto the public sidewalks. Nor are they shorn of those interests when they step from the sidewalks into their automobiles. . . .

Accordingly, we hold that except in those situations in which there is at least articulable and reasonable suspicion that a motorist is unlicensed or that an automobile is not registered, or that either the vehicle or an occupant is otherwise subject to seizure for violation of law, stopping an automobile and detaining the driver in order to check his driver's license and the registration of the automobile are unreasonable under the Fourth Amendment. This holding does not preclude the State of Delaware or other States from developing methods for spot checks that involve less intrusion or that do not involve the unconstrained exercise of discretion. Questioning of all oncoming traffic at roadblock-type stops is one possible alternative.

We hold only that persons in automobiles on public roadways may not for that reason alone have their travel and privacy interfered with at the unbridled discretion of police officers. The judgment below is affirmed.

So ordered.

### *Batson v. Kentucky,* 476 U.S. 79 (1986)

*The Supreme Court's decision in this case represents an extension of the long-established position of the Court that systematic exclusion of people of a particular race from jury duty is a violation of the Constitution. Here, the Court applied this principle to peremptory challenges. Prosecutors and defense attorneys are both granted a limited number of peremptory challenges (i.e., the opportunity to strike a potential juror from the jury pool for no particular reason whatsoever) for any given trial. Traditionally, the right of criminal lawyers on both sides of the case to exercise their peremptory challenges without any oversight has always been upheld.*

*In Batson, however, the Supreme Court said that exclusion of people from the jury, even through a peremptory challenge, was not constitutional if the exclusion was because of race. The Supreme Court did not require that attorneys have a good reason for excluding people. Indeed, the reasons could be quite silly—as always—except that the reason had to be race neutral. This opinion represents one of the Court's more contemporary statements outlawing racial profiling during the trial process.*

JUSTICE POWELL delivered the opinion of the Court.

This case requires us to reexamine that portion of Swain v. Alabama, 380 U.S. 202 (1965), concerning the evidentiary burden placed on a criminal defendant who claims that he has been denied equal protection through the State's use of peremptory challenges to exclude members of his race from the petit jury. Petitioner, a black man, was indicted in Kentucky on charges of second-degree burglary and receipt of stolen goods. On the first day of trial in Jefferson Circuit Court, the judge conducted voir dire examination of the venire, excused certain jurors for cause, and permitted the parties to exercise peremptory challenges. The prosecutor used his peremptory challenges to strike all four black persons on the venire, and a jury composed only of white persons was selected. Defense counsel moved to discharge the jury before it was sworn on the ground that the prosecutor's removal of the black veniremen violated petitioner's rights under the Sixth and Fourteenth Amendments to a jury drawn from a cross section of the community, and under the Fourteenth Amendment to equal protection of the laws. Counsel requested a hearing on his motion. Without expressly ruling on the request for a hearing, the trial judge observed that the parties were entitled to use their peremptory challenges to "strike anybody they want to." The judge then denied petitioner's motion, reasoning that the cross-section requirement applies only to selection of the venire and not to selection of the petit jury itself. The jury convicted petitioner on both counts.

In Swain v. Alabama, this Court recognized that a "State's purposeful or deliberate denial to Negroes on account of race of participation as jurors in the administration of justice violates the Equal Protection Clause." This principle has been "consistently and repeatedly" reaffirmed in numerous decisions of this Court both preceding and following Swain. We reaffirm the principle today. More than a century ago, the Court decided that the State denies a black defendant equal protection of the laws when it puts him on trial before a jury from which members of his race have been purposefully excluded. Strauder v. West Virginia. That decision laid the foundation for the Court's unceasing efforts to eradicate racial discrimination in the procedures used to select the venire from which individual jurors are drawn. In Strauder, the Court explained that the central concern of the recently ratified Fourteenth Amendment was to put an end to governmental discrimination on account of race. Exclusion of black citizens from service as jurors constitutes a primary example of the evil the Fourteenth Amendment was designed to cure. . . .

Purposeful racial discrimination in selection of the venire violates a defendant's right to equal protection because it denies him the protection that a trial by jury is intended to secure. "The very idea of a jury is a body . . . composed of the peers or equals of the person whose rights it is selected or summoned to determine; that is, of his neighbors, fellows, associates, persons having the same legal status in society as that which he holds." The petit jury has occupied a central position in our system of justice by safeguarding a person accused of crime against the arbitrary exercise of power by prosecutor or judge. Those on the venire must be "indifferently chosen" to secure the defendant's right under the Fourteenth Amendment to "protection of life and liberty against race or color prejudice."

Racial discrimination in selection of jurors harms not only the accused whose life or liberty they are summoned to try. Competence to serve as a juror ultimately depends on an assessment of individual qualifications and ability impartially to consider evidence presented at a trial. A person's race simply "is unrelated to his fitness as a juror." (Frankfurter, J., dissenting). As long ago as Strauder, therefore, the Court recognized that by denying a person participation in jury service on account of his race, the State unconstitutionally discriminated against the excluded juror.

The harm from discriminatory jury selection extends beyond that inflicted on the defendant and the excluded juror to touch the entire community. Selection procedures that purposefully exclude black persons from juries undermine public confidence in the fairness of our system of justice. Discrimination within the judicial system is most pernicious because it is "a stimulant to that race prejudice which is an impediment to securing to [black citizens] that equal justice which the law aims to secure to all others." . . .

In Strauder, the Court invalidated a state statute that provided that only white men could serve as jurors. We can be confident that no State now has such a law. The Constitution requires, however, that we look beyond the face of the statute defining juror qualifications and also consider challenged selection practices to afford "protection against action of the State through its administrative officers in effecting the prohibited discrimination." Thus, the Court has found a denial of equal protection where the procedures implementing a neutral statute operated to exclude persons from the venire on racial grounds, and has made clear that the Constitution prohibits all forms of purposeful racial discrimination in selection of jurors. While decisions of this Court have been concerned largely with discrimination during selection of the venire, the principles announced there also forbid discrimination on account of race in selection of the petit jury. Since the Fourteenth Amendment protects an accused throughout the proceedings bringing him to justice, the State may not draw up its jury lists pursuant to neutral procedures but then resort to discrimination at "other stages in the selection process."

Accordingly, the component of the jury selection process at issue here, the State's privilege to strike individual jurors through peremptory challenges, is subject to the commands of the Equal Protection Clause. Although a prosecutor ordinarily is entitled to exercise permitted peremptory challenges "for any reason at all, as long as that reason is related to his view concerning the outcome" of the case to be tried . . . the Equal Protection Clause forbids the prosecutor to challenge potential jurors solely on account of their race or on the assumption that black jurors as a group will be unable impartially to consider the State's case against a black defendant. . . .

Since the ultimate issue is whether the State has discriminated in selecting the defendant's venire, however, the defendant may establish a prima facie case "in other ways than by evidence of long-continued unexplained absence" of members of his race "from many panels." Cassell v. Texas, 339 U.S. 282, 290 (1950) (plurality opinion). In cases involving the venire, this Court has found a prima facie case on proof that members of the defendant's race were substantially underrepresented on the venire from which his jury was drawn, and that the venire was selected under a practice providing "the opportunity for discrimination." Whitus v. Georgia, supra, at 552; see Castaneda v. Partida, supra, at 494; Washington v. Davis, supra, at 241; Alexander v. Louisiana, supra, at 629–631. This combination of factors raises the necessary inference of purposeful discrimination because the Court has declined to attribute to chance the absence of black citizens on a particular jury array where the selection mechanism is subject to abuse. When circumstances suggest the need, the trial court must undertake a "factual inquiry" that "takes into account all possible explanatory factors" in the particular case. Alexander v. Louisiana, supra, at 630.

Thus, since the decision in Swain, this Court has recognized that a defendant may make a prima facie showing of purposeful racial discrimination in selection of the venire by relying solely on the facts concerning its selection in his case. These decisions are in accordance with the proposition, articulated in Arlington Heights v. Metropolitan Housing Development Corp., that "a consistent pattern of official racial discrimination" is not "a necessary predicate to a violation of the Equal Protection Clause. A single invidiously discriminatory governmental act" is not "immunized by the absence of such discrimination in the making of other comparable decisions." 429 U.S., at 266, n. 14. For evidentiary requirements to dictate that "several must suffer discrimination" before one could object, McCray v. New York, 461 U.S., at 965 (MARSHALL, J., dissenting from denial of certiorari), would be inconsistent with the promise of equal protection to all.

In deciding whether [purposeful discrimination in jury selection has taken place], the trial court should consider all relevant circumstances. For example, a "pattern" of strikes against black jurors included in the particular venire might give rise to an inference of discrimination. Similarly, the prosecutor's questions and statements during voir dire examination and in exercising his challenges may support or refute an inference of discriminatory purpose. These examples are merely illustrative.

We have confidence that trial judges, experienced in supervising voir dire, will be able to decide if the circumstances concerning the prosecutor's use of peremptory challenges creates a prima facie case of discrimination against black jurors.

Once the defendant makes a prima facie showing [of discrimination], the burden shifts to the State to come forward with a neutral explanation for challenging black jurors. Though this requirement imposes a limitation in some cases on the full peremptory character of the historic challenge, we emphasize that the prosecutor's explanation need not rise to the level justifying exercise of a challenge for cause. But the prosecutor may not rebut the defendant's prima facie case of discrimination by stating merely that he challenged jurors of the defendant's race on the assumption—or his intuitive judgment—that they would be partial to the defendant because of their shared race.

The State contends that our holding will eviscerate the fair trial values served by the peremptory challenge. Conceding that the Constitution does not guarantee a right to peremptory challenges and that Swain did state that their use ultimately is subject to the strictures of equal protection, the State argues that the privilege of unfettered exercise of the challenge is of vital importance to the criminal justice system.

While we recognize, of course, that the peremptory challenge occupies an important position in our trial procedures, we do not agree that our decision today will undermine the contribution the challenge generally makes to the administration of justice. The reality of practice, amply reflected in many state- and federal-court opinions, shows that the challenge may be, and unfortunately at times has been, used to discriminate against black jurors. By requiring trial courts to be sensitive to the racially discriminatory use of peremptory challenges, our decision enforces the mandate of equal protection and furthers the ends of justice. In view of the heterogeneous population of our Nation, public respect for our criminal justice system and the rule of law will be strengthened if we ensure that no citizen is disqualified from jury service because of his race. . . .

In this case, petitioner made a timely objection to the prosecutor's removal of all black persons on the venire. Because the trial court flatly rejected the objection without requiring the prosecutor to give an explanation for his action, we remand this case for further proceedings. If the trial court decides that the facts establish, prima facie, purposeful discrimination and the prosecutor does not come forward with a neutral explanation for his action, our precedents require that petitioner's conviction be reversed.

It is so ordered.

### *United States v. Sokolow,* 490 U.S. 1 (1989)

*The case of Sokolow was heard by the Supreme Court during the height of the drug war in the United States. Indeed, as discussed earlier in the book, the use of profiles to identify potential criminals was expanded and popularized by the successful use of drug courier profiles. Such a profile was used in this case.*

*Here, the Supreme Court made it clear that profiling is a permissible police tactic for generating the reasonable suspicion required for an investigatory stop and detention. It reaffirmed its position in Prouse that the discretionary reliance on hunches is not enough for the officer to detain. Profiles that are built upon articulable facts and probabilities and that do not rely primarily on the protected status of a suspect—particularly race or ethnicity—are however acceptable and indeed valuable.*

CHIEF JUSTICE REHNQUIST delivered the opinion of the Court.

Respondent Andrew Sokolow was stopped by Drug Enforcement Administration (DEA) agents upon his arrival at Honolulu International Airport. The agents found 1,063 grams of cocaine in his carry-on luggage. When respondent was stopped, the agents knew, inter alia, that (1) he paid $2,100 for two airplane tickets from a roll of $20 bills; (2) he traveled under a name that did not match the name under which his telephone number was listed; (3) his original destination was

Miami, a source city for illicit drugs; (4) he stayed in Miami for only 48 hours, even though a round-trip flight from Honolulu to Miami takes 20 hours; (5) he appeared nervous during his trip; and (6) he checked none of his luggage. A divided panel of the United States Court of Appeals for the Ninth Circuit held that the DEA agents did not have a reasonable suspicion to stop respondent, as required by the Fourth Amendment. We take the contrary view.

This case involves a typical attempt to smuggle drugs through one of the Nation's airports. On a Sunday in July 1984, respondent went to the United Airlines ticket counter at Honolulu Airport, where he purchased two round-trip tickets for a flight to Miami leaving later that day. The tickets were purchased in the names of "Andrew Kray" and "Janet Norian" and had open return dates. Respondent paid $2,100 for the tickets from a large roll of $20 bills, which appeared to contain a total of $4,000. He also gave the ticket agent his home telephone number. The ticket agent noticed that respondent seemed nervous; he was about 25 years old; he was dressed in a black jumpsuit and wore gold jewelry; and he was accompanied by a woman, who turned out to be Janet Norian. Neither respondent nor his companion checked any of their four pieces of luggage.

After the couple left for their flight, the ticket agent informed Officer John McCarthy of the Honolulu Police Department of respondent's cash purchase of tickets to Miami. Officer McCarthy determined that the telephone number respondent gave to the ticket agent was subscribed to a "Karl Herman," who resided at 348-A Royal Hawaiian Avenue in Honolulu. Unbeknownst to McCarthy (and later to the DEA agents), respondent was Herman's roommate. The ticket agent identified respondent's voice on the answering machine at Herman's number. Officer McCarthy was unable to find any listing under the name "Andrew Kray" in Hawaii. McCarthy subsequently learned that return reservations from Miami to Honolulu had been made in the names of Kray and Norian, with their arrival scheduled for July 25, three days after respondent and his companion had left.

He also learned that Kray and Norian were scheduled to make stopovers in Denver and Los Angeles.

On July 25, during the stopover in Los Angeles, DEA agents identified respondent. He "appeared to be very nervous and was looking all around the waiting area." App. 43–44. Later that day, at 6:30 P.M., respondent and Norian arrived in Honolulu. As before, they had not checked their luggage. Respondent was still wearing a black jumpsuit and gold jewelry. The couple proceeded directly to the street and tried to hail a cab, where Agent Richard Kempshall and three other DEA agents approached them. Kempshall displayed his credentials, grabbed respondent by the arm, and moved him back onto the sidewalk. Kempshall asked respondent for his airline ticket and identification; respondent said that he had neither. He told the agents that his name was "Sokolow," but that he was traveling under his mother's maiden name, "Kray."

Respondent and Norian were escorted to the DEA office at the airport. There, the couple's luggage was examined by "Donker," a narcotics detector dog, which alerted on respondent's brown shoulder bag. The agents arrested respondent. He was advised of his constitutional rights and declined to make any statements. The agents obtained a warrant to search the shoulder bag. They found no illicit drugs, but the bag did contain several suspicious documents indicating respondent's involvement in drug trafficking. The agents had Donker reexamine the remaining luggage, and this time the dog alerted on a medium-sized Louis Vuitton bag. By now, it was 9:30 P.M., too late for the agents to obtain a second warrant. They allowed respondent to leave for the night, but kept his luggage. The next morning, after a second dog confirmed Donker's alert, the agents obtained a warrant and found 1,063 grams of cocaine inside the bag.

Respondent was indicted for possession with the intent to distribute cocaine in violation of 21 U.S.C. 841(a) (1). The United States District Court for Hawaii denied his motion to suppress the cocaine and other evidence seized from his luggage, finding that the DEA agents had a reasonable suspicion that he was involved in drug trafficking when they stopped him at the airport. Respondent then entered a conditional plea of guilty to the offense charged.

The United States Court of Appeals for the Ninth Circuit reversed respondent's conviction by a divided vote, holding that the DEA agents did not have a reasonable suspicion to justify the stop. The majority divided the facts bearing on reasonable suspicion into two categories. In the first category, the majority placed facts describing "ongoing criminal activity," such as the use of an alias or evasive movement through an airport; the majority believed that at least one such factor was always needed to support a finding of reasonable suspicion. In the second category, it placed facts describing "personal characteristics" of drug couriers, such as the cash payment for tickets, a short trip to a major source city for drugs, nervousness, type of attire, and unchecked luggage. The majority believed that such characteristics, "shared by drug couriers and the public at large," were only relevant if there was evidence of ongoing criminal behavior and the Government offered "[e]mpirical documentation" that the combination of facts at issue did not describe the behavior of "significant numbers of innocent persons." Ibid. Applying this two-part test to the facts of this case, the majority found that there was no evidence of ongoing criminal behavior, and thus that the agents' stop was impermissible. The dissenting judge took the view that the majority's approach was "overly mechanistic" and "contrary to the case-by-case determination of reasonable articulable suspicion based on all the facts." We granted certiorari to review the decision of the Court of Appeals because of its serious implications for the enforcement of the federal narcotics laws. We now reverse.

The Court of Appeals held that the DEA agents seized respondent when they grabbed him by the arm and moved him back onto the sidewalk. The Government does not challenge that conclusion, and we assume—without deciding—that a stop occurred here. Our decision, then, turns on whether the agents had a reasonable suspicion that respondent was engaged in wrongdoing when they encountered him on the sidewalk. In Terry v. Ohio, we held that the police can stop and briefly detain a person for investigative purposes if the officer has a reasonable suspicion supported by articulable facts that criminal activity "may be afoot," even if the officer lacks probable cause.

The officer, of course, must be able to articulate something more than an "inchoate and unparticularized suspicion or 'hunch.'" The Fourth Amendment requires "some minimal level of objective justification" for making the stop. INS v. Delgado (1984). That level of suspicion is considerably less than proof of wrongdoing by a preponderance of the evidence. We have held that probable cause means "a fair probability that contraband or evidence of a crime will be found," and the level of suspicion required for a Terry stop is obviously less demanding than that for probable cause.

The concept of reasonable suspicion, like probable cause, is not "readily, or even usefully, reduced to a neat set of legal rules." We think the Court of Appeals' effort to refine and elaborate the requirements of "reasonable suspicion" in this case creates unnecessary difficulty in dealing with one of the relatively simple concepts embodied in the Fourth Amendment. In evaluating the validity of a stop such as this, we must consider "the totality of the circumstances—the whole picture." As we said in Cortez:

> The process does not deal with hard certainties, but with probabilities. Long before the law of probabilities was articulated as such, practical people formulated certain common-sense conclusions about human behavior; jurors as factfinders are permitted to do the same—and so are law enforcement officers.

The rule enunciated by the Court of Appeals, in which evidence available to an officer is divided into evidence of "ongoing criminal behavior," on the one hand, and "probabilistic" evidence, on the other, is not in keeping with the quoted statements from our decisions. It also seems to us to draw a sharp line between types of evidence, the probative value of which varies only in degree. The Court of Appeals classified evidence of traveling under an alias, or evidence that the suspect took an evasive or erratic path through an airport, as meeting the test for showing "ongoing criminal activity." But certainly instances are conceivable in which traveling under an alias would not reflect ongoing criminal activity: for example, a person who wished to travel to a hospital or clinic for an operation and wished to conceal that fact. One taking an evasive path through an airport might be seeking to avoid a confrontation with an angry acquaintance or with a creditor. This is not to say that each of these types of evidence is not highly probative, but they do not have the sort of ironclad significance attributed to them by the Court of Appeals.

On the other hand, the factors in this case that the Court of Appeals treated as merely "probabilistic" also have probative significance. Paying $2,100 in cash for two airplane tickets is out of the ordinary, and it is even more out of the ordinary to pay that sum from a roll of $20 bills containing nearly twice that amount of cash. Most business travelers, we feel confident, purchase airline tickets by credit card or check so as to have a record for tax or business purposes, and few vacationers carry with them thousands of dollars in $20 bills. We also think the agents had a reasonable ground to believe that respondent was traveling under an alias; the evidence was by no means conclusive, but it was sufficient to warrant consideration. While a trip from Honolulu to Miami, standing alone, is not a cause for any sort of suspicion, here there was more: surely few residents of Honolulu travel from that city for 20 hours to spend 48 hours in Miami during the month of July.

We do not agree with respondent that our analysis is somehow changed by the agents' belief that his behavior was consistent with one of the DEA's "drug courier profiles." A court sitting to determine the existence of reasonable suspicion must require the agent to articulate the factors leading to that conclusion, but the fact that these factors may be set forth in a "profile" does not somehow detract from their evidentiary significance as seen by a trained agent.

We hold that the agents had a reasonable basis to suspect that respondent was transporting illegal drugs on these facts. The judgment of the Court of Appeals is therefore reversed, and the case is remanded for further proceedings consistent with our decision.

It is so ordered.

### *Whren v. United States* (1996)

*No case has received as much attention within the context of discussions about racial profiling, and other unlawful profiling, as has the present case. The facts in Whren are as follows: Plainclothes police officers were on patrol in a neighborhood considered to be a "high drug area." The officers observed a vehicle in which Whren was a passenger. The vehicle stopped at a stop sign for an unusually long period of time. The vehicle then made the turn without signaling and sped off. The police officers stopped the vehicle, using the unlawful turn as the basis for the stop. Upon approaching the vehicle, officers observed crack cocaine being held by passenger Whren.*

*Whren argued that the officers used the minor traffic violation to investigate other crimes for which they had no probable cause. He urged the Supreme Court to require demonstration that a reasonable officer would make a traffic stop for the purpose of enforcing the traffic violation in question in any given traffic stop situation. The Supreme Court ruled unanimously that the traffic stop and subsequent arrest and prosecution of Whren were legal. Where probable cause exists that a traffic violation has occurred, police are not required to demonstrate that they did not have ulterior motives in the stop.*

JUSTICE SCALIA delivered the opinion of the Court.

In this case we decide whether the temporary detention of a motorist who the police have probable cause to believe has committed a civil traffic violation is inconsistent with the Fourth Amendment's prohibition against unreasonable seizures unless a reasonable officer would have been motivated to stop the car by a desire to enforce the traffic laws.

On the evening of June 10, 1993, plainclothes vice-squad officers of the District of Columbia Metropolitan Police Department were patrolling a "high drug area" of the city in an unmarked car. Their suspicions were aroused when they passed a dark Pathfinder truck with temporary license plates and youthful occupants waiting at a stop sign, the driver looking down into the lap of the passenger at his right. The truck remained stopped at the intersection for what seemed an unusually long time—more than 20 seconds. When the police car executed a U-turn in order to head back toward the truck, the Pathfinder turned suddenly to its right, without signaling, and sped off at an "unreasonable" speed. The policemen followed, and in a short while overtook the Pathfinder when it stopped behind other traffic at a red light. They pulled up alongside, and Officer Ephraim Soto stepped out and approached the driver's door, identifying himself as a police officer and directing the driver, petitioner Brown, to put the vehicle in park. When Soto drew up to the driver's window, he immediately observed two large plastic bags of what appeared to be crack cocaine in petitioner Whren's hands. Petitioners were arrested, and quantities of several types of illegal drugs were retrieved from the vehicle.

Petitioners were charged in a four-count indictment with violating various federal drug laws, including 21 U.S.C. Section(s) 844(a) and 860(a). At a pretrial suppression hearing, they challenged the legality of the stop and the resulting seizure of the drugs. They argued that the stop had not been justified by probable cause to believe, or even reasonable suspicion, that petitioners were engaged in illegal drug-dealing activity; and that Officer Soto's asserted ground for approaching the vehicle—to give the driver a warning concerning traffic violations—was pretextual. The District Court denied the suppression motion, concluding that "the facts of the stop were not controverted," and "[t]here was nothing to really demonstrate that the actions of the officers were contrary to a normal traffic stop."

Petitioners were convicted of the counts at issue here. The Court of Appeals affirmed the convictions, holding with respect to the suppression issue that, "regardless of whether a police officer subjectively believes that the occupants of an automobile may be engaging in some other illegal behavior, a traffic stop is permissible as long as a reasonable officer in the same circumstances could have stopped the car for the suspected traffic violation."

The Fourth Amendment guarantees "[t]he right of the people to be secure in their persons, houses, papers, and effects, against unreasonable searches and seizures." Temporary detention of individuals during the stop of an automobile by the police, even if only for a brief period and for a limited purpose, constitutes a "seizure" of "persons" within the meaning of this provision. An automobile stop is thus subject to the constitutional imperative that it not be "unreasonable" under the circumstances. As a general matter, the decision to stop an automobile is reasonable where the police have probable cause to believe that a traffic violation has occurred.

Petitioners accept that Officer Soto had probable cause to believe that various provisions of the District of Columbia traffic code had been violated. They argue, however, that "in the unique context of civil traffic regulations" probable cause is not enough. Since, they contend, the use of automobiles is so heavily and minutely regulated that total compliance with traffic and safety rules is nearly impossible, a police officer will almost invariably be able to catch any given motorist in a technical violation. This creates the temptation to use traffic stops as a means of investigating other law violations, as to which no probable cause or even articulable suspicion exists. Petitioners, who are both black, further contend that police officers might decide which motorists to stop based on decidedly impermissible factors, such as the race of the car's occupants. To avoid this danger, they say, the Fourth Amendment test for traffic stops should be, not the normal one (applied by the Court of Appeals) of whether probable cause existed to justify the stop; but rather, whether a police officer, acting reasonably, would have made the stop for the reason given.

Petitioners contend that the standard they propose is consistent with our past cases' disapproval of police attempts to use valid bases of action against citizens as pretexts for pursuing other investigatory agendas. We are reminded that in Florida v. Wells (1990), we stated that "an inventory search must not be used as a ruse for a general rummaging in order to discover incriminating evidence"; that in Colorado v. Bertine (1987), in approving an inventory search, we apparently thought it significant that there had been "no showing that the police, who were following standard procedures, acted in bad faith or for the sole purpose of investigation"; and that in New York v. Burger (1987), we observed, in upholding the constitutionality of a warrantless administrative inspection, that the search did not appear to be "a 'pretext' for obtaining evidence of . . . violation of . . . penal laws." But only an undiscerning reader would regard these cases as endorsing the principle that ulterior motives can invalidate police conduct that is justifiable on the basis of probable cause to believe that a violation of law has occurred. In each case we were addressing the validity of a search conducted in the absence of probable cause. Our quoted statements simply explain that the exemption from the need for probable cause (and warrant), which is accorded to searches made for the purpose of inventory or administrative regulation, is not accorded to searches that are not made for those purposes.

. . . Not only have we never held, outside the context of inventory search or administrative inspection (discussed previously), that an officer's motive invalidates objectively justifiable behavior under the Fourth Amendment; but we have repeatedly held and asserted the contrary. In United States v. Villamonte-Marquez (1983), we held that an otherwise valid warrantless boarding of a vessel by customs officials was not rendered invalid "because the customs officers were accompanied by a Louisiana state policeman, and were following an informant's tip that a vessel in the ship channel was thought to be carrying marihuana." We flatly dismissed the idea that an ulterior motive might serve to strip the agents of their legal justification. In United States v. Robinson (1973), we held that a traffic-violation arrest (of the sort here) would not be rendered invalid by the fact that it was "a mere pretext" for a narcotics search and that a lawful post-arrest search of the person would not be rendered invalid by the fact that it was not motivated by the officer-safety concern that justifies such searches. In rejecting the contention that wiretap evidence was subject to exclusion because the agents conducting the tap had failed to make any effort to comply with the statutory requirement that unauthorized acquisitions be minimized, we said that "[s]ubjective intent alone . . . does not make otherwise lawful conduct illegal or unconstitutional." We described Robinson as having established that "the fact that the officer does not have the state of mind which is hypothecated by the reasons which provide the legal justification for the officer's action does not invalidate the action taken as long as the circumstances, viewed objectively, justify that action."

We think these cases foreclose any argument that the constitutional reasonableness of traffic stops depends on the actual motivations of the individual officers involved. We of course agree with petitioners that the Constitution prohibits selective enforcement of the law based on considerations such as race. But the constitutional basis for objecting to intentionally discriminatory application of laws is the Equal Protection Clause, not the Fourth Amendment. Subjective intentions play no role in ordinary, probable-cause Fourth Amendment analysis.

Recognizing that we have been unwilling to entertain Fourth Amendment challenges based on the actual motivations of individual officers, petitioners disavow any intention to make the individual officer's subjective good faith the touchstone of "reasonableness." They insist that the standard they have put forward—whether the officer's conduct deviated materially from usual police practices, so that a reasonable officer in the same circumstances would not have made the stop for the reasons given—is an "objective" one.

But although framed in empirical terms, this approach is plainly and indisputably driven by subjective considerations. Its whole purpose is to prevent the police from doing under the guise of enforcing the traffic code what they would like to do for different reasons. Petitioners' proposed standard may not use the word "pretext," but it is designed to combat nothing other than the perceived "danger" of the pretextual stop, albeit only indirectly and over the run of cases. Instead of asking whether the individual officer had the proper state of mind, the petitioners would have us ask, in effect, whether (based on general police practices) it is plausible to believe that the officer had the proper state of mind.

Why one would frame a test designed to combat pretext in such fashion that the court cannot take into account actual and admitted pretext is a curiosity that can only be explained by the fact that our cases have foreclosed the more sensible option. If those cases were based only upon the evidentiary difficulty of establishing subjective intent, petitioners' attempt to root out subjective vices through objective means might make sense. But they were not based only upon that, or indeed even principally upon that. Their principal basis—which applies equally to attempts to reach subjective intent through ostensibly objective means—is simply that the Fourth Amendment's concern with "reasonableness" allows certain actions to be taken in certain circumstances, whatever the subjective intent. But even if our concern had been only an evidentiary one, petitioners' proposal would by no means assuage it. Indeed, it seems to us somewhat easier to figure out the intent of an individual officer than to plumb the collective consciousness of law enforcement in order to determine whether a "reasonable officer" would have been moved to act upon the traffic violation. While police manuals and standard procedures may sometimes provide objective assistance, ordinarily one would be reduced to speculating about the hypothetical reaction of a hypothetical constable—an exercise that might be called virtual subjectivity.

Moreover, police enforcement practices, even if they could be practicably assessed by a judge, vary from place to place and from time to time. We cannot accept that the search and seizure protections of the Fourth Amendment are so variable and can be made to turn upon such trivialities. The difficulty is illustrated by petitioners' arguments in this case. Their claim that a reasonable officer would not have made this stop is based largely on District of Columbia police regulations which permit plainclothes officers in unmarked vehicles to enforce traffic laws "only in the case of a violation that is so grave as to pose an immediate threat to the safety of others." This basis of invalidation would not apply in jurisdictions that had a different practice. And it would not have applied even in the District of Columbia, if Officer Soto had been wearing a uniform or patrolling in a marked police cruiser. . . .

In what would appear to be an elaboration on the "reasonable officer" test, petitioners argue that the balancing inherent in any Fourth Amendment inquiry requires us to weigh the governmental and individual interests implicated in a traffic stop such as we have here. That balancing, petitioners claim, does not support investigation of minor traffic infractions by plainclothes police in unmarked vehicles; such investigation only minimally advances the government's interest in traffic safety, and may indeed retard it by producing motorist confusion and alarm—a view said to be supported by the Metropolitan Police Department's own regulations generally prohibiting this practice. And as for the Fourth Amendment interests of the individuals concerned, petitioners point out that our cases acknowledge that even ordinary traffic stops entail "a possibly unsettling show of authority"; that they at best "interfere with freedom of movement, are inconvenient, and consume time" and at worst "may create substantial anxiety . . ." That anxiety is likely to be even more pronounced when the stop is conducted by plainclothes officers in unmarked cars. . . .

Petitioners urge as an extraordinary factor in this case that the "multitude of applicable traffic and equipment regulations" is so large and so difficult to obey perfectly that virtually everyone is guilty of violation, permitting the police to single out almost whomever they wish for a stop. But we are aware of no principle that would allow us to decide at what point a code of law becomes so expansive and so commonly violated that infraction itself can no longer be the ordinary measure of the lawfulness of enforcement. And even if we could identify such exorbitant codes, we do not know by what standard (or what right) we would decide, as petitioners would have us do, which particular provisions are sufficiently important to merit enforcement. For the run-of-the-mine case, which this surely is, we think there is no realistic alternative to the traditional common-law rule that probable cause justifies a search and seizure.

Here the District Court found that the officers had probable cause to believe that petitioners had violated the traffic code. That rendered the stop reasonable under the Fourth Amendment, the evidence thereby discovered admissible, and the upholding of the convictions by the Court of Appeals for the District of Columbia Circuit correct.

Judgment affirmed.

In this chapter, summaries of pertinent academic studies along with a list and description of various books are provided for those interested in researching further the issue of criminal justice profiling.

## Academic Studies

In the pages that follow, readers are able to examine several studies, from the 1990s through the present day, that in some way relate to profiling in the criminal justice system. The list is not exhaustive but represents a good sample of the type of research being done and that has been done in this area.

Interestingly, relatively few studies have actually been conducted on profiling specifically—particularly regarding actors other than the police. Instead, many studies have set out to examine inequities that may exist in the criminal justice system. According to most of the contemporary criminal justice and criminological research findings, these inequities typically form along racial and gender lines. Many of the research efforts summarized in the following pages relate to disparities felt between races and gender at the charging or sentencing phase of the criminal justice system.

---

A Georgia Department of Juvenile Justice officer guards a classroom at Atlanta's Metro Regional Youth Detention Center. Many critics of profiling argue that teenaged blacks and Hispanics are too often targeted by the police and the justice system. Defenders of law enforcement respond by saying that the police are just focusing on where the crime actually is, and all too often teenaged minorities are involved. (AP Photo/David Goldman)

Most of that research indeed found that unequal treatment does exist when race or gender is taken into account. Although most researchers do not suggest a purposeful bias, as profiling would necessarily require, they argue that bias does exist nonetheless and constitutes a serious problem for a system that claims to put everyone on equal footing before the law.

The popularity of profiling-related studies has ebbed and flowed in the halls of academe. There was a lot of scholarly interest in the subject in the late 1990s and early 2000s. However, in the years after the 9/11 attacks in 2001, there was a precipitous decline in interest in this topic by public policy makers and scholars alike. That's not to say that no research was done; but it definitely slowed down. Then, with the election of Barak Obama bringing race relations to the forefront of discussion again, and given the propensity that he had for weighing in on national race-related stories and controversies (such as the 2009 arrest of black Harvard Professor Henry Louis Gates at his home by Cambridge police officers who mistook him for a burglar, or the 2012 killing of Trayvon Martin, whom Obama said could be his own son), interest in profiling and disparate treatment in the justice system has been resurrected. We should expect to see a growing number of published studies in the future.

The following studies are ordered alphabetically by lead author.

Benda, Brent, and Nancy Toombs. Religiosity and Violence: Are They Related after Considering the Strongest Predictors? *Journal of Criminal Justice* 28, pp. 483–496 (2000).

> Much attention has been paid in this handbook and in the scholarly literature to the interaction of race and, to a lesser (but still significant) extent, gender. But profiling can, of course, involve a variety of suspect variables beyond race and gender. One such variable is the religious background of people under scrutiny. If you ask the average police officer on the street to describe the role religion plays in the officer's enforcement actions, you

would get the answer "none." For one thing, the religious background of suspects is not typically known. For another, the religious background, if known, has typically not yet been associated with frequent and particular violations. There is no sense in the law enforcement community that drug use is a Catholic problem, for example. There is no sense that Lutherans make up an inordinate share of prostitutes. Religious background, except for certain types of offenses and cases commonly associated with domestic and international terrorism, is not seen as relevant.

In this study, the authors set out to examine the relationship, if any, between religion and general crime. In doing so, the authors administered a 150-question survey to approximately 600 men housed at the only adult boot camp correctional facility in Arkansas. The questionnaire, among other things, measured religious background, intensity of faith, church attendance, family background, age, and number and type of past criminal acts.

Through regression analysis, the researchers found that church attendance, which was affirmatively defined as attending church more than once a month, was not significantly related to criminal activity. Attending church predicted neither criminal activity nor a lack of crime. Religiosity, however, was found to be significantly and *inversely* related. That is to say, as the religious convictions and personal commitment to one's faith went up, the number and severity of criminal acts went down. Although the authors made no claim that the lack of religious conviction in people makes them more likely to offend, it does appear from the study that the presence of religious conviction makes one less likely to offend.

This finding is particularly interesting given the belief by some in society that devoutly religious people are problematic in the modern, indeed postmodern, United

States. The anecdotal stories of Baptist televangelists involved in sex scandals and fraud, radicalized Catholics bombing abortion clinics, or devout American Muslims engaging in terror are just that—anecdotes. These offenses and events have happened, but the research suggests that they are anomalies. In fact, religious people tend to be law abiding and therefore of little or no concern to the police. Perhaps that's why police officers don't spend too much time running a check on license plates in church parking lots on Sunday looking for people with outstanding warrants. Perhaps police officers have always known what this study purports—religious folks are generally not the problem.

Crawford, Charles. Gender, Race, and Habitual Offender Sentencing in Florida. *Criminology* 38, no. 1, pp. 263–280 (2000).

In this study, gender was added to the mix in examining sentencing practices and potential disparities. In particular, 1,103 female offenders who were eligible for enhanced penalties under Florida's habitual offender statute in fiscal year 1992–1993 we reanalyzed and compared against 9,960 male habitual offenders previously studied by the author in 1998.

Under the habitual offender law in Florida, an offender can receive harsher penalties at sentencing than he or she would otherwise be eligible for if the offender had been convicted of two prior felonies within five years of a current felony conviction. All three felonies must be unrelated to each other, that is, three separate offenses.

Of the 1,103 females eligible for sentencing as habitual offenders, only 66 women were so sentenced. This represents only 6 percent of the eligible female offenders, compared to 20 percent of the eligible men who were sentenced as habitual offenders according to the author's 1998 study. This does suggest that women in Florida are not as aggressively sentenced as men are.

About two-thirds of the women and 70 percent of men sentenced as habitual offenders were African American. In fact, the study indicated that after controlling for (i.e., taking into account) the prior records of the offenders, the seriousness of the crime, the type of crime, and the Florida county in which the sentencing took place, black women were almost twice as likely to be sentenced as habitual offenders as white women.

In sum, the state of Florida appears to avoid targeting women for habitual offender sentencing compared to eligible male offenders. If either gender has a claim that they are subject to profiling in sentencing, this study would suggest it is men. The study also suggested that when the habitual offender law is used against women, however, it is possibly discriminatorily used against black women as opposed to white women.

De Lisi, Matt, and Bob Regoli. Race, Conventional Crime, and Criminal Justice: The Declining Importance of Skin Color. *Journal of Criminal Justice* 27, no. 6, pp. 549–557 (1999).

The authors in this study wanted to examine the truthfulness of the common claim in criminal justice academic literature that racial discrimination explains why blacks are arrested, prosecuted, convicted, and imprisoned in numbers disproportionate to their percentage of the U.S. population.

Going into the study, the authors noted that there was no doubt that blacks were overrepresented participants in the criminal justice system. According to the U.S. Department of Justice, the incarceration rate per 100,000 adults in 1996 was 289 for whites and 1,860 for blacks. The chance of a black male going to prison in his lifetime was 29 percent, whereas for white males, it was only 4 percent. Black women were also more likely than white women to be incarcerated in their lifetimes—seven times more likely, to be exact.

These troubling statistics provided the backdrop for the authors' study in exploring the answers to five research questions. They were:

1. Is police discretion racially biased, resulting in higher black arrests?

2. Is the arrest setting an example of the practice of racial bias?

3. Are incarceration rates indicative of racial bias?

4. What do racial victimization rates say about racial bias?

5. Is the war on drugs biased against blacks?

To answer these questions, the authors conducted a secondary analysis of existing data.

In answering question #1, the authors examined two studies relating to driving under the influence of alcohol (DUI) arrests. It was thought by the authors that DUI enforcement represents an area of significant police discretion. If there were a general tendency or desire within the law enforcement community to discriminate against blacks, one would expect to see greater proportions of blacks arrested for DUI, where police discretion is greatest. The authors, however, did not see a disproportionate level of black arrests. In fact, whites were nine times more likely than blacks to be arrested for DUI.

Regarding the second question, the authors found that arrest data show most arrests emerging out of police response to calls. Police respond to 911 calls, disturbances, and drug-related calls by witnesses. Further, the handling of these calls is frequently hampered by the intoxicating effects of drugs and alcohol among those they are dealing with. In such chaotic and fluid situations as a domestic disturbance involving a drunk, combative boyfriend, the police have little opportunity to be racially selective in whom they arrest.

Regarding question #3, the authors again found that claims of racism's being behind the incarceration rates of blacks were spurious. The authors examined several studies, some of which supported the notion of disparate treatment against blacks, whereas others suggested harsher treatment (relatively) against whites. For example, one study showed that blacks were more likely than whites to be released from jail without having to post money for bond. Another study showed the average elapsed time from conviction to execution in death penalty cases between 1977 and 1996 was 110 months for whites and 117 months for blacks. The authors noted, however, there is compelling evidence that blacks are improperly sentenced to death at higher rates than whites.

Question #4 relates to the race of the victim and suggests that the criminal justice system, if it were racist, would ignore victims of color. But according to the authors, the aggressive drug and street crime campaigns of urban law enforcement agencies benefit minority potential victims or actual victims at far greater rates than white victims or potential victims. The authors demonstrated that blacks were more likely to be victimized than whites and therefore the intensification of police efforts, if absent, would demonstrate a lack of interest in the well-being of minorities.

Finally, in answering question #5, the authors examined studies relating to the harsher penalties associated with crack cocaine over powder cocaine. Crack tends to be the form of choice for black cocaine users, whereas powder tends to be used more by whites. The authors argued that harsher treatment of crack cocaine by the law is not necessarily rooted in racism.

Crack is a more transitory and compulsive drug than powder cocaine, said the authors. Its trafficking is also associated with more violence and tends to involve and affect younger people.

Therefore, there are alternative public policy explanations for the harsher treatment of crack cocaine than simply institutional racism.

In discussing the findings, the authors pointed out that the racial gap in state prisons in 1932 was four black prisoners to every one white prisoner, when accounting for their representation in the total population. In 1979, the gap was eight to one. And in 1999, there were more than 500,000 blacks in state prisons and just less than 400,000 whites; blacks comprise only 13 percent of the U.S. population whereas whites comprise 82 percent. The authors asked the rhetorical question: Does this mean the United States is more racist as a society today than it was in the 1930s? Clearly, something other than racism alone must explain these incarceration rates. From their evaluation of the research questions posed previously, the authors determined that the contemporary criminal justice system is essentially fair to minorities. Further, the unspoken implication is conveyed that some minority communities, and African Americans in particular, have a crime problem that must be addressed from within.

Griffin, Timothy, and John Wooldredge. Judges' Reactions to Sentencing Reform in Ohio. *Crime & Delinquency* 47, no. 4, pp. 491–512 (2001).

As mentioned previously, a very hot topic in the general realm of criminal justice profiling is the way convicted offenders who are persons of color are treated by the system at the point of sentencing. Although we often debate the predisposition of police officers to discriminate against minorities, we rarely talk about the predisposition of judges to do the same. And yet, if discrimination or bias does exist in sentencing, judges are necessarily implicated.

In this study, the authors sought to gauge the feelings that Ohio judges had concerning recent sentencing reforms. Traditionally and predictably, judges tend to vigorously defend their autonomy and discretion in sentencing offenders. Reforms put in place as a check against potential bias necessarily reduce judicial discretion. The authors wanted to test this assumption.

The reform effort, known as Senate Bill 2 and implemented by the Ohio Criminal Sentencing Commission in 1996, did several things. The key element affecting judicial discretion, however, was the implementation of presumptive sentences (i.e., judges would be expected to follow the recommended sentence within the guidelines and would have to justify not doing so). Also, "truth-in-sentencing" was a key provision. Offenders would be required to serve the majority of the sentence they received.

The authors crafted a survey and sent it out to 221 judges who presided over felony cases in Ohio courts. A total of 138 usable surveys were eventually returned. The survey measured the degree to which judges viewed the reforms favorably or unfavorably, along with specific elements of the reforms.

The majority of judges who responded to the survey believed that the guidelines diminished judicial authority (68%), did not feel their input was considered in the reform process by the Ohio Criminal Sentencing Commission (66%), and did not feel the commission understood the perspective of judges (70%). Interestingly, a majority (55%) responded, however, that the new sentencing guidelines were good for the sentencing process. The 45 percent who did not believe the guidelines were appropriate tended to be against them because of their perceived undue restriction on judicial discretion. Additional statistical analysis demonstrated a significant correlation between the fear of losing judicial authority and a belief that punishment for offenders was not being achieved. This makes sense given that the reforms proscribed a presumptive sentence of community service for less serious offenders.

It was not surprising to the authors that judges would be somewhat reluctant to give up their absolute autonomy in sentencing, even for the noble cause (in part) of ensuring equal application of the law through standardization. The slight majority that generally believed the reforms to be a good idea suggested, however (optimistically perhaps), that judges can be persuaded to passively if not actively endorse self-limiting reforms. To the extent that bias exists at the sentencing phase of the criminal justice system, reforms such as those in Ohio remain among the best hopes for change.

Hackney, Amy, and Jack Glaser. Reverse Deterrence in Racial Profiling: Increased Transgressions by Nonprofiled Whites. *Law & Human Behavior* 37, no. 5, pp. 348–353 (2013).

Most of the arguments made in favor of racial profiling relate in some way to the notion that profiling is intended to go where the crime is. In other words, criminal justice officials pay extra attention to race—particularly racial minorities—because of the disproportionate share of crime that comes from minority communities. Few researchers have bothered to ask what the effect of racial profiling might be on majority (i.e., white) behaviors. This study sought to examine this very question. The researchers hypothesized that whites, who routinely escape the attention of the police and other branches of the criminal justice system, may engage in more criminality given their own knowledge that they are paid less attention.

The researchers in this study attempted to replicate on a smaller scale the dynamics of having a choice whether to commit unlawful activity. They did this by offering a test to different groups of college students, some white and some black. Prior to the administration of the tests to each group, students were told that others had been prone to cheat on the test in the past and that proctors would be monitoring the students closely. Then, the monitors proceeded to give extra attention to black students (or to white students in different groups).

The results of the study showed that white students when tested with blacks cheated more when black students where scrutinized than any other group and scrutiny combination. In other words, as white test takers became convinced that blacks were the focus of the monitoring by proctors, many chose to cheat. This did not happen to the same degree when black students observed white students being profiled through undue monitoring and negative attention.

The study supports the hypothesis that whites may engage in greater rates of unlawful activity when the criminal justice system overtly focuses its attention and effort to repress crime on minorities. Obviously, the study must be replicated. The authors acknowledge that without further study which does a better job of operationalizing criminal activity (as opposed to ethical choices in a testing environment), their broader hypothesis regarding whites and crime cannot be completely affirmed.

Hebert, Christopher. Sentencing Outcomes of Black, Hispanic, and White Males Convicted under Federal Sentencing Guidelines. *Criminal Justice Review* 22, no. 2, pp. 133–156 (Autumn 1997).

In this study, the author attempted to fill a void perceived to exist in the literature on sentencing disparities. Although much had been written about black and white offenders, little had been done to consider Hispanic offenders side by side with black and white offenders. Given the growth of the Hispanic population in the United States, the author thought that this was an important gap to fill.

The data set relied upon by the author to study sentencing disparities was rooted in federal drug offenses for the calendar year 1989. By choosing to examine the sentences for federal drug law violations, the author was able to examine a set of crimes that is relatively new in U.S. jurisprudence. Also, drug violations tend to be more regulatory in nature and therefore *mens rea*, that is, a criminal state of mind, was less relevant. Rather, federal sentencing guidelines simply call for a certain sentence for a certain amount of a particular drug. If bias in sentencing existed, it would be easy to identify in this context.

The author examined 5,557 single-count drug charges (i.e., cocaine, marijuana, and opiates) through records maintained by the U.S. Sentencing Commission. After analysis of the data, the author concluded that blacks and Hispanics were *not* more likely than whites to be imprisoned for drug offenses generally; African Americans convicted of cocaine offenses and Hispanics convicted of marijuana offenses, however, *were* more likely than whites convicted of the same offenses to be sentenced to imprisonment. Additionally, African Americans were more likely to receive longer sentences than white offenders.

Three weaknesses of the study, as acknowledged by its author, center on limitations of the U.S. Sentencing Commission data. First, they did not reflect criminal history scores of the offenders. Federal sentencing guidelines and the guidelines of every state in the union provide for higher penalties for prior offenders, with sentences progressively harsher the more serious the offender's criminal history.

A second shortcoming was that the data did not reflect downward departures from the guidelines for those who cooperated with authorities. Under federal sentencing guidelines, an offender will likely receive less than the normally prescribed penalty if that offender helps the police and/or prosecution in a significant way. These data take no account of that.

Third, the data sometimes miscoded crack cocaine as "other drug" rather than as cocaine. Given that the penalties for crack cocaine are harsher than for powder cocaine, some opportunity was missed in the study to observe an anticipated disparity between black and white cocaine users given that blacks tended to use crack cocaine, whereas whites tended to use powder.

Despite these weaknesses, there was general support from the study for the assertion that persons of color are treated differently than whites at the sentencing phase of federal drug offenses, which by design is supposed to be rather mechanical and uniform in its application.

Henderson, Martha, Francis Cullen, Liqun Cao, Sandra Lee Browning, and Renee Kopache. The Impact of Race on Perceptions of Criminal Justice. *Journal of Criminal Justice* 25, no. 6, pp. 447–462 (1997).

Almost as important as the question of whether the criminal justice system is discriminatory against minorities is the perception by minorities of whether the criminal justice system discriminates against them. Research has shown that perception matters. Perception is reality for those holding to the perceptions. A person's perception that crime is at an all-time high and that it is unsafe to walk to the store dramatically affects the quality of life for that person, whether or not the perception is consistent with the facts.

Consequently, an important question when considering the issue of whether criminal justice profiles and treats people differently according to their group affiliation is the perception that people have regarding the fairness of the system. The present study attempted to gauge just that.

In this study, the authors administered a telephone survey to 240 Cincinnati, Ohio, residents about their perceptions of the criminal justice system. Whites totaled 136 of the respondents; blacks totaled 104. Females slightly outnumbered males: 53 percent to 47 percent. All income and education levels were represented.

A number of interesting findings about perceptions of police practice and the courts emerged from the survey. For example, 95 percent of blacks indicated that police officers on patrol are more likely to stop black motorists in white neighborhoods, as opposed to white motorists in black neighborhoods or treating all motorists the same. Whites were evenly split on this question, with 47 percent believing blacks would more likely be stopped and 47 percent believing that black and white motorists would be treated the same.

When asked whom an officer would more likely give a ticket to after pulling a speeding vehicle over, 46 percent of blacks believed that black motorists would most likely get the ticket, whereas 50 percent of blacks believed that whites and blacks would be treated the same. The vast majority of whites (93%) believed that blacks and whites would be ticketed in equal proportions after being pulled over for speeding.

Blacks also perceived inequity from the courts. A full 80 percent of black respondents believed that a black person would likely be sentenced to jail for shoplifting. Only 2 percent believed whites were more likely to receive jail time for the same offense. Seventeen percent believed blacks and whites would be treated the same. On the other hand, 59 percent of whites believed that both races would be treated the same.

Eighty-nine percent of blacks surveyed believed that a black person convicted of murder was more likely to receive the death penalty. Forty-one percent of whites agreed with them; 50 percent of whites thought both races would face the death penalty in equal proportions.

As the authors pointed out, the results of the survey pointed to a "deep and persistent racial cleavage in perceptions of racial injustice in the criminal justice system" (p. 455). This cleavage makes achieving common ground between the races on criminal justice matters truly a daunting task, for the very assumptions about the system are dramatically different. It is hard to meet in the middle with an opposing viewpoint when you are not on the same planet.

The implications of this study certainly include the fact that officials in the criminal justice system have a long way to go in winning the trust and confidence of minorities. Simply sending a police officer to a community meeting, or visiting a black church once a year on Martin Luther King Day, is not going to bridge this gap.

Higgins, George, Shaun Gabbidon, and Gennaro Vito. Exploring the Influence of Race Relations and Public Safety Concerns on Public Support for Racial Profiling During Traffic Stops. *International Journal of Police Science & Management* 12, no. 1, pp. 12–22 (2010).

This study sought to examine how race relations in the United States and concerns over public safety and crime contribute to public support for racial profiling, to the extent support exists.

The researchers tested two hypotheses which seemed reasonable and logical in light of previous studies. First, it was hypothesized that survey respondents who believe that race relations in the United States was poor would more likely believe that racial profiling during traffic stops is both widespread and unjustified. Second, it was hypothesized that survey respondents who had concerns about crime and personal safety would be more likely to support racial profiling than respondents who had no such concerns.

The study relied on Gallup survey data from a poll in 2004 in which 800 blacks, 500 Hispanics, and 700 whites were randomly sampled. Within the survey instrument, different questions were pooled together to measure the constructs of attitudes toward race relations and attitudes concerning crime and safety. In addition to race, several other demographic and geographic variables were analyzed as well.

The authors found through this study that the public's view of race relations in the United States contributed to their belief that racial profiling is widespread (but not justified). However, interestingly, the public's concern about crime and public safety did not contribute significantly to support (or lack of support) for racial profiling. In other words, the first hypothesis was partially supported and the second hypothesis was neither supported nor disproved. The authors conclude that more effort should be made by public officials to improve race relations in the United States, and that further investigation of these two hypotheses is needed.

Higgins, George, Wesley Jennings, Kareem Jordan, and Shaun Gabbidon. Racial Profiling in Decisions to Search: A Preliminary Analysis Using Propensity-Score Matching. *International Journal of Police Science & Management* 13, no. 4, pp. 336–347 (2011).

The purpose of this study was to explore the degree to which racial and ethnic backgrounds of motorists contribute to a police officer's decision to search a motor vehicle on a traffic stop. This research expands on previous studies that posed similar questions with regard to race and ethnicity's influence on police officer decision making.

The raw data for the study came from the Police-Public Contact Survey administered by the Bureau of Justice Statistics nationally in 2006 as a supplement to the National Crime Victimization Survey. Through a statistical procedure called score-matching, the authors were able to gauge the relationship of race, ethnicity, and other variables to the experience of having been stopped for traffic violations, equipment violations, and having had one's vehicle searched on a stop.

The authors found that ethnicity did not play a significant role in the decision to search a motor vehicle on a traffic stop. However, race was related to this decision. In particular, blacks were more likely than whites to have their vehicles searched during a routine traffic stop for moving or equipment violations. Interestingly, Hispanics were found to not be any more likely than whites to have their vehicles searched. The authors conclude that officer decision making with regard to searching stopped vehicles may well be influenced by persistent stereotypes of criminality attached to blacks.

Koons-Witt, Barbara A. The Effect of Gender on the Decision to Incarcerate before and after the Introduction of Sentencing Guidelines. *Criminology* 40, no. 2, pp. 297–328 (2002).

A research article discussed later entitled "Gender Bias and Juvenile Justice Revisited" by John MacDonald and Meda Chesney-Lind cites other studies and their research in Hawaii to suggest that females may be treated unfairly at least during certain phases of the criminal justice process. When bias exists against one group or another at the sentencing phase, then talk of establishing or reforming sentencing guidelines invariably comes up.

In the present study, the author sought to determine if the establishment of sentencing guidelines did anything to make the sentencing process fairer in Minnesota. In particular, the author examined the decision to put female offenders behind bars before and after the introduction of sentencing guidelines in Minnesota.

Unlike some other studies, the author first recognized the existence of prior research indicating that women tend to be treated more leniently than men when judges have maximum discretion in sentencing—particularly in urban felony courts. This is not to say there isn't sexism in the criminal justice system, however. Scholars suggest the leniency is afforded especially to those women who meet the gender role expectations of a paternalistic, chivalrous, patriarchal system. In particular, women who live up to their gender roles by being mothers of children are especially likely to receive leniency at sentencing, whereas fathers of children are not.

In testing whether or not the sentencing guidelines have adequately created an equal application of sentences for equal offenses, the author posed two primary research questions: (1) Were Minnesota's female offenders sentenced more leniently than male offenders prior to the establishment of sentencing guidelines, but not after? (2) Did having dependent children result in more lenient sentences for women than for men, both before and after the creation of the guidelines?

Minnesota's sentencing guidelines were adopted in May 1980. The guidelines were intended to uniformly regulate the decision to impose imprisonment and the duration of such imprisonment. The objective of the guidelines was to maintain equality and proportionality in sentencing while assuring that deserving people were still punished.

In this study, the author compiled data from the Minnesota Sentencing Guidelines Commission and the presentencing investigation reports of Hennepin and Ramsey counties (the counties of Minneapolis and St. Paul, respectively). Data for drug and property offenses during three separate time periods were considered (including before, immediately after, and well after the installation of the guidelines).

Interestingly, several significant findings held true across all three periods of time. For one, women were always more likely to be incarcerated than men. Also, men were more likely to have criminal histories and to have committed more serious offenses. And women were more likely to have dependent children than were men.

The authors also found that women, even with dependent children, were more likely to be sentenced to incarceration in the immediate aftermath of the guidelines as compared to similarly situated women before the guidelines. This suggests that the guidelines initially served to turn a blind eye to circumstances that had previously mattered in determining sentencing. By the third time period, however, that is, after the guidelines had been around a while, women with dependent children were incarcerated at no greater rates than before the guidelines. This suggests that judges grew increasingly comfortable returning to making chivalrous decisions, even if it meant departing from the guidelines.

In sum, the answer to the first research question posed by the author is "no." Women were not treated more leniently than men before but not after the guidelines. Rather, women were treated more leniently before and after the guidelines. The guidelines did not correct the gender inequity of sentencing against men. The second question's answer is "yes": having dependent children helped women to receive more lenient sentences in relation to men, both before and after the guidelines. In relation to themselves, however, women were treated most harshly during the immediate period after the establishment of guidelines. That development, depending on one's perspective, could be viewed as a time that was harmful to women and dependent children or as a time when the gender gap at least closed a bit regarding sentencing disparity.

Lahm, Karen. Equal or Equitable: An Exploration of Educational and Vocational Program Availability for Male and Female Offenders. *Federal Probation* 64, no. 2, pp. 39–46 (2000).

Although considerable scholarly effort has been devoted to the existence of inequalities between male and female offenders within the criminal justice system leading up to and including sentencing, there is another body of literature that has examined the quality of programs available to male and female offenders once imprisoned. Historically, very valid claims have been levied against prison officials for devoting more resources per prisoner to males for their rehabilitation than to females.

Researchers in the 1970s found female prisons to be characterized by inadequate health care, stereotypical job training (e.g., programs to learn sewing or secretarial skills instead of how to fix electronic components or manufacturing). In light of the past research, and with the female prison population in the United States growing rapidly, the author sought to examine the current status of educational and training programs for female prisoners.

In this study, the author was able to survey 474 correctional institutions, including 47 female-only institutions, in 30 states. The survey simply assessed the presence or absence of various types of educational and vocational programs that prisoners can take part in. The results of the author's findings suggest that opportunities for female prisoners have dramatically increased over the past 30 years.

Specifically, the results showed that 100 percent of both male and female institutions offered general education/high school equivalency programs. Furthermore, female institutions offered greater opportunities than did the male institutions regarding college education, managerial skill training, technical and sales training, service training, and operator/fabricator training. The two areas of training that favored the male institutions were production and farming/forestry/fishing.

The author found that female institutions are offering equal or even superior training and educational opportunities as compared with male prisons. The author also noted with dismay, however, the lingering presence of stereotypical training programs at the female prisons in addition to the other opportunities. The author may be failing to consider the possibility that some women may *want* to learn how to sew or clean or type. Although the author was correct in noting that many of the jobs women

train for in prison result in low-paying positions once released and back in society, the same is clearly true of male
prisoners who are released. The matriculation of released
prisoners into society at the lower socio-economic rungs
is likely a problem across gender.

Lundman, Richard, and Robert Kaufman. Driving while Black:
Effects of Race, Ethnicity, and Gender on Citizen Self-Reports
of Traffic Stops and Police Actions. *Criminology* 41, no. 1, pp.
195–220 (2003).

> The findings in this study concerned the perceptions of
> minorities regarding their risk for being subject to police
> action because of their race or ethnicity. The researchers
> in this study posed similar questions to those, in part,
> of Ronald Weitzer and Steven Tuch, in "Perceptions of
> Racial Profiling," which is discussed later—that is, what
> do citizens perceive as the basis for police actions taken
> against them. Unlike the Weitzer and Tuch project, how-
> ever, this study did not limit the comparison racially by
> only considering whites and blacks. Instead, the study as-
> sessed the opinions of whites, blacks, and Hispanics.
>
> In the present research, the authors sought to answer
> three specific questions:
>
> 1. Are African American men, compared to white men,
>    more likely to report being stopped by police for traf-
>    fic violations?
> 2. Are African American and Hispanic drivers less likely to
>    report that police had a legitimate reason to stop them?
> 3. Are African American and Hispanic drivers less
>    likely to report that police acted properly during an
>    encounter?
>
> Researchers Lundman and Kaufman set out to answer
> these questions by consulting and analyzing data from a
> section of the 1999 National Crime Victimization Survey

conducted by the U.S. Department of Justice. This section, titled "Contacts between Police and the Public," hereinafter will be referred to as CBPP.

The data Lundman and Kaufman had to work with were very comprehensive. The survey, conducted nationally, required that participants be at least 16 years old. The CBPP portion of the survey focused on the participants' contacts with the police in the previous 12 months. Over 80,000 subjects were randomly selected for this study; of those, 7,034 (8.7%) reported that they had been pulled over by law enforcement at least once in the past year in which they were the driver.

For these respondents, additional questions were then asked concerning the number of stops they had, the nature of the stops, and their perceptions concerning the legitimacy of the stops and the properness of police actions. The researchers also captured data concerning a variety of possible explanatory factors specific to the driver. These factors, which were controlled for, included:

- history of police contact with the driver;
- geographic location (large city, small town, etc.);
- social class of the driver;
- age of the driver;
- gender of the driver;
- race/ethnicity of the driver; and
- race/ethnicity of the driver by gender.

Using regression analysis, the researchers in this study made several determinations. These included the following:

- Drivers with previous stops were less likely to report legitimate reasons for the stops.
- Drivers in larger geographic settings were less likely to report legitimate reasons for stops than those in smaller settings.

- African Americans and Hispanics were much less likely than whites to report legitimate reasons for stops and to report that police acted properly during stops and encounters.

From these findings, Lundman and Kaufman concluded that police were indeed more likely to use traffic stops as pretexts for pulling over minorities. They argued that despite the serious threats to validity in self-report surveys, the overwhelming difference in responses between African Americans and Hispanics on the one hand and whites on the other cannot be dismissed; where there is smoke, there's fire.

Although some scholars could argue that the methodology of the study did not permit sweeping conclusions about what the police are doing and why they are doing it, the study demonstrated—once again—the undeniable perception that minorities have concerning the legitimacy of policing services they receive. Law enforcement does not fare well in the eyes of minority communities in the United States, especially in urban areas.

The cliché "perception is reality" may not hold up against rigorous scientific inquiry. After all, for the scientist—even the social scientist—reality is reality. But that fact is of little solace to those who understand that community cooperation with the police hinges on quality of life and service satisfaction—important intangibles that do indeed revolve around perceptions. Perhaps perception is reality after all.

MacDonald, John, and Meda Chesney-Lind. Gender Bias and Juvenile Justice Revisited: A Multiyear Analysis. *Crime & Delinquency* 47, no. 2, pp. 173–195 (2001).

A considerable amount of research exists concerning race and the criminal justice system. Many of the preceding studies are sampled from that body of literature. This study focuses on gender bias in the criminal justice system. Specifically, the authors examined the extent of gender bias existing in the juvenile justice system in Hawaii. Based on prior research, the authors entered this study with the theory that female juveniles, once found to be delinquent by a juvenile court, tend to be punished more severely than male juvenile delinquents.

To test this theory, the authors examined data that had been collected by the Hawaii State Judiciary and provided to the National Juvenile Court Data Archive. The data set covered all delinquency cases in the state of Hawaii from 1980 to 1991. In total, 85,692 cases were included for analysis in the study.

As with some of the previously discussed studies, a regression analysis was used to assess the relationship of several variables, including gender, to the severity of punishment one receives. Other variables considered included race/ethnicity, geographic location within Hawaii, urban versus rural areas, the year of adjudication, and so on. Of the 85,000-plus cases examined, 30 percent (nearly 26,000) involved female offenders. From the raw data, the authors noted that in most cases, boys were more likely than girls to be referred to juvenile court for property and violent offenses. The tendency was to handle female delinquency more informally at the early stages of the process.

The analysis showed that once boys and girls who were in the system were found to be delinquent (the juvenile court term for "guilty"), however, girls were treated more harshly. For the authors, this demonstrated a built-in anti-female bias in Hawaii's juvenile justice system. Efforts were taken to control for all relevant factors. If it is true that females are given a pass at the frontend of the system while boys are not, however, then perhaps the females making it all the way through to sentencing for their delinquent acts are there precisely because they are more deserving of harsher punishment (otherwise, informal measures to address their misconduct would have been pursued).

In any case, the study certainly does raise the possibility of institutional bias against female offenders, at least in Hawaii, despite the common perception that females always get off more easily for their offenses by the criminal justice system.

Miller, Kirk. The Institutionalization of Racial Profiling Policy: An Examination of Antiprofiling Policy Adoption among Large Law Enforcement Agencies. *Crime & Delinquency* 59, no. 1, pp. 32–58 (2013).

Most studies relating to police profiling examine the conditions and perceptions at the time of the encounter between the police and citizens—particularly minority citizens. The present study, however, takes more of an institutional and structural approach. The author sought to uncover the factors associated with police departments actually adopting policies against racial profiling.

The study tested several hypotheses—some relating to the environment that the police agencies find themselves in, and some relating to the nature of the police organization. In some cases, the hypotheses were incompatible with one another. One environmental hypothesis is that the community's police department policies will reflect the wishes of its citizens. Therefore, as the proportion of blacks goes up as a percentage of the community, the likelihood of a department implementing an antiprofiling policy goes up. However, another environmental hypothesis tested by the author was that as the threat of crime goes up, and when positively associated with larger numbers of blacks in the community, the likelihood of implantation of an antiprofiling policy will go down (while the use of aggressive policing tactics go up). An organizational hypothesis tested in this study was the notion that police departments would be more likely to adopt antiprofiling policies as organizational pressure develops to "get with the times" and keep up with the latest innovations in policing, including community policing. This element is more or less about organizational peer pressure.

The author relied on data collected from a Bureau of Justice Statistics survey in which over 800 law enforcement agencies participated. Through logistic models testing, the author found that neither environmental hypothesis explained a department's decision to implement antiprofiling policies. However, the adoption of community policing strategies and the use of public satisfaction surveys was deemed to be significantly and positively related to the implementation of antiprofiling policies. The implication is that organizational commitment, which is necessary for community policing, is an important component to the implementation of antiprofiling policies.

Mosher, Clayton. Predicting Drug Arrest Rates: Conflict and Social Disorganization Perspectives. *Crime & Delinquency* 47, no. 1, pp. 84–104 (2001).

Many studies focus on the discretion that takes place by criminal justice officials—particularly judges—at the time of sentencing. And yet profiling is generally associated with law enforcement actions. The present study examines exactly that: law enforcement actions in the field. The author of this research examined 1989 data on illegal drug possession and trafficking arrests against the backdrop of socio-economic data from the 1990 census in a sample of U.S. cities.

Drug enforcement reached its zenith in the late 1980s and early to mid-1990s.

In light of the heightened intensity of enforcement brought on by the war on drugs, many scholars had been concerned about a disproportionate application of the drug enforcement activities against minorities. In 1996, there were approximately 1,500,000 arrests for drug offenses in the United States. That comes to 1,078 arrests per 100,000—about one-and–a-half times the arrest rate of the second-highest crime category: larceny/theft. Interestingly, in California, more than 80 percent of adults arrested for drug violations in the late 1980s were black or Hispanic. In New York State, more than 90 percent were minorities; and in Baltimore, black juveniles were arrested at nearly 100 times the arrest rate for whites. Do these figures amount to a clear case of police bias?

Within the parameters of this study, the authors were able to examine the arrest rates for drug possession and drug trafficking by race against the community variables of geographic region of the country, police-to-population ratio, gender and age makeup, percentage of high school graduates, percentage of population employed, average income, and others.

Using a statistical process known as regression analysis involving the variables listed previously, the author found that racial composition of a particular city, even after controlling for all the other community variables, was the strongest predictor of drug arrest rates for that city. Essentially, the greater the black or Hispanic population, the greater were the drug offense arrest rates. Given that other studies cited by the author demonstrated a greater rate of possession by whites compared to minorities and a basically equal rate of drug dealing between the races, the author suggested that a bias exists in police culture that favors enforcement actions against persons of color. The study reinforced the author's position that U.S. drug laws are being used by authorities to control racial minorities in America.

Pratt, Travis. Race and Sentencing: A Meta-Analysis of Conflicting Empirical Research Results. *Journal of Criminal Justice* 26, no. 6, pp. 513–523 (1998).

This study differs from others in that it amounts to a study of the studies. The researcher here conducted a meta-analysis (i.e., a grand analysis) of prior research concerning the impact race has on sentencing. As the author noted, prior research over the years had suggested any one of three possibilities explaining the relationship between races in sentencing.

The first explanation is the differential involvement perspective. This perspective says that African Americans are overrepresented in the prisons and receive harsher sentences because they are involved in more crimes than are whites and their crimes are more serious. Theorists who believe this would not deny the existence of racial bias in sentencing in the past. They would argue that at some point in contemporary history, however, the criminal justice system became sufficiently professional, formal, and bureaucratic to eliminate or severely mitigate against overt racism within the system.

The second perspective that emerges from the literature is the direct-impact perspective. This approach says that racial bias does indeed exist and exists on purpose, with the goal of keeping minorities powerless and oppressed. This position amounts to a very cynical view of the U.S. criminal justice system, seeing it really as a tool to maintain the power elite's institutions and values in place.

Finally, the interactionist perspective claims that race does play a role in sentencing, but not in isolation. Rather, race in interaction with other variables and varied contexts has been found to be statistically significant in predicting sentences for offenders.

In the study, the author set out to examine the contradictory research findings that propped up the three different perspectives. In doing so, the author attempted to pool the data from prior research and analyze the overall effect of race on sentencing while considering legally relevant variables (e.g., prior criminal history, severity of crime, etc.). The analysis examined the data from race and sentencing studies contained in sociological and criminal justice academic journals from 1974 to 1996. The author noted and accounted for the fact that the earlier studies tended to be less statistically rigorous than the latter studies. In total, 48,251 cases were examined from 47 studies.

The author performed regression analysis to determine the effects of race, prior criminal history, and seriousness of the offense on sentencing outcomes. The results showed that race and prior criminal history had a relatively small effect on the sentencing outcomes. The severity of the offense, however, had a very large effect on the variance in sentencing. Put another way, the variations in sentences the people received most often could be explained primarily by the respective difference in the severity of crimes.

The author noted that his findings do not suggest that there is no racial bias in the criminal justice system or in the sentencing process specifically. The evidence from this study, however, supported the idea that legally relevant factors play the greatest role in sentencing outcomes.

Ragatz, Laurie, and Brenda Russell. Sex, Sexual Orientation, and Sexism: What Influence Do These Factors Have on Verdicts in a Crime-of-Passion Case. *Journal of Social Psychology* 150, no. 4, pp. 341–360 (2010).

This research is a departure from most of the other studies highlighted in this chapter. Most of the studies summarized in the chapter relate to the conduct and decision-making of criminal justice officials—judges, correctional officials, and especially police officers—or the perceptions that the public has regarding the decisions of those same officials. Unlike those studies, the present research explored how bias might influence the decisions of laypersons involved in the criminal justice system. In particular, the study sought to explore how the gender and sexual orientation of a defendant may influence those called upon to render a verdict. The researchers hypothesized that "jurors" would be most lenient with heterosexual female defendants.

In the study, 458 people were convenience-sampled to participate in the study. Females were 36 percent and males were 64 percent of the participants. They were read descriptions of the elements of murder and the lesser charges of voluntary and involuntary manslaughter and completed an instrument to demonstrate they understood these elements. They were also administered the Ambivalent Sexism Inventory which measured both hostile and benevolent sexism. Then the participants were read a scenario describing a crime-of-passion homicide in which the victim is the amorous partner of the perpetrator and is caught by the perpetrator having sex with another person.

The study confirmed the researchers' hypothesis that juries were more sympathetic and lenient to female heterosexual offenders. They concluded that some of this leniency has its roots in benevolent sexism (i.e., prison is no place for a lady). However, that benevolence did not extend to homosexual females. The results further suggested that jurors, both male and female, did not appear to believe that homosexual infidelity was as serious as heterosexual infidelity and therefore did not warrant such a violent response by the perpetrator.

Schbley, Ayla Hammond. Toward a Common Profile of Religious Terrorism: Some Psychosocial Determinants of Christian and Islamic Terrorists. *Police Practice & Research* 7, no. 4, pp. 275–292 (2006).

While most in academia have rejected the notion that profiling along racial, ethnic, or religious lines is useful or productive, some scholars have attempted to improve profiling techniques rather than simply discard the practice altogether. This is particularly true in the wake of the 9/11 terror attacks, as well as many domestic acts of terrorism which have been perpetrated in the United States over the past couple decades. The author in this study sought to examine psychological and sociological traits of both Christian and Islamic terrorists to look for commonalities which might contribute to the construction of a profile instrument which could predict a willingness to kill perfect strangers for a cause.

The study is a qualitative one. The author's data is drawn from interviews and the analysis of FBI and court-ordered psychological profiles drawn up of seven religiously (Christian) motivated terrorists in custody. The author concedes that his findings are not generalizable as they lack experimental conditions. Nevertheless, the author believes that he is on to something worth further research. In particular, he found that Christians who suffered one or more mental and personality disorders may be at risk for transforming from mere zealotry into self-sacrificial terroristic acts if they experience religious dogma-induced depression.

Son, In Soo, Mark Davis, and Dennis Rome. Race and Its Effects on Police Officers' Perceptions of Misconduct. *Journal of Criminal Justice* 26, no. 1, pp. 21–28 (1998).

In contrast to studies that focus on the perceptions of minorities toward the criminal justice system, the present study flipped that around. Here, the authors conducted a survey of 718 Ohio police officers to determine if race played a role in how they perceived the seriousness of another officer's misconduct toward a suspect. It was hypothesized by the authors that if the police were biased against minorities, then they would view misconduct directed against minorities as less serious than misconduct directed against white citizens.

To measure police perceptions about misconduct and the influence race has on those perceptions, the researchers developed a survey that included 35 short stories or vignettes. In each vignette, a hypothetical police officer engaged in some form of misconduct. Examples of misconduct included drug use, theft from a crime scene, forcing a confession, and so on. Fewer than one-third of the vignettes made any reference to the race of the suspect or officer in the scenario. This was considered an important design feature in the study because the researchers did not want the officers to know the purpose of the survey.

In contradiction to the anticipated results of the study, the researchers found that the citizen's race in each of the vignettes did not play a significant role when officers characterized the seriousness of the misconduct. Rather, the acts of misconduct of the officers in the vignettes and the consequences of the actions played the greatest role in determining how seriously the survey respondents viewed the misconduct. Another factor was the suspect's behavior toward the officer in each vignette. This is consistent with other research that shows officers are harsher with uncooperative citizens than they are with cooperative ones.

The authors noted the cycle that exists when minorities, who presume the existence of police bias, manifest that bias in the form of uncooperativeness. This, of course, is met with harsher tactics, which then only serve to reinforce the idea that it is all about bias.

Thomson, Ernie. Discrimination and the Death Penalty in Arizona. *Criminal Justice Review* 22, no. 1, pp. 65–76 (Spring 1997).

The author of this study noted that many other studies had been conducted concerning suspected patterns of racial bias in death sentences. Considerable focus has fallen on southern states where the history of racial tension is obvious. Studies on death penalty bias have also been conducted in nonsouthern states, however, and have found similar bias.

In this study, the author examined whether racial and ethnic discrimination in death sentences occurs in the state of Arizona, which has many ethnic groups represented among its population. In particular, the author sought to find out whether African Americans and Hispanics were more likely to be sentenced to death for capital offenses than were white offenders, particularly if the victims were white.

To answer this research question, the author examined the racial and ethnic characteristics of reported homicides in Arizona from 1982 to 1991 and compared that data against the racial or ethnic characteristics of death row inmates in 1993 who were convicted during the 1982–1991 time frame. As the author acknowledged, he made no attempt to evaluate the role that prosecutorial, judicial, or jury discretion played in the sentence. Instead, he focused on the gross "beginning to end disparities."

The study's findings suggested that in Arizona, white murderers were more likely to receive the death penalty than minority murderers. Further, murderers of all ethnic backgrounds were more likely to receive the death penalty if their victims were white.

When the data are taken in combination, the study found that minorities were three times more likely to receive the death penalty if they murdered white victims as opposed to minority victims. And white murderers were twice as likely to receive the death penalty if their victims were white as opposed to minority victims.

The implication of the study is that an inequitable profiling of sorts takes place at sentencing in homicide cases—the profile relates to the victim rather than the offender. The author admitted the study's limitations with regard to details of those homicides, however. Not all homicides are capital offenses eligible for the death penalty. Aggravating circumstance must accompany the crime to elevate it to a capital offense.

Most murders are intraracial—that is, murderers tend to kill victims of the own race. This makes sense given that most murderers and the victims know each other.

Typically, the victim is a family member, domestic partner, friend, coworker, or acquaintance of the murderer. On the other hand, most capital offenses, such as those involving murder combined with rape, or murder during a liquor store robbery, are stranger crimes. Further, white individuals are more likely to be in a position to fall prey to a stranger-committed, capital murder because of their socioeconomic status in relation to minorities. Regardless of whether the offender is white, black, or Hispanic, the store owner who is robbed and shot is quite often white. These unforeseen variables may explain some of the tendency to favor capital sentences when white victims are involved—perhaps the killings tended to be capital offenses when those victims were involved.

In any case, the study reminds us of the need to be vigilant in avoiding unfair discrimination against suspects but also in unfairly elevating the value of some victims over others when otherwise the crimes are equally abhorrent.

Weitzer, Ronald, and Steven Tuch. Perceptions of Racial Profiling: Race, Class, and Personal Experience. *Criminology* 40, no. 2, pp. 435–456 (2002).

This study represents a research effort directly aimed at broadening our understanding of racial profiling by the police. The authors noted early in the article that very little existed in scholarly literature concerning the experiences people have had with profiling or their perceptions of it. One exception is the police-public contact survey conducted by the U.S. Department of Justice (DOJ) in 1999. That study found that blacks were more likely than whites or Hispanics to report being stopped by the police in 1999. Of those citizens stopped by the police, blacks and Hispanics were more likely than whites to report being ticketed, arrested, or searched during the stop. They were also more likely to indicate that officers had used force or threatened to use force during the stop. That study relied on survey respondents who had reported being stopped by the police. The present study sought to expand the DOJ one by analyzing perceptions of police actions according to the wider population.

The data analyzed by the authors came from a 1999 nationwide Gallup survey of 2,006 U.S. residents. The authors restricted their analysis to the 903 whites and 961 blacks who took part in the survey. The survey questionnaire polled respondents about their attitudes toward racial profiling and the police. Additionally, demographic and background data were obtained (e.g., education level, income range, gender, where they lived, etc.).

When asked about the use of racial profiling to stop motorists because the police perceive certain racial groups as more likely to be engaged in criminal activity, 94 percent of blacks and 84 percent of whites disapproved of the practice. Among whites, women tended to be slightly more disapproving then men. When asked if they thought the practice was widespread, 82 percent of blacks and 60 percent of whites believed that it was.

When the survey respondents were asked if they had ever been stopped by the police because of their race or ethnic background, 40 percent of blacks said they had. Only 5 percent of whites reported being stopped by the police because of race or ethnicity. The percentage of blacks reporting being stopped by the police went up when just considering males and in particular, the 18 to 34 age range. Seventy-three percent of black males in that age group reported having been stopped because of their race.

The authors pointed out that this last statistic was consistent with other studies that showed young black males more frequently encountered law enforcement. Lost on the authors, ironically, is the fact that these statistics suggest that racial profiling—taking police action solely because of a suspect's race—is not occurring. Race is not the sole criteria if age and gender are playing a significant role.

Profiling may indeed be taking place, but not racial profiling. Otherwise, one would expect to see equal percentages claiming victimization of racial profiling by blacks across variables of age, gender, location, and so on.

In any event, the study highlighted the fact that prior personal experiences with law enforcement significantly help shape people's attitudes toward the police and police practice. Officers need to be reminded that however mundane a traffic stop or other minor offense encounter may be for them, such an encounter is a significant event in the lives of most people. Police officers must do their best to demonstrate fairness, professionalism, and solid, legal tactics to leave a lasting favorable impression on members of the public, regardless of race.

Williams, Marian, and Jefferson Holcomb. Racial Disparity and Death Sentences in Ohio. *Journal of Criminal Justice* 29, pp. 207–218 (2001).

In this research, the authors analyzed data from the Supplemental Homicide Report (SHR) for the state of Ohio from 1981 to 1994. The SHR is a database of information gathered by the FBI from police departments around the country. Although not every police agency submits data, the vast majority of police agencies of any size or consequence submit data to be counted in the SHR. The SHR reflects the number of homicides that took place in any particular jurisdiction, along with specific information about the homicides. This information includes details about the homicide, the classification of the homicide, information about the offenders, and information about the victims. The data from the SHR were then matched against Ohio death penalty information from the same period of time using data from the Office of the Ohio Public Defender.

In their analysis, the authors found that from 1981 to 1994, only 4 percent of the 6,441 cases in which the death sentence could have been imposed actually saw the death sentence handed down. White killers were more likely than black killers to receive the death penalty (5% to 3% respectively). Not unlike the results shown in Ernie Thomson's study, "Discrimination and the Death Penalty in Arizona," however, murders involving white victims were twice as likely to result in a death sentence for the offender as were murders with victims of color. Additionally, blacks who killed whites were five times more likely to receive the death penalty than were blacks who killed blacks. Not surprisingly, offenders who killed multiple victims of any race were significantly more likely to receive the death sentence than were those who killed only one victim. Further, male offenders who killed female victims were more likely to receive a death sentence than those who murdered male victims. Also, older offenders were more likely than younger offenders to be sentenced to death.

Once again, a significant profiling question that emerges from this study is whether or not offenders are sentenced according to profiles of the victims. The victim's race and gender in these cases seem to have a relationship to the sentencing outcome. Although a relationship may exist, this falls short of claiming causation. There may be additional intervening variables that affect the sentencing outcome that are also related to the variables of victim race and gender. In other words, when A is seen to be related to B, as in this study, further analysis is needed before we can say if A causes B, or B causes A, or C causes A and B. From this study, by the authors' own admission, we just don't know.

## Books

In this section of the chapter, the titles and descriptions of various books are provided. The majority of books that one can find on profiling tend to address specifically the issue of racial profiling. Unfortunately, few books have been produced that confront the criminal justice system's intentional reliance on suspect gender, sexual orientation, or religion in making decisions or arriving at conclusions (although some of the titles which do exist made it to the following list). What follows is a selected list of books that may be of interest to someone who desires to research a variety of criminal justice profiling issues. As with the academic articles, the books are listed in alphabetical order by author.

Alexander, Michelle. *The New Jim Crow: Mass Incarceration in the Age of Colorblindness.* New York: New York Press. 2012. 336 pp. ISBN: 978-1595586438.

> The author of this book is a well-known law professor at Ohio State University and a civil rights activist. She posits that, despite America's belief that we are in an era of color-blindness (especially in light of Barak Obama's election), there remains a real racial caste system in the United States with African Americans at the bottom. Through the war on drugs and other pretexts, the criminal justice system has targeted black men and relegated them to second class citizenship. The prison system is a powerful tool in this process, according to Alexander. Just as with Jim Crow laws, blacks who traverse this system have many of their constitutional rights impinged upon. This is especially true of the right to vote, as felons are disenfranchised from suffrage.

Bartol, Curtis R., and Ann M. Bartol. *Criminal & Behavioral Profiling.* Thousand Oaks, CA: SAGE. 2012. 368 pp. ISBN: 1-41298-308-8.

> Curtis and Ann Bartol are well-established and widely recognized experts in the area of criminal behavior and behavioral profiling. This particular publication is their latest to address the issue. The book provides an excellent

overview of different types of criminal profiling, including crime scene profiling, geographic profiling through mapping, and psychological profiling. With all these types of profiling, the object is to develop a suspect. This book also has a chapter on suspect-based profiling. With this type of profiling, clues from the individual prompt investigators to narrow in on that person as a suspect. Computer-aided passenger screening at airports is an example of this and is discussed. The book concludes with the current state of the use of profiling evidence in court.

Bhui, Hindpal Singh, ed. *Race and Criminal Justice.* London: SAGE. 2009. 240 pp. ISBN: 978-1412945554.

This is a reader which offers a comprehensive overview of the interaction of race and ethnicity in the criminal justice system. It is comprehensive in that it spans the criminal justice system and includes chapters relating to policing, prosecutions, prisons, and community corrections measures such as probation. It also examines the issue of immigration and crime. Interestingly, the book is focused on the British experience in these areas. American readers, prior to reading this book, may be unaware of the extent to which the British are wrestling with many of the same issues regarding criminal justice, race, and ethnicity as the United States. The book also explores another issue which is not unique to the United Kingdom but rather is common to all of Western Europe: the influx of Muslim immigrants from Africa and the Middle East, and their often rocky assimilation into Western societies—particularly post-9/11.

Bireda, Martha. *Eliminating Racial Profiling in School Discipline.* Lanham, MD: Scarecrow Press. 2002. 128 pp. ISBN: 0-8108-4201-7.

This book examined the question of why suspensions, expulsions, and other sanctions are so high for African

American students, particularly males. Although the book focused on the secondary education setting, there are parallels to the perceived problem of profiling by the criminal justice system. The book examined cultural assumptions that contribute to the higher rate of punitive interventions against black males. The reader may find these assumptions to likewise be at work in the decisions made by justice officials.

Bucerius, Sandra M., and Michael Tonry, eds. *The Oxford Handbook of Ethnicity, Crime, and Immigration.* New York: Oxford University Press. 2013. 960 pp. ISBN: 0-19985-901-9.

This book is an edited works relying on many scholars in the areas of criminology, sociology, psychology, law, political science, and other social science fields. The editors themselves contribute to the book. Tonry is a very well-known legal and criminological scholar at the University of Minnesota Law School and his written or edited many books. Given the heightened debate on immigration, undocumented aliens, and the clarion call from the political right for the federal government to police America's borders, the material in the book is especially timely. Each chapter covers a topic relating to the intersection of immigration and minority ethnicity with the criminal justice system. The chapters all provide an overview of their topics, a critical analysis, and discussion of controversies and key research. Some of the chapters consist of case studies relating to immigrants, minorities, and the criminal justice system.

Douglas, John, Ann Burgess, Alan Burgess, and Robert Ressler. *Crime Classification Manual: Standard System for Investigating and Classifying Violent Crimes.* rev. ed. San Francisco: Jossey-Bass, 1997. 400 pp. ISBN: 0-7879-3885-8.

Although last published in 1997, this book is appropriate to list here because it remains a classic in the field of profiling and offender classification. John Douglas is a founding father of the practice as employed in criminal investigative work. The book focused on the criminal intent of offenders and delivered a mechanism for developing a suspect profile within the context of violent crimes. The authors in particular examined the offender "signatures" commonly left behind at violent crime scenes. The book devotes attention to serial types of violent crime, including homicides, sexual offenses, and arson. The book is intended to be a reference manual for criminal justice and forensic mental health practitioners.

Epp, Charles R., and Steven Maynard-Moody. *Pulled Over: How Police Stops Define Race and Citizenship.* Chicago: University of Chicago Press. 2014. 272 pp. ISBN: 978-0226113999.

This interesting book is focused entirely on the encounters that occur during a police stop. The authors note that 12 percent of Americans are stopped by the police each year, and the percentage is nearly double for racial minorities. The authors explore the history of police investigative stops and critically evaluate their value as a law enforcement tool. In analyzing current data on the subject, the authors find that police stops cause greater mistrust and less communication to occur between minorities and the police. They note that this turns out to be true even with the police are respectful and courteous throughout their encounters with citizens. The authors argue that with the new wave of anti-immigration sentiment and the clamor for border security, Hispanics are likely to follow in the footsteps of African Americans as a group who experiences discriminatory policing on a large scale. The authors conclude by attempting to offer practical suggestions for police reform which are effective for crime control while honoring civil liberties.

Fredrickson, Darin, and Raymond Siljander. *Racial Profiling: Eliminating the Confusion between Racial and Criminal Profiling and Clarifying What Constitutes Unfair Discrimination and Persecution.* Springfield, IL: Charles C. Thomas Publishing, 2002. 170 pp. ISBN: 0-398-07255-8.

> This text attempted to distinguish between legitimate criminal profiling techniques and the controversial practice of racial profiling. The position of the authors in this book was that profiling is a legitimate police technique but that bias and prejudice in police officers can spoil or pollute the process and therefore diminish the practice's legitimacy. Solutions, according to the authors, can be found in understanding the issue thoroughly and through hiring unbiased police officers and enforcing stringent anti-bias policies. Legal remedies, such as consent decrees between police departments and the federal justice department, were also explored.

Fridell, Lorie, Robert Lunney, Drew Diamond, and Bruce Kubu. *Racially Biased Policing: A Principled Response.* Washington, DC: Police Executive Research Forum. 2001. To download this book, go to: http://www.cops.usdoj.gov/Publications/RaciallyBiasedPolicing.pdf

> The book critically examined the issue of racially biased policing, encouraging law enforcement administrators to recognize its existence generally and the potential damage it can cause within a department and community. Chapter 4 is key in that it offered up model policies for governing police conduct in this regard. Police executives were advised to embrace the policies in whole or in part, as the needs of their particular departments dictate.

Harris, David. *Good Cops: The Case for Preventive Policing.* New York: New York Press. 2005. 352 pp. ISBN: 978-1565849235.

> The author of this book is one of the leading thinkers on the issue of racial profiling and police practice. His books

are frequently cited in studies and by government officials who take dim view of discriminatory police practices. Here, Harris puts forth a new policing model, what he terms as "preventive policing," based on leadership, accountability to the public, and explicit collaboration with the community. The author highlights a number of cities where this policing model has been successfully implemented, including Detroit, Boston, and San Diego. He notes that preventive policing has reduced crime in the areas where it has been embraced. And it has done so while also respecting the civil rights of the community members.

Harris, David. *Profiles in Injustice: Why Racial Profiling Cannot Work.* New York: New Press. 2003. 320 pp. ISBN: 1-56584-818-7.

This book is another well-known and well-regarded book by David Harris, a law professor at the University of Pittsburgh. This publication was one of the earliest books confront head-on the arguments made by law enforcement that profiling is a useful and effective police tool. Profiling is used to a greater or lesser degree by local police officers, state troopers, and federal customs and border officials in their respective law enforcement roles, and many argue for the practice. Harris attempted to refute arguments favoring profiling by calling into question the ethical and legal problems that profiling generates. Harris also produced statistical evidence, however, to demonstrate that profiling, apart from questions of legality or morality, was simply ineffective as a law enforcement tool. The book also included a chapter on profiling in the wake of the September 11 terrorist attacks.

Heumann, Milton, and Lance Cassak. *Good Cop, Bad Cop: Racial Profiling and Competing Views of Justice.* New York: P Lang. 2003. 246 pp. ISBN: 0-82045-829-5.

This book, which was an instant classic on racial profiling when it was first published, provides an excellent history of profiling and explains how it transformed from an acceptable police practice to go after drug couriers into a widely condemned practice. Details about profiling for drug couriers in the airports and on the highways are provided. The debate over profiling, including arguments for both sides, is also presented and includes a cost-benefit analysis for the practice. The implications of profiling by law enforcement in the wake of 9/11 are also discussed.

Holmes, Ronald, and Stephen Holmes. *Profiling Violent Crimes: An Investigative Tool.* 3rd ed. Thousand Oaks, CA: Sage. 2002. 299 pp. ISBN: 0-761-92593-7.

This is the third edition of what many call a classic work in criminal profiling. The text focused on behavioral and psychological profiling in solving violent crimes. The authors have included a new chapter since previous editions, which addresses crimes and the occult. The dark role that unconventional religious sects and Satanism can play in certain crimes was explored thoroughly.

Sexual crimes, and particularly the psychological profile of pedophiles, were also examined. The book is intended to be resource for the criminal justice practitioner, as well as for students destined for careers in investigating violent and often bizarre crimes.

Jackson, Janet, and Debra Bekerian, eds. *Offender Profiling: Theory, Research, and Practice.* Indianapolis, IN: Wiley Publishing. 1998. 254 pp. ISBN: 0-471-97565-6.

This text is a compilation of works by several authors whose expertise lies in profiling as an investigative tool. Some of the chapters in this book focus on the role of personality theories in developing offender profiles, the use of databases in investigatory profiling, and geographic profiling. Although this type of profiling cannot be equated with racial profiling or gender profiling per se, the criteria of race, gender, culture, geography, and other objective factors are potential component parts in developing an offender profile. This text, through its contributors, helped distinguish unlawful and unethical profiling based on prejudice from profiling based on objective observations and facts.

Kocsis, Richard, ed. *Criminal Profiling: International Theory, Research and Practice.* Totowa, NJ: Humana Press. 2007. 413 pp. ISBN: 978-1-60327-146-2.

Richard Kocsis is a forensic psychologist and one of the world's leading experts on behavioral profiling. He was one of the first scholars to scientifically test the validity of psychological and other forms of profiling. Indeed, some of his studies were not well-received by many profiling consultants, as the validity of some techniques had doubt cast upon them by Kocsis' research. In this book, Kocsis assembles several scholars and practitioners to contribute chapters on a wide range of profiling practices, including behavioral profiling, geographic profiling, pattern analysis, and offense-specific profiling in murder, sex assault, and terrorism cases. A large section of the book is set aside for chapters which specifically challenge the validity and reliability of profiling techniques—not to persuade readers to abandon profiling as a tool, but to improve profiling practices.

Malkin, Michelle. *In Defense of Internment: The Case for Racial Profiling in World War II and the War on Terror.* Washington, DC: Regnery Publishing. 2004. 376 pp. ISBN: 0-89526-051-4.

This book represents one of the more controversial books highlighted in this chapter. The thesis of the book, which was written shortly after the 9/11 attacks, is that sometimes racial, ethnic, and/or religious profiling is necessary to keep the country safe. It is authored by Michelle Malkin, a leading conservative political commentator. However, the tenor of this book is much more like an academic, historical account of the topic than a pundit's talking points. Malkin makes her case not by focusing on the 9/11 terror attack; rather she examines the internment of Japanese Americans and resident aliens during World War II. It should be noted that Malkin herself is not white—she was born to Filipino parents. Through historical documents relating to internment, not just of those of Japanese descent but also German and Italian descent, she argues that the relocation effort and the creation of residential camps was a reasonable step to protect American military facilities from sabotage. She goes on to state that the collective guilt over the whole episode is misguided. Then, from there, Malkin defends the policy of President George Bush to round up and detain illegal immigrants of Arab decent in the days and weeks after 9/11.

The book is very well supported by original sources and certainly does a very good job of defending a position that is rarely defended—specifically, that the security of the nation requires that profiling along racial, ethnic, and religious lines is rational and should be done. If one is interested in an earnest and articulate presentation of the arguments for profiling in a time of crisis or war, this book fits the bill.

Marks, Kenneth. *Driving while Black: Highways, Shopping Malls, Taxi Cabs, Sidewalks: How to Fight Back if You Are a Victim of Racial Profiling.* New York: Broadway Publishing. 2000. 272 pp. ISBN: 0-7679-0549-0.

This publication is framed as a handbook for surviving police encounters. Its premise is that class, age, race, and dress (such as baggy pants or baseball caps on sideways) are factors in who will have encounters with the police, whether one's objective behavior warrants such an encounter or not. It also speaks to readers who believe they have been discriminated against in other ways outside of the criminal justice system, such as cab drivers failing to stop for a black man on the corner in favor of a white man farther down the street, or a black person being persistently followed by mall or store security when browsing. The book provided guidance on what actions can be taken when one believes one's civil rights have been violated.

Milovanovic, Dragon, and Katheryn Russell, eds. *Petit Apartheid in the U.S. Criminal Justice System.* Durham, NC: Carolina Academic Press. 2001. 124 pp. ISBN: 0-89089-951-7.

This publication took a theoretical approach to explaining the relationship of African Americans to the criminal justice system. Contributions from different authors form the various chapters of the book. The chapters included discussions of racial profiling in the drug war, the perspective of African American officers in policing other African Americans, the interest in law enforcement held by African Americans, and how "petit apartheid" is manifested at the macro as well as micro levels.

Mogul, Joey L., Andrea J. Ritchie, and Kay Whitlock. *Queer (In)Justice: The Criminalization of LGBT People in the United States.* Boston: Beacon Press. 2011. 216 pp. ISBN: 978-0-80705116-0.

This book is one of the few presented in this chapter which explores the lesbian, gay, bisexual, and transgender (LGBT) perspective on the criminal justice system. It examines for readers the experiences of LGBT people as suspects of crime, as defendants on trial, as prisoners in our correctional system, and as victims of crime. In exploring these issues, the authors consider some stereotypes associated with gay crime, including the notion of "lethal lesbians," "gleeful gay killers," "deceptive gender benders," "disease spreaders," and other characterizations. Through the accounts of LGBT people who have experienced the criminal justice system, the authors conclude that the system reinforces racial and gender inequalities in American society.

Muhammad, Khalil Gibran. *The Condemnation of Blackness: Race, Crime, and the Making of Modern Urban America*. Cambridge, MA: Harvard University Press. 2011. 392 pp. ISBN: 0-67406-211-6.

> This publication weaves for readers a detailed history of blacks in America and how criminal statutes were used early in America's history to subjugate them. The history of Jim Crow laws and practices is explored, as is their manifestation in urban areas of northern states in the form of racist law enforcement. The indispensability of promulgating the notion of black criminality around the turn of the 20th century in order to keep blacks in their place is discussed. To be sure, the author has a critical agenda. But he delivers a very compelling historical account of the plight of blacks in relation to the justice system in the United States and how that experience has shaped America into what we see today.

Nance, Malcolm W. *Terrorist Recognition Handbook: A Practitioner's Manual for Predicting and Identifying Terrorist Activities*. 3rd ed. Boca Raton, FL: CRC Press. 2013. 439 pp. ISBN: 1-46655-457-6.

> This book was first published in 2003. It was driven by the desire to understand our enemies after 9/11. In subsequent editions, it has been updated to reflect the latest information about terror threats against Americans on American soil. The book spends considerable amounts of space to discuss who terrorists are, how terror groups are organized, what they believe, and why they embrace terror tactics. The author also introduces the reader to how terrorists train and select targets for the campaigns they wage. A full six chapters are devoted to the recognition and detection of terrorists, terror attacks, and tactics

through what is effectively a form of profiling and pattern analysis. The book is especially useful for law enforcement officers and other public officials who, as a part of their jobs, must confront the issue of terrorism on the home front.

Nelson, David Erik. *Racial Profiling.* Detroit: Greenhaven Press. 2009. 264 pp. ISBN: 0-73774-223-2.

The author of this book tackles the regularly asked questions about racial profiling, including whether it exists, should it be used in the fight against terrorism, is profiling effective, and what are the negative consequences that come from it. The book attempts to offer balanced treatment of the subject by advancing opposing viewpoints.

Pampel, Fred C. *Racial Profiling.* New York: Facts on File Publishing. 2004. 284 pp. ISBN: 0-81605-592-0.

This book offers readers a general overview of the issue of racial profiling. It also spends considerable portions of the book covering key legal cases involving racial profiling, including but not limited to the Justice Department's suit of the New Jersey State Police in the late 1990s. A guide to research on the topic of profiling is offered along with a thorough bibliography.

Peterson, Dana, and Vanessa R. Panfil, eds. *Handbook of LGBT Communities, Crime, and Justice.* New York: Springer. 2014. 587 pp. ISBN: 1-46149-187-8.

This publication is a scholarly, research-oriented exploration of sexual orientation, gender identity, and gender expression in patterns of offending, excluding sex work. The book delves into the experiences of LGBT offenders with the police, the courts, and correctional institutions. In doing so, the book reviews the scholarly literature relating to LGBT criminology. It also advances the latest research on the dynamics of the criminal justice system's interaction with members of the LGBT community. The book serves as a solid foundation for exploring LGBT criminology further.

O'Reilly, James. *Police Traffic Stops and Racial Profiling: Resolving Management, Labor, and Civil Rights Conflicts.* Springfield, IL: Charles C. Thomas Publishing. 2002. 304 pp. ISBN: 0-398-07295-7.

> The book is broken into four main parts. The first part addressed the issue of racial profiling within the specific context of traffic stops. The legal standards necessary for police encounters and detentions were explained, along with the political ramifications that accompany the practice of racial profiling. The second part of the book looked at the multitude of remedies for the practice of profiling, as advocated by civil rights activists, the courts, and politicians. The third part of the text addressed in detail the role of politics and elected officials in responding to racial profiling. Additionally, the role that the police unions play, as a political constituency, was addressed. Last, the book offered preventative steps that police administrations and communities can take to avoid the controversy that invariably comes with the practice of profiling.

Turvey, Brent. *Criminal Profiling: An Introduction to Behavioral Evidence Analysis.* 4th ed. Oxford, UK: Academic Press. 2011. 679 pp. ISBN: 0-12385-243-9.

> This book, first published in 1999, is now in its fourth edition. It is considered one of the premier textbooks on behavioral profiling. It is suitable as a text for working criminal investigators as well as would-be sleuths. This text teaches the deductive reasoning approach to investigative work, covering case types such as homicides, arson, stalking, and sex offenses. Turvey's deductive

profiling approach treats criminal profiling as an investigative process that requires the investigator to gain a genuine understanding of behavioral and environmental contributions to criminality. This book does not examine profiling from a racial, gender, religious, or sexual orientation consciousness, except insofar as these characteristics inform the investigator about cultural or environmental issues of relevance in a particular instance of criminality.

Vogel, Robert. *Fighting to Win.* Nashville: Turner Publishing. 2001. 248 pp. ISBN: 1-56311-627-8.

In this book, famed Florida law enforcer Robert Vogel described his career as a Florida state trooper and then as a sheriff. Vogel explained his effort to fight drug trafficking throughout his career and addressed the controversy surrounding the practice of profiling. Vogel defended the practice of profiling drug runners as an effective and ethical law enforcement tool. He attempted to debunk the criticisms that his brand of profiling was racist and unfair. The bulk of his book discussed his ultimately successful legal fight with his critics and with the U.S. Department of Justice over the practice of profiling.

Walker, Samuel, and Carol Archbold. *The New World of Police Accountability.* 2nd ed. Thousand Oaks, CA: SAGE. 2014. 320 pages. ISBN: 978-1452286877.

In this publication, Samuel Walker and Carol Archbold examine police accountability vis-à-vis encounters with members of the public involving the use of force, searches and seizures, alleged racial discrimination, and other aspects of policing. The authors thoroughly explain the federal government's role in rooting out unconstitutional behavior through "pattern or practice" investigations of law enforcement agencies and the use of consent decrees. The authors explore early intervention systems which might be put in place within a police organization to identify officer misconduct before it becomes problematic and systemic. Of particular interest to police administrators is a chapter on using risk management strategies to increase police accountability and decrease liability.

Walker, Samuel, Cassia Spohn, and Miriam DeLone. *The Color of Justice: Race, Ethnicity, and Crime in America.* 5th ed. Belmont, CA: Wadsworth. 2011. 560 pp. ISBN: 1-11134-692-5.

This book, in an updated fifth edition (having first been published in 1996), remains a scholarly classic on the subject of race, ethnicity, and criminal justice. The authors are all highly esteemed criminal justice professors and criminological theorists. The book is rich with theories of crime that relate to race, ethnicity, and inequality. The book is also replete with facts and figures and a offers a chapter on the myths and realities regarding the race and ethnicity of offenders and victims alike. Predictably, the book covers policing and race. But especially helpful are the several chapters that relate to prosecution decisions, adjudication, and sentencing. The book also includes chapters relating to disparities in correctional institutions, the imposition of the death penalty, and minority juvenile offenders. For the most part, the authors present a balanced and straight-forward discussion of the issues.

Williams, Mary, ed. *Discrimination.* San Diego: Greenhaven Press. 2002. 200 pp. ISBN: 0-7377-1226-0.

This is a compilation of essays addressing the degree of discrimination in society being felt by racial minorities, women, and homosexuals. Although the book is not exclusively devoted to discrimination within the context of the U.S. criminal justice system, a number of the essays do touch pervasive discrimination by justice officials.

Further, the general discussions and arguments that emerged from the various essays have relevance to the justice system if only because the justice system is made up of people, and it is in the hearts of people, either because of malice or unwitting ignorance, that the roots of discrimination are found.

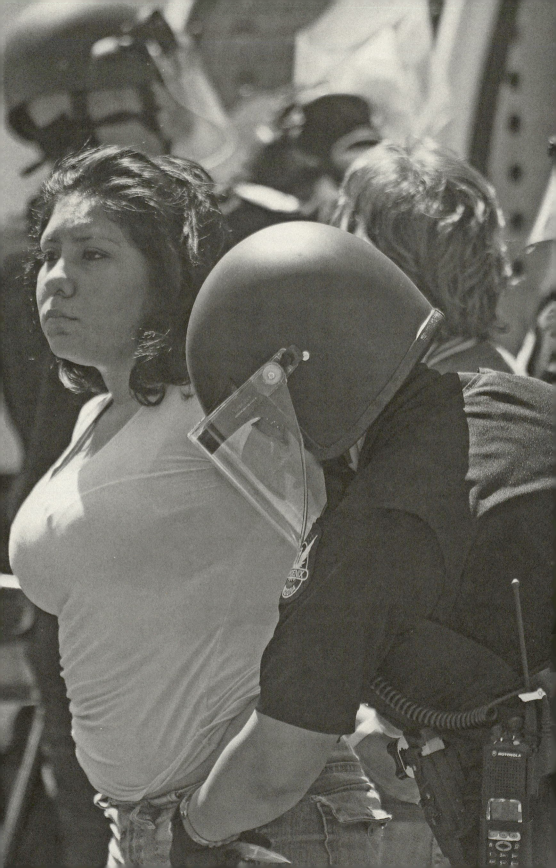

The purpose of this chapter is to provide a timeline of significant events that relate directly or indirectly (but significantly) to the issue of criminal profiling. Many elements of the timeline also appear elsewhere in this book. Even so, events are presented here with brief explanations in order to present an overall, albeit abbreviated, picture of the relevant history behind profiling in the criminal justice system along race, gender, and other lines.

**1704**  South Carolina legislatively establishes the first slave patrol in the American colonies. The slave patrols serve in a law enforcement capacity with the primary duties of searching slave quarters for contraband, dispersing slave gatherings, and generally safeguarding communities from marauding slaves by patrolling the roads.

**1727**  Virginia legislatively establishes a slave patrol similar to South Carolina's.

**1753**  North Carolina legislatively establishes a slave patrol similar to South Carolina's.

**1764**  Cesare Beccaria publishes *Essay on Crimes and Punishments*, which articulates the themes of what is now known as classical criminology. The thrust of this criminological theory is that

A protester is arrested in Phoenix, Arizona, during a public demonstration against SB1070, which became law in 2010. The law, among other things, requires police officers to verify one's immigration or residence status if the officer has reasonable suspicion to believe the suspect is in the United States illegally. (Darren Hauck/epa/Corbis) people commit crimes after making rational choices; consequently, swift and certain punishment must result from criminal deeds in order to deter people, through rationalization, from choosing criminal behavior.

**1800**    Franz Joseph Gall develops "phrenology," as published in his work *Anatomy and Physiology of the Nervous System, and of the Brain in Particular*. Phrenologists believe that mental functions, including deviant thoughts and behavior, come from localized parts of the brain. Consequently, phrenologists of the day believe that an examination of one's skull can predict inferiority among races of people and propensities to commit crime.

**1829**    Phrenology becomes a widespread theory in the United States to help explain deviance; the acceptance of the theory is due to the work of Gaspar Spurzheim, a former student of Franz Joseph Gall.

**1829**    The Metropolitan Police Act passes in the British Parliament, creating the Metropolitan Police of London. The force, known as the "Met," is headed by Sir Robert Peel and is the first modern civil police organization. It is mandated to emphasize crime prevention, community relations, maintaining order without violence to the extent possible—many of the themes of modern-day community policing.

**1850s**    Political era of policing. Law enforcement in the United States during this time is largely a tool of the political machines in power in any given city. Police officers are hired and promoted based on who they know politically and what they have done for the political bosses, whether it be financial donations, getting out the vote efforts, or similar activities. Much of the effort of law enforcement during this period is devoted to service-related duties, such as soup kitchens, driving ambulances, and so on, as these activities are politically popular.

**1857**    *Dred Scott v. Sandford*. The U.S. Supreme Court rules that blacks whose ancestors were brought to America as slaves were not included in the Constitution when it mentioned the "people of the United States" or "citizens." Because they were a "subordinate and inferior class of beings, who had been subjugated by the dominant race . . . they had no rights or privileges" under the Constitution, even in slave-free territories and states.

**1860s**    Laws emerge throughout the South in the United States to keep blacks and whites separated. State legislatures throughout the former Confederacy pass laws requiring dining facilities, recreational facilities, public transportation seating, bathrooms, drinking fountains, and a host of other accommodations to be separated for use according to race. Blacks are not permitted to use "whites only" accommodations, nor are whites permitted to use "colored" accommodations, although there is rarely a desire for the latter, since accommodations for blacks are always substandard. These laws requiring separate accommodations are known as "Jim Crow" laws.

**1866**    Ku Klux Klan (KKK) is formed as a fraternal organization in Pulaski, Tennessee. Its members are former officers of the Confederate Army. In short order, the group gains popularity and membership grows. The scope of its purpose also grows beyond the bounds of fraternity. The KKK becomes a group of marauders who intimidate, assault, terrorize, and murder newly freed blacks.

**1868**    The Fourteenth Amendment to the Constitution of the United States is ratified, thus giving all people born or naturalized in the United States the rights of citizenship. States are prohibited from depriving any person of life, liberty, or property without due process of law.

**1871**    The Ku Klux Act passes in the U.S. Congress and is signed into law. The law calls for civil and criminal sanctions against any persons who would infringe upon another's civil rights and gives the government the authority to use force to intervene against those who would deny others their civil rights.

**1875**    The Civil Rights Act of 1875 passes in the U.S. Congress and is signed into law. This law makes it a criminal and civil offense to deny other people, regardless of race or previous condition of servitude, full and equal enjoyment of public accommodations, advantages, facilities, theaters, public conveyances on land and water, and other places of amusement. The law also prohibits discrimination in jury selection for state and federal courts on the basis of race and color. The law is to be enforced by U.S. marshals and violations prosecuted in federal courts.

**1876**    Cesare Lombroso publishes *Criminal Man* and presents the theory of atavism. This theory argues that criminals are born to be criminals because of primitive and savage biological traits. This Darwinian theory was widely accepted in the United States in the late 19th century and the first half of the 20th century and was used by some in criminal justice to justify oppressing certain peoples, such as African Americans, to prevent their inevitable criminal deeds.

**1879**    *Strauder v. West Virginia*. The U.S. Supreme Court rules that a criminal defendant who is a racial minority is denied his equal protection rights under the law when members of his race are purposefully excluded from the jury. The West Virginia law that says only white males can serve as jurors is declared unconstitutional because of the racial litmus test of being white. Not addressed is the issue of whether limiting jurors to males is permissible. The court's silence on the issue allows that practice to continue.

**1886**    *Yick Wo v. Hopkins*. The U.S. Supreme Court rules that prosecutors may not consider the race of a criminal suspect when deciding whether to charge someone. Prosecutors maintain discretion in charging decisions and are permitted even some degree of caprice in their decisions, as long as race in no way enters into the decision-making process.

**1896**    *Plessy v. Ferguson*. The U.S. Supreme Court rules that Jim Crow laws are constitutionally permissible as long as the separate accommodations for blacks are equal to those for whites. Further, the Court rules that the Fourteenth

Amendment's Equal Protection Clause does not require social equality among the races; it only requires political equality.

**1905**   August Vollmer becomes town marshal, and then police chief, for the city of Berkeley, California. He is widely regarded as the father of professional policing in the United States. Vollmer is among the first law enforcement administrators to require formal academic police training for rank and file officers. He is also known for putting his officers in patrol cars, and later, putting radios in those patrol cars, to enhance police presence and response times.

**1910s**   Progressive era of policing begins to emerge. Law enforcement in the United States during this period largely moves away from overt political influence in favor of reforms that are taking place in government generally. In particular, police organizations begin to move autonomous authority into the position of police chief, personnel are selected and promoted on the basis of merit, professional training is required of officers, and the emphasis for police becomes law enforcement rather than service.

**1920**   The Nineteenth Amendment to the U.S. Constitution is ratified, granting women the constitutional right to vote in federal, state, and local elections.

**1940**   *Cantwell v. Connecticut.* The U.S. Supreme Court rules that the criminal prosecution and conviction of three Jehovah's Witnesses for sharing the faith without a solicitation license and for breaching the peace is unconstitutional. The court rules that criminal laws, when applied to constrain legitimate religious practice, violate the First Amendment's No Establishment Clause.

**1942**   In the wake of war declared against Japan by the United States, President Franklin Roosevelt issues an executive order authorizing the creation of military zones that persons of Japanese descent may not enter. These military zones cumulatively include the entire West Coast of the United States to a depth inland of about 40 miles. During the war, approximately

112,000 persons of Japanese descent are involuntarily relocated from the West Coast to war relocation camps run by the U.S. military.

**1944**   *Korematsu v. United States*. The U.S. Supreme Court rules that the prosecution of a U.S. citizen of Japanese descent for entering a prohibited military zone—in this case, Korematsu's home—was constitutional. Korematsu's rights under the Fourteenth Amendment were not violated by his prosecution. The court also rules, however, that once Japanese Americans' loyalty to the United States can be ascertained, they may no longer be held involuntarily in the military relocation camps.

**1947**   A report is published by President Harry Truman's Committee on Civil Rights. The report declares that every citizen, regardless of race, is entitled to four basic rights: to be safe and secure in their person, to freely exercise the privileges of citizenship and civic duty, to be free in conscience and expression, and to have equal opportunity. The committee goes on record to acknowledge that the first right—to be safe and secure in one's person—is severely threatened, particularly for minorities, by the practices of arbitrary arrest and police brutality.

**1954**   *Brown v. Board of Education of Topeka*. The U.S. Supreme Court rules that "separate but equal" is inherently unequal and therefore unconstitutional. This ruling reverses the precedent set in *Plessy v. Ferguson*, which upheld racial segregation law in the South. In this case, the Court determines that even when facilities, opportunities, curriculum, and other amenities are in fact equal in quality, which is rare, there is still inequality because of the social harm minorities succumb to that is caused by segregation.

**1957**   Civil Rights Act of 1957. This, the first civil rights act to be passed by Congress since 1875, creates the U.S. Commission on Civil Rights. The purpose of the commission is to investigate voting rights violations and denial of equal protection under the law. The act also clarifies the qualifications to be a federal juror, reinforcing the fact that race, ethnicity, and religion should have no part in disqualifying one for jury duty. Finally, certain criminal penalties are prescribed for violating the act.

**1961**   *Hoyt v. Florida.* The U.S. Supreme Court rules that a Florida law that systematically excludes women from becoming jurors does not invalidate the murder conviction by an all-male jury of a female accused of killing her husband. The Court is asked by Hoyt to apply the standard of "strict scrutiny" to Florida's law—customary when a "suspected class" is involved—but it refuses. Instead, the Court applies only the "ordinary equal protection scrutiny" standard. Hoyt's conviction is upheld.

**1961**   *Mapp v. Ohio.* The U.S. Supreme Court rules that evidence obtained by police without a search warrant, when such a warrant is required, must be excluded from use at trial. Thus, the exclusionary rule now applies to all levels of law enforcement, not just to federal law enforcement as it had since the 1920s. Exemplifying the dramatic impact of this case on police practice, in the year prior to Mapp, New York City police officers do not bother to obtain even one search warrant. In the year following Mapp, the same department obtains over 800 warrants.

**1963**   Martin Luther King Jr. delivers his famous "I have a dream" speech from the steps of the Lincoln Memorial in Washington, D.C., to over 200,000 people in attendance. In his speech, he references the police brutality suffered by blacks in the South as well as in the urban North.

**1964**   The Twenty-Fourth Amendment to the U.S. Constitution is ratified. This amendment outlaws any poll tax or other tax imposed on prospective voters for the right to vote. Leading up to this amendment, poll taxes had been an effective means in southern states for excluding blacks, who were generally poorer than whites, from voting.

**1964**   Freedom summer. Civil rights activists from college campuses in the North, along with black activists living in the South, seek to educate eligible black Mississippi voters on how to vote and get them registered to vote. A massive voter registration campaign is waged. Early in the campaign, three civil rights workers—Michael Schwerner, Andrew Goodman, and James Chaney—are arrested by local law enforcement in Neshoba County, Mississippi. They are released after posting bond and disappear. The Federal Bureau of Investigation later finds their fire-scorched vehicle and their murdered bodies in a rural swamp. The murders are the work of the local Ku Klux Klan. The sheriff and a deputy are among those charged with violating the civil rights of Schwerner, Goodman, and Chaney. The sheriff is eventually acquitted; the deputy and other local Klan members are convicted.

**1964**    The Civil Rights Act of 1964 passes in the U.S. Congress and is signed into law by President Lyndon Johnson. The purpose of the act is to eliminate racial segregation and other forms of discrimination. The act addresses discrimination in voting, employment, education, and segregation in public facilities. The act authorizes the U.S. attorney general to take legal action on behalf of individuals who are discriminated against. The act also prohibits federal funds from going to any organization that discriminates. Finally, the act creates the Equal Employment Opportunity Commission to ensure that the right to fair employment is not infringed upon because of one's race, color, religion, sex, or national origin. Hiring and firing decisions based on these criteria are outlawed. Exceptions exist for religious and Indian organizations.

**1965**    *Griswold v. Connecticut.* The U.S. Supreme Court rules that a right to privacy exists in the U.S. Constitution despite not being expressly mentioned therein. The Court reasons that a right to privacy can be found in the "penumbra" of the Fourteenth Amendment's rights of due process and equal protection. In this case particularly, the court finds that a state law making it a crime to prescribe or use contraceptives is unconstitutional. The Court says married couples

have a right to privacy with respect to their sexual and repro-
ductive choices.

**1968**    *Terry v. Ohio.* The U.S. Supreme Court rules that it
is permissible for police officers to temporarily stop and detain persons, without a warrant, when an officer has reasonable
suspicion that a particular person is engaged in, or about to
be engaged in, committing a crime. This investigatory detention must be brief unless probable cause is developed through
the encounter so that an arrest can be made. The Court also
rules that a pat down of the suspect for weapons is permissible
without warrant if reasonable suspicion exists that the suspect
is armed.

**1968**    The Omnibus Crime Control and Safe Streets Act of
1968 is passed in the U.S. Congress and signed into law. This
legislation, among many other things, authorizes the U.S. attorney general to pursue civil litigation against those persons
or organizations, including state and local governments, who
discriminate against others on the basis of race, color, national
origin, gender, or religion. The act also establishes the Law
Enforcement Assistance Administration, which over time provides more than $7 billion to police agencies and institutions
of higher education to research and develop better, more professional police practices.

**Late 1960s**    U.S. airlines and law enforcement team up to
develop a profile of potential air hijackers, or "skyjackers." The
need for developing such a profile is great during this time as
a rash of hijackings take place. In 1968, 18 U.S. airliners are
hijacked. In 1969, more than 30 U.S. airliners are hijacked.
The federal government also creates its Air Marshal program to
put armed law enforcement officers on board selected flights to
deal with hijackings should they arise.

**1972**    *Yoder v. Wisconsin.* The U.S. Supreme Court rules that
a state law requiring school attendance for children through
the 12th grade is unconstitutional in that it unlawfully requires Amish children to attend. The Court rejects a lower

court decision that requires a practice of a religious group to be central and inseparable in that group's theology before First Amendment protections would kick in. A lower court has said that for the Amish, having children not attend school after the eighth grade is essentially a community lifestyle issue, not an inherently religious one. The Supreme Court, however, simply says a practice must be "rooted in religious belief," as is the Amish's communal and simple lifestyle, to be protected by the First Amendment.

**1972**  *Eisenstadt v. Baird.* The U.S. Supreme Court rules that the constitutional right to privacy afforded to a married couple in *Griswold v. Connecticut* extends to unmarried heterosexual couples as well.

**1975**  Freda Adler publishes *Sisters in Crime*, which is the major early work in feminist criminology. This publication sets out to explain the differences in crime rates between men and women. Adler explains the differences as largely being due to the lack of opportunity for women in society. Just as women are denied equal access to legitimate endeavors, likewise the same lack of access throughout society inhibits their ability or desire to pursue illegitimate endeavors.

**1975**  *Taylor v. Louisiana.* The U.S. Supreme Court rules that the jury selection laws in Louisiana, which require women to register an interest in being considered for jury duty whereas men are simply drawn from the county rolls, is unconstitutional as it has the effect of systematically excluding women. This decision effectively reverses *Hoyt v. Florida.*

**Late 1970s**  The community policing model of law enforcement emerges to compete with, if not replace, the professional model of policing. With community policing, an emphasis is placed on building relationships between police officers and members of the community being policed. Partnership is a key concept, as opposed to the more standoffish and neutral approach to the public inherent to the profession model. An additional emphasis is placed on problem solving by officers and community members; abandoned is the strictly reaction orientation of the professional model.

**1979** *Delaware v. Prouse.* The U.S. Supreme Court rules that the decision to stop a black motorist without observing a traffic or equipment violation is unconstitutional under the Fourth Amendment's protection against unreasonable searches and seizures. In this case, the Court declares once and for all that stopping people for reasons ranging from an officer's outright racial bias to an officer's legitimately felt hunch is unacceptable absent an objectively observable violation.

**1982** James Q. Wilson and George Kelling, both criminologists, publish *Broken Windows*, which theorizes that visible urban decay fosters criminal activity. Consequently, if one wants to deter and reduce crime in one's neighborhood, one needs a neighborhood that appears to care. Broken windows need to be fixed; abandoned vehicles need to be towed; garbage needs to be picked up. And police need to aggressively pursue nuisance offenders, such as prostitutes, truants, vagrants, panhandlers, and petty drug dealers.

**1985** Crack cocaine explodes on the scene as the illegal drug of choice in New York City. It is a smokable form of cocaine that is cheap and very addictive. In the coming months and years, crack use and addiction spread throughout the United States—particularly in the urban inner cities.

**1986** The Anti-Drug Abuse Act is passed by the U.S. Congress and signed into law by President Ronald Reagan. This legislation signals the beginning of the War on Drugs. Drug dealers and drug cartels become federal law enforcement's public enemy number one. The act devotes nearly $2 billion to fight the drug epidemic. It allocates nearly $100 million to build new prisons, $200 million for drug education, and $241 million for drug treatment programs. The act creates mandatory minimum federal prison sentences for drug offenses. Crack cocaine, used more by minorities and the poor, draws stiffer penalties than powder cocaine, used more commonly by the white middle and upper class. The federal prison population grows exponentially in the coming years as a result of low-level drug offenders being sentenced to mandatory federal prison terms.

**1986**    *Bowers v. Hardwick.* The U.S. Supreme Court upholds the conviction of two homosexuals who were charged with sodomy. The Court refuses to extend the Fourteenth Amendment's implied right of privacy from *Griswold v. Connecticut* to consenting adults engaged in sodomy.

**1986**    *Batson v. Kentucky.* The U.S. Supreme Court overturns the conviction of a black defendant because the prosecutor had used his right of peremptory challenges to exclude blacks from the jury. In this case, the prosecutor fails to articulate that there is some other reason besides the race of the prospective jurors that causes him to exclude all blacks. The Court states that although peremptory challenges can be based on almost any reason, race cannot be a factor in peremptory challenges.

**1989**    Volusia County, Florida, Sheriff Bob Vogel establishes the Selective Enforcement Team to interdict drug trafficking on Interstate 95, which runs north/south through the county and connects Miami, Florida, to the Mid-Atlantic and Northeast. In three years, the team seizes $8 million in forfeitable cash from drug offenders and untold scores of drugs heading for market. Vogel and his Selective Enforcement Team are controversial, as almost immediately after the team is created, there appears to be racial bias against blacks and Hispanics in the decision by officers of whom to stop.

**1989**    *U.S. v. Sokolow.* The U.S. Supreme Court rules law enforcement's development and use of drug courier profiles is permissible in developing reasonable suspicion to warrant an investigatory detention. The Court states that profiles consisting of many factors, and not based solely or primarily on race, are constitutional.

**1991**    *Powers v. Ohio.* The U.S. Supreme Court rules that a racially discriminatory use of peremptory challenges to exclude blacks from a jury is unconstitutional even when the accused on trial is white. Racially motivated peremptory challenges are unconstitutional regardless of the similarity or difference in race between those prospective jurors excluded and the person on trial. Powers's murder conviction is reversed, and he is granted a new trial.

**1991**    Motorist Rodney King flees from the California Highway Patrol and the Los Angeles Police Department in a motor vehicle at speeds of over 110 miles per hour. His vehicle is cut off by squads and the chase ends. During the attempt to subdue King, Los Angeles police officers Lawrence Powell, Theodore Briseno, and Timothy Wind and Sgt. Stacey Koon are videotaped delivering more than 50 baton blows before handcuffing King.

**1992**    The four Los Angeles police officers in the Rodney King beating are tried in California district court for use of excessive force and assault against King. Sgt. Stacey Koon and Officers Timothy Wind and Theodore Briseno are acquitted on all charges. Officer Lawrence Powell is acquitted on all but one charge, about which the jury could not reach a decision. The acquittals lead to a race riot in South Central Los Angeles. The riots result in the deaths of 52 people, 7,000 arrests, and more than $1 billion in damaged property.

**1993**    Los Angeles police officers Lawrence Powell, Timothy Wind, and Theodore Briseno and Sgt. Stacey Koon are tried in federal court for violating Rodney King's civil rights. Sgt. Koon and Officer Powell are convicted and sentenced to 30 months in federal prison. Officers Wind and Briseno are acquitted.

**1994**    Rodney King sues the City of Los Angeles and LAPD officers Powell, Wind, Briseno and Sgt. Koon in civil court for violating his civil rights. The city of Los Angeles stipulates liability and is ordered to pay King $3.8 million. The civil jury finds none of the four officers liable and awards King zero dollars in damages from each officer.

**1994**    *J.E.B. v. Alabama*. The U.S. Supreme Court extends the logic the Court articulated in *Batson v. Kentucky* to the issue of gender. The Court rules that, just as race cannot be used as a basis for peremptory challenges to prospective jurors, neither can gender.

**1994**    The Violent Crime Control and Law Enforcement Act passes the U.S. Congress and is signed by President Bill Clinton. The act is a sweeping omnibus crime bill with a wide range of provisions including enhancing the federal death penalty, enhancing the protection of women against domestic violence, fine-tuning antiterrorism laws, establishing the Police Corps training program, allocating grants for community policing initiatives, and strengthening the U.S. Department of Justice in addressing the issue of police misconduct. In particular, the Special

**1994**    Litigation Section of the Justice Department is empowered under Title 42 to pursue civil relief when police officers individually or collectively as a department engage in a pattern and practice of misconduct and civil rights violations.

**1995**    Five Philadelphia police officers are convicted of fabricating evidence against African Americans in that city. The convictions call into question approximately 1,500 prosecutions involving those officers.

**1996**    *Romer v. Evans.* The U.S. Supreme Court rules that Amendment 2 to Colorado's constitution, which prohibits governmental bodies from adopting special laws protecting homosexuals from discrimination, violates the Equal Protection Clause of the Fourteenth Amendment of the U.S. Constitution. The Court finds that singling out a group, in this case homosexuals, and banning them from seeking additional protections while all other groups may still lobby for additional protections is unconstitutional.

**1996**    *Whren v. U.S.* The U.S. Supreme Court rules that the motives of police officers for stopping a motorist are irrelevant if an actual violation of the law, no matter how minor, is observed. In other words, police may use traffic and equipment violations as bases for a stop, even though the police may have little interest in traffic enforcement and may be fishing for more serious offenders. The Court refuses to adopt a standard for officers that would require no pretext before a stop could be made.

**1996** New Jersey Superior Court judge Robert E. Francis throws out 19 drug-possession cases, concluding that state troopers patrolling the New Jersey Turnpike had improperly singled out and stopped black motorists.

**1997** Under the authority granted to it in the Violent Crime Control and Law Enforcement Act of 1994, the U.S. Justice Department enters into consent decrees with the following police agencies in order to monitor reforms to which the police agencies agree: Steubenville, Ohio, Police Department; Pittsburgh, Pennsylvania, Police Department. In agreeing to the conditions of the consent decree, the police departments avoid further litigation against the federal government.

**1998** Four African American males driving a rented van on the New Jersey Turnpike are pulled over by state troopers. During the traffic stop, the troopers open fire on the van, wounding three, two critically. No drugs or contraband are found, and no charges are filed against the four occupants of the van. The state awards the four occupants nearly $13 million in a civil settlement. The troopers involved in the incident are convicted of making an unlawful stop. The troopers go on record, saying that racial profiling is the policy of the New Jersey State Police.

**1999** The New Jersey state legislature passes a resolution asking or the U.S. attorney general to investigate allegations of racial bias and profiling by the New Jersey State Police. The resolution notes that the New Jersey attorney general's office is not in a position to be impartial, thus requiring federal review.

**1999** The U.S. Department of Justice settles a lawsuit against the New Jersey State Police, resulting in a consent decree whereby a federal monitor oversees the effort by the state police to implement 97 agreed-upon reforms, including providing additional training to troopers on civil rights, installing computer tracking systems for tracking traffic stop data, and installing video cameras in every squad car.

**1999**   The Traffic Stops Statistics Study Act is introduced in the Senate and the House. The bill requires the U.S. attorney general to conduct a nationwide study of traffic stops by law enforcement officers. The study would seek to identify the violations for which motorists were stopped, motorist identifier information (race, gender, ethnicity, and approximate age), number of occupants in vehicles stopped, whether searches were conducted by the officers, duration of the stops, and disposition of the cases. Federal funds would be appropriated to help state and local governments pay for the study. The bill does not pass.

**2000**   New Jersey governor Christine Todd Whitman causes some controversy when she is photographed frisking a black man while out on patrol with a state trooper. The black man has been stopped for suspicious activity but is not ultimately arrested as no law has been violated.

**2000**   U.S. Department of Justice enters into a consent decree with the Montgomery County, Maryland, Police Department in order to monitor reforms to which the agency agrees. In agreeing to the conditions of the consent decree, the police department avoids further litigation against the federal government.

**2000**   The U.S. Senate Judiciary Committee holds hearings to investigate the issue of racial profiling and its pervasiveness in American society. Senator John Ashcroft, who later becomes the U.S. attorney general, chairs the hearings. Victims of racial profiling are called to testify, as are police officers and other law enforcement officials with varying views on the issue.

**2001**   President George W. Bush, in his first address to a joint session of Congress, decries the practice of racial profiling by law enforcement officers. He further pledges to help end the practice of racial profiling in the United States.

**2001**  A Cincinnati police officer shoots and kills Timothy Thomas, an unarmed 19-year-old black man. The city erupts into rioting. Later, Officer Steve Roach is charged with the death of Thomas but is acquitted. The incident sparks a U.S. Justice Department investigation.

**2001**  U.S. Department of Justice enters into consent decrees with the following police agencies in order to monitor reforms to which the agencies agree: Highland Park, Illinois, Police Department; Washington, D.C., Metropolitan Police Department; Los Angeles Police Department. In agreeing to the conditions of the consent decree, the police departments avoid further litigation against the federal government.

**2001**  Four U.S. airliners are hijacked. Two airliners are flown into the twin towers of the World Trade Center in New York City, one airliner is flown into the Pentagon, and one airliner crashes in rural Pennsylvania when passengers attempt to retake the jet. It is believed that the last jet was heading for the White House or the U.S. Capitol building. Nineteen men of Arab descent accomplish the four hijackings. In the wake of this disaster, Americans begin to question the wisdom of disbanding racial profiling. In the days, weeks, and months following the tragedy, Arab visitors, immigrants, and Arab Americans are scrutinized by law enforcement and intelligence officials, as well as by regular (and now wary) Americans.

**2001**  The U.S. Patriot Act passes both houses of Congress and is signed into law by President George W. Bush. The law, among other things, makes it easier for federal law enforcement officers to conduct covert surveillance operations against suspected terrorists. Civil liberties groups decry the law and predict that the government will use it to infringe upon the rights of Arab Americans and Muslims. Supporters of the law respond that Americans will not tolerate another 9/11 and that the law is not race- or religion-specific. Further, supporters note that it would be unreasonable to ignore the fact that those who attacked the United States on 9/11 were all indeed Arab and were all Muslims.

**2002**    U.S. Department of Justice enters into consent decrees with the following police agencies in order to monitor reforms to which the agencies agree: Detroit Police Department; Buffalo, New York, Police Department; Columbus, Ohio, Police Department; Cincinnati, Ohio, Police Department. In agreeing to the conditions of the consent decree, the police departments avoid further litigation against the federal government.

**2003**    *Lawrence v. Texas.* U.S. Supreme Court rules that consenting adults have a constitutional right to sexual privacy. This applies to heterosexual and homosexual conduct. The ruling overturns the long-standing decision in *Bowers v. Hardwick.* In doing so, the antisodomy laws of 13 states are invalidated.

**2003**    The Department of Justice issues a policy for all of federal law enforcement that bans criminal justice profiling that is based solely or primarily on race or ethnicity—even where such profiling would otherwise be permitted by the Constitution and by-laws. Although the Supreme Court in Whren said that motives of officers do not matter, this directive requires federal law enforcement officers to act according to pure and racially neutral motives. Using race or ethnicity by federal officers absent specific and trustworthy information that a suspect of a particular race or ethnicity is involved in a crime, or operating while holding to generalized racial or ethnic stereotypes, is forbidden.

**2003**    The University of Minnesota School of Law releases a landmark study. The study involves the tracking of traffic stop information from 65 urban, suburban, and rural Minnesota law enforcement agencies. The study shows that white motorists are stopped less frequently than black, Hispanic, or Native American motorists. White motorists who are stopped, however, more frequently possess drugs or other contraband than do minorities. These findings hold true for urban, suburban, and rural contexts. Although debate rages around the methodological soundness of the study, it goes a long way toward dispelling the notion that minority motorists are stopped more because they more often than whites are in possession of contraband.

**2009**    The Matthew Shepard and James Byrd, Jr. Hate Crimes Prevention Act is passed in Congress and signed into law by President Barak Obama. The law expands the authority of the U.S. Department of Justice to investigate and prosecute violent crimes motivated by bias against another person on the basis of perceived race, national origin, religion, sexual orientation, gender identity, or disability.

**2010**    The Support Our Law Enforcement and Safe Neighborhoods Act (aka SB 1070) is passed by the Arizona Legislature and signed by Governor Jan Brewer. The law effectively makes it a crime to be in the State of Arizona while in the United States illegally. It authorizes Arizona peace officers to stop and question persons the officers had reasonable suspicion to believe were illegal aliens in order to verify their status. Supporters of the law believe that it is a necessary step for Arizona to take in light of weak immigration enforcement, particularly along the Arizona border, by federal authorities. Critics of the law worry that it will encourage the racial profiling of individuals who appeared to be Hispanic. The law's passage prompts demonstrations against it in cities around the country. There are also several organized boycotts of Arizona. The state, however, remains committed to the law in light of its popularity with voters within the state. In 2012, the U.S. Supreme Court rules that key elements of the law are unconstitutional because of the federal government's exclusive authority to regulate immigration under the Constitution, which the Court noted is supreme over state laws.

**2010**    U.S. Department of Justice enters into a consent decree with the Indianapolis Police Department in order to monitor reforms regarding discriminatory enforcement.

**2011**    U.S. Department of Justice enters into a consent decree with the Seattle Police Department in order to monitor reforms regarding the use of force abuses and discriminatory enforcement.

**2012**    On February 26, Trayvon Martin, a black teenage male, is shot and killed by George Zimmerman, an adult Hispanic male. Martin is shot while walking through a neighborhood where Zimmerman is a part of the Neighborhood Watch. The shooting spawns a nationwide public debate about profiling. It is widely believed that Martin was targeted for attention by Zimmerman simply because Martin is black and was wearing a dark hoodie sweatshirt. Zimmerman defenders argue that Zimmerman was indeed following Martin as a suspicious person, while at the same time on the phone with the police, but that the confrontation between the two was a result of Martin becoming the aggressor. After local prosecutors decline to charge Zimmerman because they believe it to be a case of self-defense, a special prosecutor later charges Zimmerman with murder after considerable pressure is felt to do so from the media coverage and the outcry from the black community. Zimmerman is eventually acquitted of all charges, having presented evidence at trial that Martin was indeed the initial physical aggressor.

**2012**    U.S. Department of Justice enters into consent decrees with the New Orleans Police Department, the Warren (OH) Police Department and the East Haven (CT) Police Department in order to monitor reforms regarding corruption, use of force abuses, a practice of unlawful searches, and discriminatory enforcement.

**2013**    A federal court rules as unconstitutional the decade-long policy of the New York Police Department to stop and frisk suspects of minor offenses whenever such encounters can be legally justified. The court finds that the NYPD policy is disproportionately applied to racial and ethnic minorities. It further finds that the reasonable suspicion calculations are evidently flawed on the part of officers because so few of the encounters actually result in the development of probable cause of a crime.

**2014**  Attorney General Eric Holder, with the support of President Barak Obama, lobbies Congress for changes to the federal sentencing guidelines regarding drug offenses. He proposes the "all drugs minus two" guideline adjustment. This adjustment would allow judges to sentence drug offenders to lower sentences (two steps lower on the sentencing grid), thereby allowing many drug offenders to leave prison sooner or to avoid prison altogether. The proposal is widely supported by members of the black and Hispanic advocacy communities as black and Hispanics are disproportionately punished for drug offenses. This proposal, in concert with Attorney General Holder's policy of not challenging marijuana legalization efforts in various states, is seen as the beginning of an official drawdown in the War on Drugs.

**2014**  The U.S. Department of Justice announces a new program to track the use of racial profiling by police and other criminal justice agencies around the country, with the goal of eliminating the practice. The DOJ allocates $4.75 million for the program.

**2014**  Michael Brown, a black 18 year old, is shot and killed by Ferguson, MO, police officer Darren Wilson. The shooting of Brown, who was unarmed at the time, spawned several days of protests and nights of rioting in the St. Louis suburb. The police report indicates that Brown was shot after he attacked Officer Wilson when the officer stopped Brown and a companion, Dorian Johnson, for walking in the street. The officer's account of self-defense differed from the testimony of Johnson and other eyewitnesses who claim Brown was shot while attempting to give up. Many who knew Brown called him the "gentle giant" who wouldn't hurt anybody. However, days after the shooting, it is learned that Brown was captured on a convenience store surveillance camera stealing a box of cigars and roughing up the clerk who attempted to stop him. This episode happened just minutes before Brown was shot by Officer Wilson. The St. Louis County Police Department investigated the shooting and the St. Louis County Attorney referred the case to a grand jury for a prosecutive determination. The U.S. Justice Department also announced that it too would investigate the Ferguson Police Department to determine if a pattern of racial profiling existed within the department.

**atavism**   The theory that criminality is rooted in primitive and savage biological traits.

**beat patrol**   A policing strategy that concentrates an officer's attention on a particular, relatively small geographic location, thus enabling the officer to become very familiar with the area and people being policed.

**behavioral profiling**   A composite of behavioral patterns observed by law enforcement and used to predict future criminality.

**Bill of Rights**   The first 10 amendments of the U.S. Constitution, most of which establish the limitations to which government is subject when infringing upon individual freedom.

**blue curtain/wall**   Terms used to describe the culturally ingrained reluctance of police officers to report on the misconduct of other police officers

**broken windows**   A strategy of policing based on the theory that failure to address the minor offenses and public nuisances in a neighborhood will lead to more serious crime problems.

**Bureau of Justice Statistics**   An agency within the U.S. Department of Justice which serves as the research arm of the federal government on criminal justice matters. In addition to conducting its own research, the Bureau of Justice Statistics offers grants to academic and professional organizations and individuals to pursue research on topics it or Congress has identified as worthy of exploration.

**Carroll search**    A permissible warrantless bumper-to-bumper search of a motor vehicle by law enforcement without the owner's consent, provided probable cause exists that the vehicle contains evidence of a crime.

**Civil Rights Act of 1964**    A federal act outlawing discrimination in housing, employment, and other areas on the basis of race, ethnicity, religion, and gender.

**civilian review board**    A panel of citizens who are organized to evaluate the legitimacy of specific police-citizen encounters and to make recommendations or impose sanctions (depending on the degree of power conferred upon a board in a particular jurisdiction).

**classical criminology**    Theories of crime rooted in the notion that people commit crimes after making a rational choice of their own free will.

**code of ethics**    A framework for what is considered appropriate, moral, and professional behavior on the part of criminal justice professionals. Police officers, prosecutors, judges, and correctional officials all have standing codes of ethics.

**code of silence**    Similar to the "blue wall" or "blue curtain"; this is an unofficial code of conduct thought to exist in many police organizations that requires officers not to divulge to the public information about conductor misconduct on the part of other officers.

**community-based policing**    Any police program in place to foster partnerships between the community and police officers for the purpose of reducing crime and the fear of crime.

**community policing**    A strategy of policing that involves connecting specific officers to specific communities and subcommittees over the long term in order to reduce crime and the fear of crime.

**conflict model**  A political philosophy that argues that criminal laws and enforcement mechanisms have been crafted by society's powerful elite and for their benefit.

**consensus model**  A political philosophy that holds to the notion that criminal laws are an expression of society's widely shared values and beliefs.

**consent decree**  An agreement that allows a police department to avoid being sued by the U.S. Justice Department for civil rights violations provided that the police department in question consents to set conditions and oversight by the U.S. Justice Department.

**crime control model**  A conceptualization of the criminal justice system that emphasizes the need for efficiency and effectiveness in catching, punishing, and incapacitating criminals.

**criminal justice profiling**  The activity of criminal justice officials strategically considering characteristics such as race, gender, religion, or sexual orientation as they make discretionary decisions in the course of their duties.

**criminal justice system**  Generally considered to be the combination of law enforcement, the courts, and the correctional system—all working (sometimes at odds with each other) toward the goal of achieving justice.

**criminal profiling**  The term generally used to describe all types of profiling utilized in the investigation of unsolved crime.

**criminogenics**  The theory that some people are just born criminals.

**cultural diversity**  A topic of periodic training for many criminal justice professionals that emphasizes a recognition that society in the United States is made up of people with many different cultural and social backgrounds that impact their behavior and their relationships with the criminal justice system.

**deadly force**  Physical force which, based on the amount or technique, would reasonable cause great bodily harm or death to the person against whom the force is being applied.

**driving while black (DWB)**   A play on the words "driving while intoxicated"; the phrase used to describe the "crime" being committed by black motorists when they are pulled over for no apparent reason by the police.

**drug courier profile**   A composite of traits identified by law enforcement as consistent with those commonly possessed by those engaged in drug trafficking.

**due process model**   A conceptualization of the criminal justice system that emphasizes the need to protect individual rights and freedoms from a potentially overzealous or mistaken government.

**ethnicity**   Generally, the combination of cultural, religious, national, and racial groupings to which one belongs to or from which one comes.

**excessive force**   The use by law enforcement or corrections officials of more force than necessary to accomplish a legitimate official task, such as placing someone under arrest.

**Federal Bureau of Investigation (FBI)**   The federal law enforcement agency with the broadest federal enforcement powers; it pioneered the use of criminal profiling to solve crime.

**Federal Tort Claims Act**   The federal law under which federal criminal justice officials may be sued for violating citizens' constitutional and civil rights. Federal officials have been eligible to be sued under this law since the landmark ruling of Bivens v. Six Unknown Drug Agents in 1971.

**Fourteenth Amendment**   Ratified in 1868, this amendment to the U.S. Constitution declared that the states were prohibited from depriving any person of life, liberty, or property without due process of law; court cases over time used the Fourteenth Amendment to apply the Bill of Rights to state and local government action.

**gender**   A person's status of being male or female physiologically.

**GLBT**   An acronym meaning "gay, lesbian, bisexual, transgender."

**incident-driven policing**    A reactive style of policing whereby officers merely respond to one incident after another with little or no effort or opportunity to develop relationships with the community.

**institutional discrimination**    The concept that consistent bias is felt by certain groups in the criminal justice system due to otherwise neutral factors, such as criminal record or family status.

**legalistic model**    A style of policing that emphasizes following the letter of the law.

**1983 action**    A lawsuit filed under the provision of 18 USC 1983, which permits citizens to sue state and local government officials, as well as local government agencies, for violating one's constitutional rights and other federally protected civil rights.

**pattern and practice investigation**    An investigation of a state or local government agency (usually a law enforcement agency) conducted by the U.S. Justice Department to determine if violations of citizens' constitutional and civil rights are recurring and systemic. When constitutional violations are a pattern or common practice in the agency, the U.S. Justice Department will require the agency to take measures to change the policies, practices, and culture within the organization.

**peremptory challenge**    The ability of a trial attorney to strike a prospective juror from hearing a case for almost any reason or no reason.

**phrenology**    A theory of crime that proposed that deviant thought and behavior were rooted in localized parts of the brain and that, therefore, an examination of one's skull could help predict future criminality.

**police brutality**    A term used to describe unlawful use of force by police officers.

**police-community relations**    A general term referring to the state of understanding and relationship between a police organization and the community it serves.

**police discretion**    The ability of police officers to make enforcement decisions in the field without consulting others higher up in the chain of command or elsewhere in the criminal justice process.

**police misconduct**    Nonprofessional, unethical, and/or unlawful conduct by police officers.

**probable cause**    A reasonable and prudent belief, supported by articulable facts, that a person has committed a crime, or that evidence of a crime may be found on a particular person or in a particular place. Both search warrants and arrests are based upon probable cause (sometimes called "reasonable cause").

**problem-oriented policing**    A policing strategy that empowers officers to determine the source of problems within their jurisdiction and take sweeping steps to solve those problems, as opposed to repeatedly reacting to the symptoms of those problems.

**prosecutorial discretion**    The ability of prosecutors to decide whom to prosecute and whom not to prosecute without consulting others in the criminal justice process.

**prosecutorial misconduct**    Unprofessional, unethical, or unlawful conduct by a prosecutor either while building a case for prosecution or while in trial.

**psychological profiling**    Drawing conclusions about unidentified criminal offenders through the analysis of psychological traits and application of psychological theories.

**race**    Distinguishing biological features among human beings that are genetically passed on from generation to generation.

**racial profiling**    The exclusive use of race by criminal justice officials in identifying criminals or potential criminal activity.

**rational basis**    This is the lowest threshold required of government agencies to justify their actions, policies, and laws. The government can be said to be acting constitutionally under a rational basis analysis if the government's actions are rationally related to a legitimate government interest. This is the relevant threshold for most things government does as they do not involve the encroachment on fundamental constitutional rights and civil liberties.

**reasonable suspicion** A reasonable belief, based on a totality of circumstances, which would lead a reasonable person to believe that a crime has been, or is about to be, committed by a particular person under suspicion. Although a lower standard of proof than probable cause, reasonable suspicion also requires articulable facts and goes beyond a mere hunch. Reasonable suspicion is required for an officer to make a brief investigatory stop of a citizen.

**religion** A belief system concerning that which governs nature and the universe.

**selective enforcement** A police and prosecutorial strategy that aggressively takes enforcement action against particular offenses deemed to be an acute problem.

**serial offender** A criminal offender who repeatedly reoffends in a similar manner, often out of compulsion.

**service model** A style of policing that emphasizes aiding the community in nonenforcement ways and building relationships.

**sexual orientation** The status of sexual preference one has toward either the same or opposite gender.

**slave patrols** A law enforcement operation in the American South during the 18th and 19th centuries devoted to curbing rebellious slave activities and conducting general patrol duties.

**social contract** The concept that the people consent to be policed by the government in exchange for protection of individual rights and liberties.

**stereotyping** A shortcut to perceiving a person or persons by relying on assumptions about groups to which they belong, whether true or untrue.

**stop and frisk** This refers to the practice of a law enforcement officer detaining someone briefly during an investigative stop and patting the person down for weapons. The authority for doing this comes from the 1968 Supreme Court case of Terry v. Ohio, in which the Court authorized investigative detentions short of arrest based on reasonable suspicion, as well as the frisking of suspects for weapons if the officer has reasonable suspicion that the suspect possesses a weapon which could be employed against the officer.

**street justice**    The term used to describe the extra legal remedies taken against criminal offenders by police officers prior to or in lieu of arrest and formal charges; generally involves unlawful use of force.

**strict scrutiny**    This is the highest threshold required of government agencies to justify their actions, policies, and laws. The government can be said to be acting constitutionally under a strict scrutiny analysis if the government can successfully demonstrate that its actions meet a compelling government interest which requires encroachment on what would otherwise be sacrosanct fundamental constitutional rights. Actions, policies, and laws which specifically consider protected classifications such as race, ethnicity, and religion generally require a strict scrutiny analysis.

**systematic discrimination**    The concept that bias is built into the very processes and mechanisms of the criminal justice system, thus resulting in consistent discrimination against certain groups of people.

**Terry search/frisk**    A permissible, brief detention and search for weapons by law enforcement if reasonable suspicion exists that a subject as a weapon and is committing or about to commit a crime. Also see "stop and frisk".

**Title 42 USC 1983**    A federal law permitting citizens to sue state and local law enforcement officers and agencies for violation of one's civil rights. Violations must occur under the "color of law." Federal officers may not be sued under this statute. However, federal officer may be sued under the Federal Tort Claims Act for constitutional and civil rights violations.

**traffic stop**    A police encounter with a citizen in which the officer requires a motorist in the targeted vehicle to pull over and yield to the officer's investigation of a traffic or equipment violation. All stops require an objective basis; in other words, an officer must have at least reasonable suspicion of an equipment violation, traffic infraction, or of a crime.

**voir dire**    The process by which prospective jurors are selected for or eliminated from jury service in a trial; the process is generally accomplished through questions asked of would-be jurors by the trial attorneys and the judge in the case.

Note: Page numbers in *italics* indicate figures and tables.

abuse and humiliation, 114
academic success, predictors of, 149
Academy of Behavioral Profiling, 195
Adler, Freda, 157, 330
African Americans
    criminal justice system and, 140–151
    incarceration rates, 132–140
aggravating factors, 67–69
Air Marshal program, 329
Alexander, Michelle, 304
amendments to the Constitution, 70–72
American Civil Liberties Union (ACLU), 188
American Civil Rights Institute, 188–189
American Revolution, 17
Americans for Effective Law Enforcement (AELE), 189

"America's Toughest Sheriff," 157–158
Amnesty International, 189
Amy, Hackney, 274–276
*Anatomy and Physiology of the Nervous System, and of the Brain in Particular* (Gall), 322
anonymous obscene communications, 114
anthrax scare, 5
Anti-Drug Abuse Act (1986), 331
anti-sodomy laws, 19, 332, 338
anti-terrorism laws, 334
apartheid, in the U.S. criminal justice system, 313
Arab Americans, 120–125
arbitrary arrest, 326
Archbold, Carol, 318
Arizona
    border control, 158
    death penalty in, 298–300

illegal aliens in, 339
SB 1070, 158
Arpaio, Joe, *154,* 157–158
arrest rates, 87–88
Ashbrook Center for Public
    Affairs, 195–196
Ashcroft, John, 336
atavism, theory of, 324
auto theft profiling, 40

bailiffs, 22
bank robberies, 114
Barnett, Ida B. Wells,
    134
Bartol, Ann M., 304
Bartol, Curtis R., 304
*Batson v. Kentucky* (1986),
    61, 63, 176, 245–251,
    332
Beccaria, Cesare, 30,
    321–322
"beginning to end dispari-
    ties," 299
behavior profiling, quasi-
    science of, 5–6
behavioral evidence analysis,
    113, 317
Behavioral Research and
    Instruction Unit (BRIU),
    113
Bekerian, Debra, 310
Benda, Brent, 268–270
Bhui, Hindpal Singh, ed.,
    305
bias-based policing, 10–11,
    143

Bill of Rights, 69–70, 183
binge drinking, 22
biological theories of crime,
    31
Bireda, Martha, 305–306
birth control, 179,
    328–329
Black, Justice Hugo, 230
black criminality, 314
black middle class, 137
Blackmun, Justice Harry,
    158–159
blackness, condemnation of,
    314
"bobby," 23
Bond, Julian, 159–160
bonded servitude, 132
border control, 158
border integrity policy, 98
border patrol, 221
Border Patrol apprehensions,
    *222*
born criminals, 31
born-traits, 32
*Bowers v. Hardwick* (1986),
    332
Bratton, Bill, 38
Brawley, Tawana, 181
breaching the peace, 325
Briseno, Theodore, 333
*Broken Windows* (Wilson and
    Kelling), 331
"broken windows" theory
    of policing, 37–38,
    186–187, 331
Brown, Henry, 160

Brown, Michael, 341
*Brown v. Board of Education*
(1954), 160, 173–174,
326
Browning, Sandra Lee,
279–281
Bucerius, Sandra M., 306
Bureau of Justice Assistance,
203
Bureau of Justice Statistics,
141, 203, 210
Bureau of Prisons, 203
bureaucracy, 53
Burger, Justice Warren E.,
160–161
Burgess, Alan, 306–307
Burgess, Ann, 306–307
Bush, George W., 97, 336
Byrd, James Jr., 339

California incarceration rates,
140–141
*Cantwell v. Connecticut*
(1940), 325
Cao, Liqun, 279–281
capital murder cases, 55
caring (asset), 149
Carlson, Daniel, 8
Carroll search, 76, 77
*Carroll v. United States*
(1925), 76
Carson, Ann, 222–223
Cassak, Lance, 309
Cato Institute, 190
Center for Constitutional
Rights, 190

Center for Equal Opportu-
nity, 191
challenges for cause, 59
*Chambers v. Maroney* (1970),
76
Champion, Dean, 52
Chaney, James, 328
character (asset), 148–149
charging decisions, 55–58
Charles, Crawford, 270–271
Chesney-Lind, Meda,
289–291
child molestation, 32
child sexual abuse, 114
Christian terrorists, 296–297.
*See also* Ku Klux Klan
(KKK)
Christopher, Hebert,
277–279
Cincinnati, Ohio, 25
Cincinnati Police Depart-
ment, 92–93
civil litigation, 91, 94–96
civil rights, U.S. Constitution
and, 69–81
Civil Rights Act (1871), 94
Civil Rights Act (1875), 323
Civil Rights Act (1957),
326
Civil Rights Act (1964), 72,
95, 175, 328
Civil Rights Complaints
in U.S. District Court:
1990–2006, 210, *211*
civil rights movement,
134–135

Civil Rights of Institu-
tionalized Persons Act
(CRIPA), 91
civil upheaval, 24
classical criminology, tenets
of, 30, 321–322
Cleary, Jim, 81, 88
Clinton, William (Bill),
161–162
cocaine, 18–19, 138–139,
144, 271–274. *See also*
crack cocaine
code of ethics, 27
Cohen, Thomas, 210
Cole, David, 60
*The Color of Justice: Race,
Ethnicity, and Crime
in America* (Walker,
Spohn, and DeLone),
318
colorblindness, 304
Commission on the Accreditation of Law Enforce-
ment Agencies (CALEA),
191
Committee on Civil Rights,
326
Community Oriented Polic-
ing Service (COPS), 162,
203
community policing model,
27–28, 38, 162,
166–167, 330–331
Community Relations Ser-
vice, 203
competence (asset), 148

*The Condemnation of Black-
ness: Race, Crime, and the
Making of Modern Urban
America* (Muhammad),
314
confidence (asset), 149
conflict model, 15–17
Confronting Discrimination
in the Post-9/11 Era, 210
Congressional Black Caucus
Foundation, 192
connection (asset), 147–148
consensual encounters, 75
consensus, government based
on, 16–17
consensus model principles,
15
consensus *versus* conflict
debate, 15
consent, of search, 75
consent decrees, 335, 336,
337, 338, 339–340
constitutional liberties, 72
Contacts between the Police
and the Public, 211,
287–289
contextual discrimination,
20
contraceptives, 328
Correctional Populations in
the United States, 2012,
215
corruption, 25, 26
crack cocaine disparities, 138,
139, 144, 150, 271–274,
331–332

crime
emerging profiling theories,
29–33
immigration and, 306
politicization of, 117
punishment and, 316
*Crime Classification Manual*
(FBI), 113
*Crime Classification Manual:*
*Standard System for Inves-*
*tigating and Classifying*
*Violent Crimes* (Douglas
et al.), 306–307
crime control, value of,
13–14
crime scene analysis, 113
crime scene patterns, 114
crime-fighting model of
policing, 27
crimes of passion, 295–296
*Criminal & Behavioral Profil-*
*ing* (Bartol and Bartol),
304
criminal behavioral profiling,
112–116
criminal investigative analysis, 113
criminal justice profiling
applications of, 21
arguments against, 81–87
arguments for, 87–90,
311–312
art of, 115
controversial nature of, 6
in court, 58–65
defined, 6–9

fictional, 113
goals of, 41
importance of studying,
9–13
inexact nature of, 114–115
by police, 21–22
political philosophy and,
14–16
potential discriminatory
effects of, 10
remedies, 91–96
at sentencing, 65–69
stereotyping and, 47–51
unintentional contradic-
tions, 12
criminal justice system
African Americans overrepresentation in, 140–151
competing goals of, 13
as a continuum, 19–20
decentralized nature of, 13
disproportionate minor-
ity contact (DMC),
141–142
"doing justice," 13–14
mental illness and the,
128–131
reform efforts, 25–26
youth proximity to,
149
*Criminal Man* (Lombroso),
324
criminal profiling. *See* criminal justice profiling
*Criminal Profiling: An Intro-*
*duction to Behavioral*

*Evidence Analysis* (Turvey), 317
*Criminal Profiling: International Theory, Research and Practice* (Kocsis), 311
criminality, rational approaches to explaining, 30
criminogenic theory of crime, 31
Cullen, Francis, 279–281

Dahle, Thorvald, 105, 107–111
data collection, 162
Davis, Mark, 297–298
De Blasio, Bill, 38
De Lisi, Matt, 271–274
death penalty, 174, 298–300, 302–303
Declaration of Independence, 17
deductive reasoning, 114
deductive reasoning approach, 317
Dees, Morris, 163–164
deindustrialization, 137
DeJong, Christina, 316
*Delaware v. Prouse* (1979), 74, 78–79, 185, 240–245, 331
"deliberate indifference," 95
DeLone, Miriam, 318
Department of Homeland Security, 203

determinate sentences, 66–67
deterrence, 66
developmental asset framework, 147, 150
developmental assets, 146–147
developmental constructs, threats to, 149
developmental systems theory, 146
Diallo, Amadou, 108, 181
Diamond, Drew, 308
differential involvement perspective, 294
direct-impact perspective, 294
discretionary enforcement. *See* police discretion
*Discrimination* (Williams), 319
"Discrimination and the Death Penalty in Arizona" (Thomson), 298–300
discrimination legislation, 72
discriminatory jury pools, 60
discriminatory laws, 18
disorganized offenders, 114
disparate incarceration by race, 144
disproportionate minority contact (DMC), 141–143, 271–274
disproportionate punishment, 30

dog searches, 76–77, 84

"doing justice," values associated with, 13–14

DOJ Civil Rights Division, 91

domestic violence, 334

"don't ask, don't tell" policy, 162

Douglas, John, 34, 164, 306–307

*Dred Scott v. Sandford* (1857), 182, 322

driving while black (DWB), 77, 135

*Driving while Black* (Marks), 312–313

"Driving while Black: Effects of Race, Ethnicity, and Gender on Citizen Self-Reports of Traffic Stops and Police Actions," 287–289

drug arrest rates, predicting, 292–293

drug courier profiling, 35–36, 39–40, 251–257, 317, 332

Drug Policy Alliance, 192

Drug Reform Coordination Network, 193

drug sentencing, 19

drug war, 140

DuBois, W.E.B., 164–165

due process, 14, 58

Durose, Matthew, 211, 221

DWB—Driving While Black, 77, 135

*Edmonson v. Leesville Concrete Company, Inc.* (1991), 62, 63

education and employment, 148

educational programs, availability of, 285–287

"The Effect of Gender on the Decision to Incarcerate before and after the Introduction of Sentencing Guidelines" (Koons-Witt), 283–285

Eighth Amendment, 71, 72

Eisenhower, Dwight, 183

*Eisenstadt v. Baird* (1972), 330

Eith, Christine, 211

*Eliminating Racial Profiling in School Discipline* (Bireda), 305–306

elitism, political philosophy of, 17–21

emancipation of slaves, 133

empathy toward others, 149

employment prospects, 148, 150

End Racial Profiling Act (2013), 215–216

England, police institutions in, 22–25

English Riot Act, 22–23

environmental assets, 150

Epp, Charles R., 307

Equal Employment Opportunity Commission, 328

equal justice concept, 9, 33, 58
"Equal or Equitable: An Exploration of Educational and Vocational Program Availability for Male and Female Offenders" (Lahm), 285–287
Equal Protection Clause, 18, 62–63
*Essay on Crimes and Punishments* (Beccaria), 30, 321
ethnic fighting, 24
ethnicity, crime and, 306, 318
ethnicity-based disparities, 141
EthnicMajority.com, 193
evolution, Darwin's theory of, 31
excessive punishment, 30
"Exploring the Influence of Race Relations and Public Safety Concerns on Public Support for Racial Profiling During Traffic Stops" (Higgins et al.), 281–283
external developmental assets, 142–143, 147

Fair Sentencing Act (2010), 144
FBI
  Behavioral Analysis Unit (BAU), 40–41
  Behavioral Science Unit (BSU), 113
  National Center for the Analysis of Violent Crime (NCAVC), 40–41
  organized/disorganized dichotomy profiling approach, 113–114
  profilers, 3–5, 34–35
  Violent Criminal Apprehension Program, 40–41
federal death penalty, 334
federal prosecutorial guidelines, 56
federal sentencing guidelines, 341
female offenders
  crimes of passion, 295–296
  criminal behavior, 157
  educational and vocational programs for, 285–287
  sentencing guidelines and, 283–285
feminist criminology, 157, 330
fictional profiling, 35
Fifth Amendment, 70, 72
*Fighting to Win* (Vogel), 317
fire setting, 114
First Amendment, 70, 72, 325
fishing expeditions, 74
"5 Cs" of positive youth development (PYD), 147–149

Florida Highway Patrol
guidelines, 109
*Florida v. Wells* (1990), 79
*Floyd, et al. v. City of New
York* (2013), 38
"Flying While Arab,"
120–125
Fourteenth Amendment, 18,
71–72, 323
Fourth Amendment, 70, 72
Francis, Robert E., 335
Fredrickson, Darin, 37, 308
free black populations,
132–133
freedom summer (1964),
327–328
Fridell, Lorie, 308

Gabbidon, Shaun, 281–283
Galati, Paul, 124
Gall, Franz Joseph, 165,
322
gang environments, 138
gender. *See also* female
offenders
crimes of passion and,
295–296
incarceration and, 141
Jane Crow laws, 235
jury selection and, 235–240
peremptory challenges and,
333–334
*Queer (In)Justice* (Mogul et
al.), 313
sentencing guidelines and,
283–285

vocational rehabilitation
and, 285–287
"Gender, Race, and Habitual
Offender Sentencing
in Florida" (Crawford),
270–271
"Gender Bias and Juvenile
Justice Revisited: A Mul-
tiyear Analysis,"
289–291
gender identity, 315–316
gender profiling, 88,
117–118
general deterrence, 66
George, Higgins,
281–283
Gerald, Rossano, 83–87
Ginsburg, Ruth Bader,
165–166
Glaser, Jack, 274–276
Glaze, Lauren, 215
global self-regard, 149
Goldstein, Herman,
166–167
*Good Cop, Bad Cop: Racial
Profiling and Competing
Views of Justice* (Heu-
mann and Cassak), 309,
316
*Good Cops: The Case for Pre-
ventive Policing* (Harris),
308
good faith actions, 96
Goodman, Andrew, 328
government, greater aims of,
9–10

government documents
Bureau of Justice Statistics,
210
Civil Rights Complaints
in U.S. District Court:
1990–2006, 210
Confronting Discrimina-
tion in the Post-9/11 Era,
210
Contacts between the
Police and the Public,
2008, 211
Correctional Populations in
the United States, 2012,
215
End Racial Profiling Act
(2013), 215–216
Guidelines Regarding the
Use of Race by Federal
Law Enforcement
Agencies, 220
Immigration Offenders in
the Federal Justice Sys-
tem, 2010, 221
Police Behavior during
Traffic and Street Stops,
2011, 221, *223*
Prisoners in 2011, 222–223
Probation and Parole in the
United States, 2011, 225,
*227*
Protecting Civil Rights:
A Leadership Guide
for State, Local, and
Tribal Law Enforcement,
227–228
Protecting the Rights of
Lesbian, Gay, Bisexual,
Transgender, and Intersex
Individuals, 228
Protecting Women's Rights,
228–229
Racial Profiling Factsheet,
229
Great Migration, 137
Greene, Steve, 136
Griffin, Timothy, 274–276
*Griswold v. Connecticut*
(1965), 159, 179, 328
Guidelines Regarding the
Use of Race by Federal
Law Enforcement Agen-
cies, 220

habitual offender sentencing,
270–271
Haitian Revolution, 133
*Handbook of LGBT Commu-
nities, Crime, and Justice*
(Peterson and Panfil),
315
Harlan, John M., 167, 236
Harlem Children's Zone
(HCZ), 150–151
Harris, David, 33, 308,
309
Harris, Eddy L., 135
hate crimes, 120–125
Hate Crimes Prevention Act
(2009), 339
hate groups, 163
Hatfill, Steven, 5–6

Heinrich, Paige, 105, 116–119
Herberman, Erinn, 215
Heumann, Milton, 309
Highland Park, Illinois, Police Department, 92
high-risk behavior patterns, 147, 150
hijacker profiling, 33–34
*Hirabayashi v. United States* (1943), 121
Hobbes, Thomas, 17, 167–168
Holcomb, Jefferson, 302–303
Holder, Eric, 19, 107, 220, 341
Holmes, Ronald, 310
Holmes, Stephen, 310
Homeland Security, 120–125
homicide profiling, 298–300
homosexuality, 19, 32, 296, 319, 332, 334, 338
Hoover, J. Edgar, 168–169
*Hoyt v. Florida* (1961), 235–240, 327
Hughes, Johnny, 88–89
Human Rights Watch, 193–194
hunches, 74

"I have a dream" speech, 171, 327
illegal immigrants, 158
immigration, ethnicity, crime and, 306

Immigration Offenders in the Federal Justice System, 2010, 221, *222*
"The Impact of Race on Perceptions of Criminal Justice" (Henderson et al.), 279–281
*In Defense of Internment: The Case for Racial Profiling in World War II and the War on Terror* (Malkin), 311
incapacitation, 66
incarceration patterns, 143
incarceration rates, 140–141, 271–274
incorporation (judicial process), 72
indentured servitude, 132
indeterminate sentences, 66–67
individual factors, of discretion, 53, 54–55
inductive reasoning, 114
inhibited assets, 146–147
institutional discrimination, 20
"The Institutionalization of Racial Profiling Policy" (Miller), 291–292
interactionist perspective, 294
internal assets, 147
International Association of Chiefs of Police (IACP), 194

International Association of Directors of Law Enforcement Standards and Training (IADLEST), 194–195
International Association of Forensic Criminologists, 195
internment, racial profiling and, 311
intraracial murder, 298–300
investigative profiling, 41
investigatory detention, 329
irrational profiling, 8–9
Islamic terrorists, 296–297
islamophobic profiling, 120–125
Ivins, Bruce, 5

Jackson, Janet, 310
Jackson, Jesse, 169–170
Jane Crow laws, 235–240
Japanese Americans, 121, 230–235, 325, 326
*J.E.B. v. Alabama* (1994), 62, 63, 159, 333
Jehovah's Witnesses, 325
Jewell, Richard, 3–5
Jim Crow era, 134–135
Jim Crow laws, 18, 137, 304, 314, 323, 324
*Judges' Reactions to Sentencing Reform in Ohio* (Griffin and Wooldredge), 274–276
judicial profiling, 42

jury selection (voir dire), 6–7, 59–65, 245–251
jury service, women and, 230, 235–240

Kaufman, Robert, 287–289
Kelling, George E., 37, 186, 331
Kennedy, Randall, 81–82
Kientz Anderson, Lauren, 106, 132–140
King, Martin Luther Jr., 170–171, 175, 327
King, Rodney, 58, 108, 171–172, 333
Kocsis, Richard, 311
Koon, Stacey, 172, 333
Koons-Witt, Barbara A., 283–285
Kopache, Renee, 279–281
*Korematsu v. United States* (1944), 230–235, 326
Koski, Connie M., 106, 120–125
Ku Klux Act (1871), 323
Ku Klux Klan (KKK), 29, 163, 323, 328
Kubu, Bruce, 308
Kyckelhahn, Tracey, 210

Lady Justice, 9, 58
Lahm, Karen, 285–287
Langton, Lynn, 221
law enforcement, 21–22, 27
Law Enforcement Assistance Administration, 329

*Lawrence v. Texas* (2003), 338

Leadership Conference on Civil Rights, 196

legal redundancy, 10

legal segregation, 136

legal sufficiency model, 56–57

Lerner, Richard, 147

Lewis, John, 172–173

LGBT criminology, 228, 313, 315

liberation theory of criminology, 157

Locke, John, 16, 17

Lombroso, Cesare, 31, 173, 324

long-term poverty, 138

Los Angeles Police Department, 92

Louima, Abner, 108, 181

Lundman, Richard, 287–289

Lunney, Robert, 308

lust and mutilation murders, 114

lynching, 134

MacDonald, John, 289–291

*mala in se* offenses/crimes, 15

*mala prohibita* offenses/crimes, 16

Malkin, Michelle, 311

management science, 27

mandatory minimum federal prison sentences, 331

mandatory school attendance, 329–330

mandatory sentencing, 66–67, 138

mandatory sentencing guidelines, 143–144

*Mapp v. Ohio* (1961), 327

Maricopa County Sheriff's Department, 158

Marks, Kenneth, 312

Marshall, Thurgood, 173–174

Martha, Henderson, 279–281

Martin, Trayvon, 47–48, 89, 107, 340

Maruschak, Laura, 225

mass incarceration, 304

Maynard-Moody, Steven, 307

McDonald, William, 97

media attention, 108, 116–119

media bias, 133

*Melendres v. Arpaio* (2013), 158

mental health profiling, 128–131

merit selection and promotion, 27

"the Met" four-part mandate, 23–24

Metropolitan Police Act (1829), 23, 322

Mfume, Kweisi, 174–175

Miller, Kirk, 291–292

Mills, C. Wright, 18
Milovanovic, Dragon, 313
Milwaukee, Wisconsin, 108–109
misconduct, perceptions of, 297–298
mitigating factors, 67–69
mob violence, 22, 24
Mogul, Joey L., 313
Montgomery bus boycott, 175
Montgomery County, Maryland, Police Department, 92
Mosher, Clayton, 292–293
Motivans, Mark, 221
motive of the offender, 114
motor vehicle searches, 76
Muhammad, Khalil Gibran, 314
Muslim Americans, 120–125

Nance, Malcolm W., 314
National Association for the Advancement of Colored People (NAACP), 160, 164–165, 175, 196
National Center for the Analysis of Violent Crime (NCAVC), 40, 113
National Commission on Crime Control and Prevention mandates, 11–12
National Crime Victimization Survey, 211, 221

National Day of Protest to Stop Police Brutality, Repression and the Criminalization of a Generation (NDP), 198
National Institute of Justice, 203
National Organization of Black Law Enforcement Executives (NOBLE), 197
national security policy, 98
National Sheriffs' Association (NSA), 198
Native Americans profiling, 110
*Neal v. Delaware* (1881), 61
neighborhood crime statistics, 136
neighborhood variables, 53–54
Nelson, David Erik, 315
Nelson, Pat, 106, 128–131
New Jersey State Police, 92, 335
*The New Jim Crow: Mass Incarceration in the Age of Colorblindness* (Alexander), 304
New Orleans Police Department, 94
*The New World of Police Accountability* (Walker and Archbold), 318
New York Police Department (NYPD), 37–38, 124

New York Transit Police, 37–38

night watchmen, 22, 24

9/11 attacks, impact of, 7, 10, 96–99, 120–125, 220, 296–297, 337

books about, 311, 314

Nineteenth Amendment, 325

*No Equal Justice* (Cole), 60

No Establishment Clause, 325

North Carolina, 28–29

Obama, Barak, 97, 220, 339

"objectively reasonable" conduct, 96

obscene communications, 114

occult and ritualistic crimes, 114

occupying military force, 38

offender personalities, 113–114

*Offender Profiling: Theory, Research, and Practice* (Jackson and Bekerian), 310

offender-victim relationships, 117–118

Office of Legislative Affairs, 203

officer aloofness, 26

Olympic Park bombing, 3–5

Omnibus Crime Control and Safe Streets Act (1968), 91, 329

Operation PUSH (People United to Serve Humanity), 169–170

order maintenance, 21

O'Reilly, James, 316

organizational variables, 53

organized offenders, 113–114

organized/disorganized dichotomy profiling approach, 113–114

"out of place" policing, 110

*The Oxford Handbook of Ethnicity, Crime, and Immigration* (Bucerius and Tonry), 306

Pampel, Fred C., 315

Panfil, Vanessa R., 315

parent-child dynamics, impaired, 147–148

parish-constable watch system, 22

Parker, Kathleen, 89

Parks, Erika, 225

Parks, Rosa, 175–176

parole violations, 141

patrol cars, 27

pedophilia, 32, 114, 310

Peel, Sir Robert, 23, 322

peer delinquency, 148–149

perceptions of misconduct, 297–298

"Perceptions of Racial Profiling: Race, Class, and Personal Experience" (Weitzer and Tuch), 300–302
peremptory challenges, 59, 245–251, 332
persecution, 308
person-context dynamics, 146
person-environment relationship, 142, 145
Peterson, Dana, 315
*Petit Apartheid in the U.S. Criminal Justice System* (Milovanovic and Russell), 313
philosophies of crime in America, 29–33
"phrenology," 165, 322
Pittsburgh Police Department, 92
plain view search, 76
Planned Parenthood Federation of America, 179
plea-bargaining, 57
*Plessy v. Ferguson* (1896), 160, 167, 174, 324, 326
pluralism, 16–17
police, primary functions of, 21–22
police accountability, 318
*Police Administration* (Wilson), 187

*The Police and Modern Society* (Vollmer), 182
Police Behavior during Traffic and Street Stops, 2011, 221
police brutality, 326
Police Complaint Center (PCC), 199
Police Corps training program, 334
police discretion, 51–55
Police Executive Research Forum (PERF), 199
Police Foundation, 200
police institutions, origins of, 22–28
police misconduct, 334
police profile categories, 33
*Police Traffic Stops and Racial Profiling: Resolving Management, Labor, and Civil Rights Conflicts* (O'Reilly), 316
Police-Public Contact Survey, 2011, *224*
policing
    political era of, 322
    Progressive era of, 325
    reform model of, 27
*Policing in the Community* (Champion and Rush), 52
political biases, 144
political equality, 324–325
political era of policing, 25
political philosophy, 14–16

poll tax, 327
positive youth development
    (PYD), 147–149
posses, 22
poverty, long-term, 138
Powell, Justice Lewis, 176,
    245
Powell, Lawrence, 172, 333
*Powell v. Alabama* (1932), 63
power elite, 17–18
*Powers v. Ohio* (1991),
    61–62, 332
Pratt, Travis, 293–295
"Predicting Drug Arrest
    Rates: Conflict and Social
    Disorganization Perspec-
    tives," 292–293
presumptive sentences, 67
pretextual stops, 109
preventative patrol, 188
preventive policing, 308
prison experience, 146
prison financing strategies,
    141
prison populations, 138
prisoner growth rate, 142
*Prisoners in 2011,* 222–223,
    *226*
privacy, right to, 328, 330,
    332, 338
proactive profiling, 36–41
probable cause, 74–75, 76,
    257–264
Probation and Parole in the
    United States, 2011, 225,
    *227*

probation officers, 144–145
professional model of polic-
    ing, 27–28, 330
professionalism, 26–27
profiled characteristics, 7
*Profiles in Injustice* (Harris),
    33, 309
profiling. *See* criminal justice
    profiling
*Profiling Violent Crimes: An
    Investigative Tool* (Holmes
    and Holmes), 310
Progressive era policing, 25
prosecutorial decision mak-
    ing, 55–58
prosecutorial profiling, 42
Protecting Civil Rights: A
    Leadership Guide for
    State, Local, and Tribal
    Law Enforcement,
    227–228
Protecting the Rights of
    Lesbian, Gay, Bisexual,
    Transgender, and Intersex
    Individuals, 228
Protecting Women's Rights,
    228–229
psychological profiling, 113
Public Agenda, 200
public interest, 108
public policy, 16–17, 150
*Pulled Over: How Police Stops
    Define Race and Citizen-
    ship* (Epp and Maynard-
    Moody), 307
punishment, 65–66

pure justice, 19, 20
*Purkett v. Elem* (1995), 63
pyramid of power, 18

*Queer (In)Justice: The Crimi-
nalization of LGBT
People in the United States*
(Mogul et al.), 313

"Race, Conventional Crime,
and Criminal Justice:
The Declining Impor-
tance of Skin Color"
(De Lisi and Regoli),
271–274
race and citizenship, 307
race and crime, 314
*Race and Criminal Justice*
(Bhui), 305
"Race and Its Effects on
Police Officers' Percep-
tions of Misconduct"
(Son, Davis, and Rome),
297–298
"Race and Sentencing:
A Meta-Analysis of
Conflicting Empiri-
cal Research Results,"
293–295
race consciousness, state-
sanctioned, 160
race data, 110
race/ethnicity
crime and, 318
developmental assets and,
147

incarceration rates,
140–150
media attention and,
117–119
unconscious stereotypes
and, 144–145
racial disparity, 55
"Racial Disparity and Death
Sentences in Ohio" (Wil-
liams and Holcomb),
302–303
racial profiling, 37, 80–83,
92, 107–111
*Racial Profiling* (Fredrickson
and Siljander), 308
*Racial Profiling* (Nelson),
315
*Racial Profiling* (Pampel),
315
racial profiling, perceptions
of, 300–302
Racial Profiling Factsheet,
229
racial profiling policy,
291–292
"racialization" of religion,
121
racialized thinking and
behaviors, 143
*Racially Biased Policing*
(Fridell, Lunney, Dia-
mond, and Kubu), 308
radio-squad cars, 26–27
Ragatz, Laurie, 295–296
Rainbow Coalition, 170
Rainbow/PUSH, 201

Rand Center on Quality Policing, 110
random checkpoints, 75
rape, occult and ritualistic crimes, 114
rational profiling, 8–9
Ray, James Earl, 171
reactive profiling, 36–41
reasonable suspicion, 73, 74, 75, 240–245, 251–257, 329
recidivism, 30, 141, 142–143, 146, 149–150
reform, 26–27
Regoli, Bob, 271–274
rehabilitation, 66
rehabilitation programs, availability of, 285–287
Rehnquist, Justice William H., 176–177, 251
religion, "racialization" of, 121
"Religiosity and Violence" (Brent and Toombs), 268–270
religious terrorism, 296–297, 311. *See also* Ku Klux Klan (KKK)
Reno, Janet, 177
Ressler, Robert, 306–307
restorative justice, 66
retribution, 66
"Reverse Deterrence in Racial Profiling" (Hackney and Glaser), 274–276
right to privacy, 328

right to vote, 327
*Ring v. Arizona* (2002), 66
riots, 22–23, 24
Ritchie, Andrea J., 313
ritualistic crimes, 114
Roach, Steve, 337
Robina Institute, 201
*Roe v. Wade* (1973), 159
Rome, Dennis, 297–298
*Romer v. Evans* (1996), 334
Rousseau, Jean-Jacques, 178
Rudolph, Eric Robert, 5
Rush, George, 52
Russell, Brenda, 295–296
Russell, Katheryn, 313

Sabol, William, 222–223
sadistic sexual assault, 114
Sanger, Margaret, 178–179
SB 1070 (Arizona), 158
Scalia, Antonin, 179–180, 257
Schbley, Ayla Hammond, 296–297
school attendance, 329–330
school discipline, 305–306
Schwerner, Michael, 328
scientific crime fighting, 27
search warrant requirement, 75
segregation, legal, 136, 323
selective enforcement, 18, 109
Selective Enforcement Team, 332

self-efficacy, 149

Sentate Bill (SB) 1070 (2010), 80

sentencing
discretion, 341
disparities, 143–144, 277–279
guidelines, 283–285
profiling at, 65–69
race and, 293–295
reform in Ohio, 274–276

"Sentencing Outcomes of Black, Hispanic, and White Males Convicted under Federal Sentencing Guidelines" (Herbert), 277–279

"separate but equal," 160, 174

serial killer profiling, 34–35

service aspect of policing, 21, 25

"Sex, Sexual Orientation, and Sexism: What Influence Do These Factors Have on Verdicts in a Crime-of-Passion Case" (Ragatz and Russell), 295–296

sex education, 179

sexual crimes, 310

sexual homicide, 114

sexual privacy, 338

sharecropping, 136

Sharpton, Alfred, 180–181

Shepard, Matthew, 339

shire reeve (sheriff), 22

shoe bomber, 99

Shtull, Penny R., 105, 112–116

Siljander, Raymond, 37, 308

*Sisters in Crime* (Adler), 157, 330

situational variables, 53, 54

Sixth Amendment, 70–71, 72

skin color, 271–274

skyjacking, 329, 337

slave patrols, 28–29, 321

slavery, 132, 136

*Smith v. Mississippi* (1896), 60

Snow, Murry, 158

*The Social Contract* (Rousseau), 178

social contract theory, 16–17, 167–168

social disorganization theory, 145–146

social equality, 324–325

socioeconomic status, 143

sociological theories of crime, 32–33

solicitation licenses, 325

Son, In Soo, 297–298

South Carolina, 10, 28–29

Southern Poverty Law Center, 163, 202

specific deterrence, 66

Spohn, Cassia, 318

Spurzheim, Gaspar, 322

St. Louis, Missouri, 110

state government agencies, 204–207

state-sanctioned race consciousness, 160

stereotypical training programs, 286

stereotyping, 47–51, 133

Steubenville, Ohio, Police Department, 92

stop and frisk policy, 38, 340

stop and search, 10

stranger crimes, 300

*Strauder v. West Virginia* (1879), 60, 324

strict constructionism, 180

"strict judicial scrutiny," 73

structural/environmental factors, 142–143, 145

subway system crime, 38

Sullivan, Daniel, *2*

Supplemental Homicide Report (SHR), 302

Support Our Law Enforcement and Safe Neighborhoods Act (2010), 80, 339

system efficiency model, 56, 57

systematic discrimination, 19–20

systematically inhibited/decreased assets, 146–147

Taney, Roger, 181–182

*Taylor v. Louisiana* (1975), 185, 330

terror profiling, 120–125

*Terrorist Recognition Handbook: A Practitioner's Manual for Predicting and Identifying Terrorist Activities* (Nance), 314

Terry search, 76, 77

*Terry v. Ohio* (1968), 74, 183, 329

theories of crime and profiling, 29–33

Thomas, Timothy, 337

Thompson, Tommy, 108

Thomson, Ernie, 298–300

"three-strikes law," 138

Title 42, 334

Tonry, Michael, 306

Toombs, Nancy, 268–270

"Toward a Common Profile of Religious Terrorism: Some Psychosocial Determinants of Christian and Islamic Terrorists" (Schbley), 296–297

traffic stops, *214*

citizenship and, 307–308

"Driving while Black," 287–289

"Exploring the Influence of Race Relations and Public Safety Concerns on Public Support for Racial Profiling During Traffic Stops," 281–283

management, labor, and
    civil rights conflicts, 316
pretextual, 109
racial profiling and,
    300–302
reasonable suspicion and,
    73–75
*Whren et al. v. United States*
    (1996), 257–264
Traffic Stops Statistics Study
    Act (1999), 336
traffic-stop patterns, 77–78
training standards, 27
Travis, Raphael, 106,
    140–151
trial sufficiency model, 56, 57
Truman, Harry S., 326
Tuch, Steven, 287, 300–302
Turvey, Brent, 317
Twenty-Fourth Amendment,
    327

unconscious stereotypes, 144
underground economy, 137,
    138, 139
unfair discrimination, 308
United States
    cronyism and corruption, 25
    modern police departments
        in, 23–25
    policing in the American
        South, 28–29
    political era, 322
    Preamble to the Constitu-
        tion, 17
    Progressive era, 25

*United States v. Sokolow*
    (1989), 36, 251–257, 332
unreasonable searches
    and seizures, 83–87,
        240–245, 259–264, 331
urban America, 314
urban density, 136–137
urban law enforcement
    model, 28–29
urban plea-bargaining, 57
U.S. Commission on Civil
    Rights, 326
U.S. Constitution, civil rights
    and, 69–81
U.S. Department of Justice
    (DOJ)
    Civil Rights Division, 91,
        93–94
    overview, 202
    prosecutorial guidelines, 56
U.S. Department of State,
    204
U.S. Patriot Act (2001), 337
Utah, 10–11

valence, of stereotypes, 48–49
vehicle searches, 76
victimization, perceived risk
    of, 117
victimization statistics, 90
vigilante groups, 29
violence, religiosity and,
    268–270
Violent Crime Control and
    Law Enforcement Act
    (1994), 11, 91, 334, 335

violent crimes
classification of, 306–307
profiling, 113, 310
Virginia, 10, 28–29
Vito, Gennaro, 281–283
vocational programs, availability of, 285–287
Vogel, Bob, 36, 332
Vogel, Robert, 317
voir dire. *See* jury selection (voir dire)
Vollmer, August, 182–183, 325
voter registration campaign, 327–328
voting rights, 325
Voting Rights Act (1965), 175

Walker, Samuel, 52–53, 318
War on Drugs, 140, 331
War on Terror, 120–125
warrantless searches, 76, 183
Warren, Earl, 183
Washington DC Police Department, 92
*Wayte v. U.S.* (1985), 58
Weitzer, Ronald, 287, 300–302
Wells, Ida B., 184
West Virginia, 10
*When Cultures Clash* (Carlson), 8

White, Justice Byron, 184–185, 241
white flight, 136
Whitlock, Kay, 313
Whitman, Christine Todd, 185–186, 336
*Whren v. United States* (1996), 77, 78, 257–264, 334
Williams, Marian, 302–303
Williams, Mary, 319
Wilson, Darren, 341
Wilson, James Q., 37, 186–187, 331
Wilson, O. W., 187–188
Wind, Timothy, 333
women. *See also* female offenders; gender
feminist criminology, 330
jury selection and, 330
voting rights of, 325
Wooldredge, John, 274–276
World War II, racial profiling and, 311

*Yick Wo v. Hopkins* (1886), 57, 324
*Yoder v. Wisconsin* (1972), 329–330

Zimmerman, George, 47–48, 89, 107, 340

## About the Author

Jeff Bumgarner, PhD, is Professor and Department Head of Criminal Justice and Political Science at North Dakota State University. He is the author or coauthor of five books and many articles and book chapters on law enforcement and other criminal justice topics. His research interests include federal law enforcement, homeland security, police practices, and criminal justice public policy. Dr. Bumgarner is a licensed peace officer in Minnesota. In addition to his many years of college teaching, he has several years of experience as a deputy sheriff, federal agent, and police chief.